T H E

REAGAN

LEGACY

T H E
REAGAN
LEGACY

SIDNEY BLUMENTHAL AND
THOMAS BYRNE EDSALL,
Editors

Pantheon Books New York

For Jackie and Mary

Library of Congress Cataloging-in-Publication Data
The Reagan legacy.
Includes bibliographies and index.
1. United States—Politics and government—1981– .
2. Reagan, Ronald.   I. Blumenthal, Sidney, 1948– .
II. Edsall, Thomas Byrne.
E876.R397   1988   973.927   87–43109
ISBN 0–394–56555–X
ISBN 0–394–75970–2 (pbk.)

BOOK DESIGN BY GUENET ABRAHAM
Manufactured in the United States of America
First Edition

CONTENTS

INTRODUCTION

The essays in this volume, by seven journalists who have spent much of the 1980s reporting on national and international affairs for a wide range of newspapers and magazines, represent an attempt to begin to evaluate the Reagan legacy in terms of its impact on politics, economics, diplomacy, law, culture, and ideology. The contributors were given a free hand to explore their own interests, with the result that there are substantial differences of opinion and interpretation in the varying assessments of what has been a major turning point in American politics: the election and reelection of the first ideologically committed conservative president since the establishment of the post–New Deal configuration of the Republican and Democratic parties.

There is clear agreement among the authors that the two terms of the Reagan presidency have profoundly altered the content and direction of political and economic life. At the same time, five of the authors have come to the conclusion that the Reagan revolution has failed in one or more ways to achieve its ultimate objectives: that it has not produced a Republican realignment of the electorate; that its leaders have not developed a long-term agenda designed to expand the conservative voting base (such as that developed by Margaret Thatcher's Conservative Party in England); that the ascendency of conservative Republicanism has not been accompanied by the emergence of genuine literary or artistic support in the larger public culture; that despite record defense expenditures, the administration has failed to achieve the restoration of American international diplomatic and military influence; and that a barrage of law-and-order rhetoric notwithstanding, the Reagan years have seen the systematic undermining, on the part of government itself, of the primacy of the rule of law.

When Reagan took office, one of his first acts was to outline conservative standards for the new administration. "It is my intention to curb the size and influence of the federal establishment," the president declared in his January 1981 inaugural address. Six months later, on the eve of congressional passage of his $749 billion tax cut, Reagan went on national television to present to the public what he saw as two choices: "One road is all too familiar to us. It leads ultimately to higher taxes. It merely brings us back full circle to the source of our economic problem, where government decides that it knows better than you what should be done with your earnings and, in fact, how you should conduct your life. The other road promises to renew the American spirit. It is a road of hope and opportunity. It places the direction of your life back in your hands where it belongs."

Now, at the close of the Reagan presidency, massive budget
and trade deficits stemming from administration policies dominate the economic debate; there is a growing recognition, among
Republicans as well as Democrats, that tax cuts have not resolved
the nation's fiscal problems, which have in fact been exacerbated
in an increasingly complex world economy. Furthermore, public-
opinion-polling data suggest that eight years after Reagan's first
inaugural address, Americans from the boardroom to the barroom
are looking more, rather than less, to government to ensure economic security.

The essays collected here analyze various aspects of the Reagan
legacy and some of the larger ideological, political, and economic
issues raised during the past decade.

Thomas Edsall, a political reporter for the *Washington Post* and
author of *The New Politics of Inequality* and *Power and Money*,
argues that the Reagan years have produced a major alteration
of the political and economic structure of the nation. Politically,
the Reagan presidency has solidified a realignment of the Mountain West states and further strengthened the Republican Party
in the South, where it is now a competitive force in local elections
in urban and suburban areas. Administration policy has accelerated the erosion of organized labor, a critically important
institution for the Democratic Party. Reagan has succeeded in
counterbalancing Democratic arguments for strengthened government services by focusing public attention on tax burdens. More
importantly, the Reagan election in 1980 and reelection in 1984
demonstrated the presence of a right-leaning coalition, dominated
by an alliance between the affluent and the religious, that has

become a force equal to what remains of the New Deal Democratic coalition.

Economically, not only has the deficit stymied the Democratic Party, but tax and domestic spending cuts have significantly redistributed after-tax income in ways rewarding the most loyal Republican voters and penalizing most Democratic voters, according to Edsall. Increased income inequity dovetails with both the growing polarization of Democratic and Republican voters on the basis of income, and with patterns of voter turnout in which the more affluent (and more Republican) segment of the electorate has gained expanding and disproportionate influence over the election process. Long-range employment trends are likely to further amplify income differences, as new jobs will increasingly require the training and education skills most lacking in the black and Hispanic communities, two key sources of Democratic support. Despite all these advantages, however, the Republican Party has not yet achieved its long-sought goal of political realignment, as the party's best chance after the 1980 election was stalled, perhaps permanently, by the recession of 1981–82.

William Schneider, resident fellow at the American Enterprise Institute, contributing editor to the *Los Angeles Times,* the *Atlantic, National Journal,* and *Public Opinion,* and coauthor of *The Confidence Gap,* argues that two major developments during the Reagan administration—the explosive budget deficit and the enactment of the 1986 tax-reform bill—have effectively prevented Democrats from reviving coalition-style politics. In addition, "the Reagan administration has changed the political consensus in both parties," as all of the 1987 Republican candidates for president can be described as "conservatives of one sort or another," and all the Democratic candidates except Senator Paul Simon and the Reverend Jesse Jackson can be described as "pragmatists 'who wanted to try new ideas.' In the Democratic Party, pragmatism means giving up the burden of defending big government."

At the same time, however, Schneider contends that the success of the Reagan administration in cutting taxes, lowering the rate of inflation, and restoring military security have had the "unintended consequence" of curtailing popular support for the conservative agenda, as the revolt against government and against heavy tax burdens has quieted. "Republicans will learn that Reaganism is a spent political force. They will gain little by promising bold new policies aimed at continuing the Reagan revolution. The Democrats will learn that Reagan has established a new institutional order. They will gain little by promising to undo that order. The mandate of the 1988 election will most likely be a weak one, more revisionist than visionary. It will be a mandate to correct the mistakes and excesses of the Reagan revolution, not to extend the revolution or destroy it."

Robert Kuttner, economics correspondent of the *New Republic,* columnist for *Business Week* and the *Boston Globe,* and author of *Revolt of the Haves, The Economic Illusion,* and *The Life of The Party,* has written an essay that focuses on the contemporary dilemma of the Democratic Party. The internationalization of the world economy has had profound political consequences, particularly for liberal and left Western political parties. "Almost by definition, the (traditional Democratic) policies of regulation, stabilization, redistribution, the recognition of trade unions, and other tricks in the postwar Keynesian kit, operate within the nation-state," Kuttner writes. The globalization of the economy has severely undermined the effectiveness of national labor, regulatory, and tax policies to reward and protect key liberal constituencies, and the political parties using these strategies are "therefore necessarily weaker politically. This has been especially true in the United States, where our 'left' party, the Democrats, has always been ideologically squeamish about challenging the primacy of the market."

Domestically, the deficits created during the Reagan years have placed the Democratic Party in a fiscal straightjacket that, Kuttner argues, has been made even more constricting by the willingness of Democrats in Congress to accept deficit-reduction targets in 1989 and 1990 that will drastically limit the capacity of the next administration to provide government services. Kuttner contends that an alternative available to Democrats is to propose a series of tax hikes of roughly $40 billion to $45 billion, falling primarily on the rich, revenues from which should be clearly linked to programs serving broad public needs. Kuttner suggests that the mortgage interest deduction be capped at 100 percent of the value of a median-priced home, providing new revenues of $10 billion to $15 billion that would then be specifically earmarked to provide breaks for those seeking to enter the home-ownership market for the first time. Similarly, Kuttner would convert the regressive Social Security tax into a progressive levy by exempting the first $4,000 in income and then eliminating the provision that excludes from the tax all income in excess of $43,000 a year, with the additional revenues to be used specifically for job-training. "Liberalism will remain in the political desert" until it regains a commitment to serve "broad majorities of wage- and salary-earning voters, who live paycheck to paycheck, and who require economic opportunity and security that only a mixed economy and an activist government can provide. . . . Whether or not Reaganism succeeded in its professed policy goals only history can judge. But it has already been remarkably successful at paralyzing the liberal impulse."

John Judis, senior editor of *In These Times,* contributor to the *New Republic,* and author of *William F. Buckley, Jr.: Patron Saint of the Conservatives,* has written an essay arguing that conservatives have successfully used the Reagan years, first, to build a cadre of ideologically committed workers equipped to staff any future right-wing administration; and, second, to build a network of organizations prepared to maintain this cadre during Democratic administrations. "Over the last two decades, conservatives have developed a political and governing elite capable of sustaining the movement," Judis writes. "During the mid and late 1970s, lobbying groups, think tanks, and political action organizations were created; during the Reagan years, conservatives have been able to get on-the-job training in running the country. As a result, a new generation of conservative leaders has emerged, capable of filling high cabinet and White House posts in a future administration."

The failure of the Republican Party to establish strong organizations at the grass-roots level, however, has deprived the conservative movement of the kind of vital support structure that liberals and the Democratic Party have received from the strong Democratic base in state and local government. In addition, the mailing lists of the conservative movement are in no way equivalent, according to Judis, to the organizational strength provided to the left by trade unions. The emergence of the religious right is, in some respects, the conservative answer to organized labor, but the newly mobilized evangelicals and fundamentalists have demonstrated strong separatist impulses, and the agenda of the religious right has often served to divide the Republican Party.

Perhaps most important, Judis argues, have been "the signs of intellectual stagnation and drift" as "the movement's thinkers [have been] increasingly unable to reformulate their ideas in light of changed experience": the 1982 recession, the 1987 stock market crash, and the emergence of a new Soviet leadership under Mikhail Gorbachev.

David Ignatius, editor of the "Outlook" section of the *Washington Post*, and author of the novel *Agents of Innocence*, spent three years covering the Mideast for the *Wall Street Journal*. "What made the military posturing and rhetorical excesses of the Reagan era so troubling was that they were accompanied by a loss of flexibility and subtlety in foreign policy," Ignatius writes. The erosion of the capacity to negotiate to America's long-term diplomatic advantage, in conjunction with stepped-up military expenditures, was reflected most clearly in the misappropriation of the authority of the National Security Council. The inability of the NSC to fulfill its basic function—that is, to bring into the Executive Branch information necessary to the resolution of competing interagency foreign-policy objectives—not only allowed bureaucratic bickering over trade policy, the Mideast, Central America, and arms control, but even more importantly, according to Ignatius, allowed antiterrorism policy to dominate the internal workings of the Reagan administration, a policy debacle culminating in the Iran-contra scandal.

Ignatius contends that the failure of the Reagan administration to develop increasingly sophisticated diplomatic tools to deal with the Soviet Union comes at a time when the new Soviet leader, Mikhail Gorbachev, is demonstrating exceptional strength in what had traditionally been the forte of the United States: flexibility, innovation, and a sophisticated use of the media. "The arms control process was the clearest sign that a role reversal had taken place in Soviet-American relations," Ignatius writes. "By 1987, the tables had turned. Now it was the Soviets who initiated the arms-control dialogue and offered concession after concession to the sullen and unyielding Americans." In the long run, the role reversal of the two superpowers suggests that the United States may begin to lose its ability to negotiate its way through conflicts and confrontations with the Soviet Union. "The tragedy of the Reagan presidency was that in rejecting diplomacy, the administration rejected the creative application of American power. The next president should understand what Reagan did not: that military force is a costly waste of money unless it serves American diplomatic goals," Ignatius concludes.

Lincoln Caplan, a contributor to the *New Yorker* and author of *The Insanity Defense and the Trial of John W. Hinkley, Jr.* and *The Tenth Justice: The Solicitor General and the Rule of Law,* argues that certain Reagan administration policies and actions constitute a fundamental challenge to the American rule of law. This has been done by elevating the role of the president, diminishing the role of the Supreme Court, and transforming the role of each branch of government under the separation of powers as defined in the Constitution.

The most theoretically radical proposal of the administration was initiated by Attorney General Edwin Meese, himself subject to a sequence of investigations concerning allegations of wrongdoing in the conduct of his personal business affairs. Meese argued that the Supreme Court's interpretation of the Constitution does not establish a "supreme Law of the Land." Meese asserted that the president is empowered to reject Supreme Court interpretations and to treat Executive Branch views as legitimate authority in determining the meaning of the law. In practice, Caplan argues, the most dramatic challenge by the Reagan administration to the rule of law came in the Iran-contra affair, when Reagan abdicated his constitutional responsibility to "take care that the laws be faithfully executed."

A less obvious, yet equally revealing, example, according to Caplan, occurred in the transformation by the administration of the office of solicitor general from "the legal conscience of the government, and a symbol of the American commitment to the rule of law" into a partisan spokesman for the president. Caplan argues that this transformation was revealed as the office of the solicitor general aggressively pursued the Reagan administration agenda in case after case involving voting rights, abortion, school discipline, and the medical treatment of the handicapped, asking the Court to overturn established precedent, to put aside established legal reasoning, and spurning the notion of the solicitor general's traditional restraint, in order to advance toward administration-articulated goals, an objective underlying calls for "judicial restraint." Caplan writes, "As the solicitor general's story indicate[s], once the president's lawyers failed to persuade Congress to turn various parts of the Reagan agenda into law, they turned to the courts as the main forum in which to pursue [Reagan's] domestic policies."

Finally, Caplan discusses the process of appointment by the Reagan administration of judges to the federal Judiciary—by 1987, over 42 percent of the federal bench—judges selected for their conservative credentials and rated less qualified overall by the bipartisan Standing Committee on the Federal Judiciary of the American Bar Association than the appointments of previous administrations. Caplan writes: "Instead of clustering at the high end of the spectrum of quality, the Reagan judges ended up at the low end. The president's team seemed to have reached the bottom of the barrel among ideologues who were candidates for appellate judgeships. Senator Daniel Patrick Moynihan, Democrat from New York, expressed his views about judicial selection in the Reagan administration in plain terms: 'There is a word for the ideological tests for the judiciary which are seemingly now in place in the White House and the Justice Department. The word is 'corruption.' ''

Sidney Blumenthal, a staff writer for the *Washington Post* and author of *The Permanent Campaign* and *The Rise of the Counter-Establishment,* describes the weakness of cultural development during the Reagan administration. "There was no spontaneous burst of truly original artistic creation that somehow could be seen as part of the larger changes Reagan sought," Blumenthal writes. He points to the "deep cultural outpouring" that accompanied and underpinned the last large-scale American political realignment—the New Deal.

Blumenthal sees, however, a distinct Reaganite aesthetic, built upon the worship of wealth and nostalgia for a past that never happened, an aesthetic that Blumenthal calls "neokitsch"— "a video-age substitute for folk culture, yet familiar . . . a vast scavenger operation, drawing upon the images of kitsch past and present . . . ripped from the context of popular culture." Among the chief practitioners of this aesthetic were the members of the Reagan family. And the chief means of neokitsch display was the public spectacle of which the ostentatious first Reagan inaugural set the pattern. "The overriding of community by class and of the homespun by show business made the Reaganite cultural realignment mainly a matter of fantasy," Blumenthal concludes.

. . .

While the authors disagree over the specific interpretation of events, over the long-range prospects for the two parties, and over consequences of the changes wrought throughout the past eight years, together these essays attempt to provide at least a preliminary insight into the most significant American political upheaval in the past fifty years. The primary achievement of the Reagan presidency has been to change the terms of the national political debate, a shift in the public discourse that this book sets out to explore and evaluate.

THE

REAGAN

LEGACY

THE REAGAN LEGACY

THOMAS BYRNE EDSALL

The two administrations of Ronald Reagan have over-
seen a fundamental shift in the balance of power in American
politics. Campaigns and policies surrounding the Reagan presidency have accelerated the strengthening of the Republican Party
as it has taken firm root in the South and Mountain West, among
the religious, and among the affluent. Nothing has been more
important than the Reagan presidency itself in the development
of a new conservative coalition providing the first effective and
substantial challenge since the Depression to the Democratic-
liberal hegemony that had dominated the nation's political and
legislative agenda. Under the direction of the Reagan White
House, Congress enacted legislation providing conclusive evidence that the political right could break the hold of the liberal
establishment on the decisions of the federal government.

The Reagan administration has, in addition, conducted a concerted attack both on the traditional use by the Democratic Party of government to expand its constituencies, and on the party's core support groups. The administration has successfully weakened the public commitment to the use of government for broad social improvement by shifting the focus of public attention to tax burdens. The administration has permitted the size of the federal deficit to grow to levels drastically constricting future Democratic attempts to restore an agenda of expanded government intervention in domestic affairs. The wounds of an already weak labor movement have been aggravated by the federal regulatory apparatus, particularly by the decisions of the politically appointed National Labor Relations Board weakening the leverage of unions in collective bargaining. The Reagan administration has altered the climate of the civil rights debate, gutting the investigative role of the Commission on Civil Rights, retreating from affirmative-action remedies, and supporting tax breaks for schools that discriminate—all without provoking politically intolerable levels of public outcry.

In terms of the basic priorities of the federal government, the Reagan administration has succeeded in what amounts, in 1986 dollars, to an annual $70 billion transfer from domestic programs (other than Social Security and Medicare) to the military, compared with spending priorities when Reagan took office.[1]* The Reagan tax initiatives have contributed to a steady increase in after-tax income inequality which has rewarded upper-income voters, who provide the strongest Republican voting margins,

---

*See Notes in the back of the book.

with by far the largest benefits from the economic recovery following the 1981–82 recession.[2] Finally, and perhaps most importantly in terms of solidifying potential gains for a right-center coalition, the administration since the recession has benefited from an impressive and sustained economic recovery. The recovery, while uneven between regions, industries, and classes, produced over 13 million new jobs from 1981 through 1986, while job growth in Europe stagnated; a boom in the stock market, pushing the Dow Jones industrial average from 776.92 in August 1982 to an all-time high of 2,722.42 in August 1987—holding nervously at 1913.63 by mid-November 1987, after a precipitous 508-point drop on October 19, 1987; a significant improvement in real family income, which rose 10.7 percent from 1982 to 1986; and has sustained low rates of inflation, averaging 3.3 percent for the first six years of the Reagan administration.[3]

Despite these major accomplishments for a conservative government—accomplishments that will alter the future course of government more substantially than did, for example, the Republican administrations of Dwight D. Eisenhower and Richard M. Nixon—the Reagan administration and the Republican Party have failed to achieve their ultimate political goal: a realignment of the electorate. Without a realignment, there can be no durable institutionalization of conservative goals, which only the creation of a new majority in the electorate can bring about.

At the end of the Reagan administration, it is perhaps most accurate to say that this country has entered a stage of political competition best described as a form of trench warfare. The struggle exists on two different fronts. On one front, each party now has a target coalition, the possibility of putting together a winning alliance. This represents a major change from the past fifty years when the "natural" majority lay with the Democratic Party. In presidential elections, the edge has progressively shifted to the Republican Party, although the GOP advantage is far more fragile than the muscular New Deal coalition that carried the Democratic Party for half a century.

On a second front—the competition for seats in the House of Representatives, the Senate, and state legislatures—the contest between the two parties has become a struggle of small gains. Unable so far to produce decisive shifts, political competition occurs along an extended battlefront, with the resources of each side spread thinly along the entire line of conflict. Unlike a political realignment in which there are massive changes in the balance of power, the current struggle between the parties is far more incremental. Each seeks to gain specific pieces of the other's territory—a House or Senate seat, a governor's mansion, control of a state legislature, and sometimes the office of county sheriff. Each party chips away at the other, seeking to make incursions and to hold ground at every point along the battle line. Major outcomes, such as control of the United States Senate, are determined by accumulating a series of individual victories, while keeping losses to a minimum. In many ways, this amounts to a war of attrition.

The contest at both levels is a kind of rifle-and-foxhole war dominated by tactical maneuvers, as opposed to the more comprehensive and strategic politics of realignment, encompassing broad shifts in public opinion. A central strategy for victory in these trenches has become the development of "wedges" designed to break up the opposition's core of support, as in the case of Republican tactics designed to encourage tensions between black and white urban voters, or Democratic maneuvers accentuating the splits between Christian activists and Republican Party regulars.

This essay will attempt to explore the forces that have worked to prevent the Republican Party from reaching majority party status, and will examine the significant shifts in domestic politics and economics that have evolved during the Reagan administration and that will remain a part of the Reagan legacy. Not only are the Democratic and Republican parties significantly different from the parties they were in 1980, but the federal government itself has changed shape, with lasting consequences for whichever party holds power in the future.

While the Republican Party has not achieved majority status and the Democratic Party has not restored its own authority, the importance of this partisan battle cannot be underestimated. If either party succeeds in shaping a new majority coalition, that coalition will effectively define the nation's economic and social policies, determining the outcome of continuing controversies ranging from the effect of the tax system on the distribution of income to the legality of abortion. The failure to resolve the struggle between the two parties is particularly reflected in the divergent policies underlying the tax measures enacted from 1981 to 1986, involving radically different approaches to the taxation of the poor and of business.

When President Reagan took office in 1981, the material to establish a new political balance of power—a realignment—was available. Looking backward, four conditions stand out: public opinion in the years preceding the 1980 election had begun to swing toward the right, against the welfare state, and the faith of

the electorate in the Democratic Party's ability to manage the
economy and international affairs had been severely eroded.[4]
Second, the fact that the Reagan victory was accompanied by the
unexpected Republican takeover of the Senate provided the momentum essential for the administration to convert power into the
building of broad popular support for a new political and legislative agenda. It was this momentum that gave Reagan de facto
control over the Democratic-controlled House in 1981, enabling
him to demand a high degree of loyalty from the Republican
minority on intensely controversial issues—a loyalty unseen in at
least a generation—and to force into the GOP voting column
southern Democrats fearful of being swept away in a conservative
Republican tide. Third, for the decade before Reagan's election,
key leaders in the business and conservative communities had set
out to build the kind of elite structures essential to any movement
or party planning a serious challenge to the liberal establishment
that dominated the nation's capital—through the creation of
think tanks, through the financing of conservative intellectuals,
particularly economists, through the establishment of ideological
political action committees, through the production of new right-
of-center journals and publications, and through the chartering of
right-wing public-interest law firms. Finally, the growing threat
of international competition in the 1970s ended what had been
an unwritten agreement or truce between organized labor and
major American corporations that had, in the decades following
the Second World War, effectively guaranteed unions both their
jobs and steady pay hikes at or above the rate of inflation.[5] This
tacit agreement had allowed major, private-sector unions to remain economically secure participants in the Democratic coalition, a status that was severely undermined when major

corporations caught the labor movement by surprise in the mid-1970s by adopting a highly effective adversarial posture in union negotiations.

For a brief moment after the 1980 election, a plurality of the electorate signaled a willingness to ally itself with the Republican Party. Perhaps most important, both Reagan and the Republican Party had begun to shape a base of support for the formation of a new conservative majority to replace the decayed New Deal coalition: an alliance of voters dominated by the affluent—the mirror opposite of the Roosevelt coalition. This core of support was strengthened by significant numbers of white working- and lower-middle-class voters disenchanted with rising marginal tax rates, high inflation, unemployment, and soaring interest rates under Jimmy Carter's Democratic administration. Republican support was strengthened further by the growing numbers of fundamentalist Christians and Catholics politicized by the issues of abortion, women's rights, school prayer, and homosexual rights.

Despite the availability of the raw material for realignment in 1980 and 1981, the eight years of the Reagan presidency, including a landslide reelection victory, have not resulted in the achievement of this core goal. The single most important factor blunting the drive toward realignment was the recession of 1981–82, when median family income dropped sharply, the unemployment rate exceeded 10 percent, and average weekly wages fell to the lowest levels since 1961.[6]

Before the recession began in late 1981, Reagan had successfully altered the fundamental direction of domestic economic policy. He won approval of two major pieces of legislation: the Economic Recovery Tax Act of 1981, cutting taxes by $747 billion over five years, disproportionately rewarding two of his most loyal constituencies, the affluent and the business community; and the Gramm-Latta budget legislation, cutting domestic spending in a way most damaging to the recipients and professional providers of health and welfare programs, two firmly Democratic constituencies.

These administration policies, in combination with a sharp increase in defense spending, were central elements of an economic realignment strategy. Not only was the fiscal structure of the federal government altered to strengthen vital elements of the Republican coalition and to weaken the economic position of beneficiaries of Democratic programs, but the flow of federal revenues—the lifeblood of any future attempt to restore Democratic support among the voters—was severely curtailed.

While the effect of the tax cut on federal revenues remains powerful—and may prove to be the the most lasting achievement of the Reagan administration—it is hard to underestimate the detrimental consequences of the recession for the long-range political goals of Reagan and the Republican Party. The basic premise of the Republican realignment strategy was to rupture the already frayed ties between the middle class and the poor, ties that were essential to the Democratic coalition. Budget cuts were targeted toward those in the bottom fifth of the income distribution,[7] and did not threaten the middle class. The middle and working classes received a tax cut, but that tax cut—the centerpiece of the GOP's divide-and-conquer strategy—amounted to an almost imperceptible one-dollar-a-week bonus during 1981 for the average nonagricultural worker.[8] Before the larger tax cuts of the second and third years of the legislation could take effect, the recession began, forcing, at least briefly, a restoration of common interest between the poor and significant sectors of the working and middle classes. In the four months after the tax bill was passed in August 1981, the number of unemployed in the United States grew by 1.34 million, reaching the highest level—8.6 percent[9]—since the depression of the 1930s.

By the time of the next congressional elections, in November 1982, the number of the unemployed reached 11.9 million. Nearly 4 million men and women lost their jobs between the day the tax bill was passed and Election Day 1982, when the unemployment rate hit 10.7 percent—and the realignment process was brought to a dead halt.

The absolutely critical ingredient in the early phases of a realignment is the acquisition and sustained possession of power. The conversion of the electorate to a new majority party, and, equally important, to a new national agenda, requires the party seeking realignment to have the power to enact its agenda for the evaluation and approval of the public. In the three previous realignments—in 1860, 1896, and 1932—the newly dominant party held both branches of Congress for fourteen to eighteen years. This long period of control allowed the ascendant party—the GOP in 1860 and 1896, the Democrats in 1932—to put into law a comprehensive legislative program. Subsequent elections not only reaffirmed support for the party in power, but also affirmed continued backing of the goals of the party and its national agenda.

For Reagan and Republicans seeking realignment, the key task in 1981 was to build beyond the tenuous control they maintained over the Democratic House, and to move steadily toward a Republican majority, a process that had started in the mid and late 1970s. In those years, the Republican and Democratic parties had begun to change their economic shape in ways that had not been seen since the 1940s, as party allegiance on the basis of income sharply intensified, the rich becoming more Republican, the poor more Democratic.[10] Although in the 1930s and 1940s these divisions had worked to the disadvantage of the GOP, since the 1950s, median family income had grown enormously, rising from $12,341 in 1947 to $24,176 in 1980, both calculated in 1981 dollars. In other words, it had become a realistic possibility to attempt to achieve a Republican realignment in part through an economic polarization of partisan allegiance—a polarization the Reagan candidacy sharply accelerated.

In seeking to institutionalize Republican strength, however, Reagan faced a Democratic House majority far more entrenched than the Democratic and Republican House majorities of the nineteenth and early twentieth centuries. Since the New Deal, House incumbents have learned to use the perquisites of office—large staffs providing constituent services, regular newsletters and other mailings, congressionally financed trips back home each weekend—to reduce the chances of defeat in every election. The percentage of competitive House districts—those with elections settled by 5 percent or less of the vote—has been reduced from 39.2 percent in 1860, 34.5 in 1896, and 30.9 in 1932, to just 15.7 percent in 1980. In other words, it is much tougher for a resurgent minority party to take over the House than it used to be.[11]

Despite these hurdles, trends were moving in the right direction for the GOP during the 1970s. The Republican Party had successfully whittled away the overwhelming 291–144 Democratic House majority of the 1974 post-Watergate 94th Congress, cutting it back over three subsequent elections to 242–190 (with three vacancies) after the 1980 election. In 1982, however, the recession reversed this process, as Democrats increased their majority to 269–166, a gain of 27 seats. This Democratic midterm victory not only for the time being ended any possible restoration of de facto Republican control through an alliance with conservative southern Democrats, but it made the House all the more impregnable to the kind of Republican takeover essential for a realignment.

The 1981–82 recession not only restored, at least briefly, a base of public support for the Democratic Party, but it provided as well a critical boost at an important practical level: fund-raising. From 1976 through 1980, the National Republican Congressional Committee had used its ten-to-one financial advantage over the Democratic Congressional Campaign Committee to identify carefully those districts likely to produce competitive elections, particularly open seats, and then to fully finance Republican nominees. In the 1980 election, for example, the GOP financial advantage reached $34.8 million to $2.8 million in terms of money spent by the House campaign committees. With the sure knowledge that the recession would guarantee a stronger Democratic majority after the 1982 election, the Democratic Congressional Campaign Committee was able to raise significantly its level of fund-raising. From 1980 to 1982, Democratic fund-raising grew from $2.8 million to $6.5 million. By 1986, the GOP advantage was reduced from 10 to 1 to 3.2 to 1, as the Republican House committee spent $41.3 million to the Democrats' $12.6 million.[12]

Just as important as the changed ratio is the fact that the Democrats are no longer overwhelmed by the technological superiority
of the GOP, and the capacity of the GOP during the late 1970s
and early 1980s to win competitive House elections on the basis
of a massive infusion of resources unmatched by the Democrats
has been sharply curtailed.

A similar, and partially successful, Democratic attempt to re-
coup from the threat of attack by better-financed Republican
candidates competing for marginal seats can be seen in the pattern of contributions by political action committees (PACs). In
1980, PAC money, which is subject to some control and direction
by the national party structures, was far better targeted in Republican races than in Democratic contests. Republican Senate and
House candidates running either for open seats or against Democratic incumbents received significantly more money from PACs
than Republican incumbents. In contrast, only about one out of
every five dollars in PAC contributions going to Democrats went
to open-seat candidates or to candidates challenging Republican
incumbents. Since most shifts take place in the open seats and in
a few challenges to vulnerable incumbents, the 1980 patterns, if
they continued, would have pointed toward a steady chipping
away of the Democratic majority in the House. In fact, however,
Democratic-oriented PACs, particularly those associated with organized labor, have shifted their contribution patterns somewhat
toward challengers and open-seat candidates, although the Democratic Party continues to permit completely safe, entrenched incumbents to absorb disproportionately large amounts of money
from the private resources available to candidates.

■ ■ ■

The changing patterns in the use of campaign money are just a small reflection of the importance of the recession to the broad network of liberal and civil rights organizations in Washington and throughout the country. In 1981, such groups as the AFL-CIO, the Leadership Conference on Civil Rights, Citizens for Tax Justice, Americans for Democratic Action, the NAACP, the National Organization for Women, and the Children's Defense Fund were all on the ropes. The 1980 election had been widely interpreted as a repudiation of their goals, and their voice in the formulation of policy had been reduced to a whisper. The 1981–82 recession not only provided the Democratic liberal left breathing room, but more importantly gave credence to the charge that Reagan administration programs threatened the economic well-being of those in the middle and lower-middle classes and placed unfair hardships on the poor. The liberal network has not regained the political stature and muscle it had before the rise of the conservative movement in the mid and late 1970s, but it has been able to sharply decelerate, and in many cases to halt, the implementation of the conservative agenda.

These factors have contributed to the conversion of what had been the steady ascendency of the Republican Party into a kind of delicate homeostasis—that is, a balance of power between the two parties. Instead of a realignment, the Republican surge of the late 1970s and early 1980s has produced a sustained period of near parity between the Democrats and Republicans. Data provided by the Wirthlin Group,[13] which conducts 16,000 to 20,000 interviews annually for the Republican National Committee, shows some fluctuation in voters' partisan identification throughout the Reagan presidency, with the Democratic advantage growing during the recession and during the initial disclosures of the

Iran-contra scandal, and the GOP picking up strength at the height of the 1984 election between Reagan and Walter F. Mondale. In the long run, however, the Democrats appear to be holding onto a modest 4-to-8-percentage-point advantage—an edge supported by the findings of *Washington Post* / ABC and *New York Times* / CBS polls. Mondale's 59–41 loss to Reagan shows, however, that this partisan advantage is entirely unreliable in presidential elections. In addition, the Democratic edge is far smaller than the 15-to-25-point advantage held by the Democrats from the 1950s, when careful measurements first began, through most of the 1970s.

Using another measurement of the degree of realignment—a measure of political power, calculated by the number of offices each party holds—the Reagan presidency has, in one respect, achieved a significant goal: the wiping out of the Democratic gains from Watergate. As of 1987, the balance of power between the Republican and Democratic parties has returned to what it was in 1972 in state and federal governments. At perhaps the most important level, the state legislatures, where the redistricting of congressional district boundaries is decided, there were 4,471 Democrats and 2,912 Republicans in 1987, almost identical to the 4,472–3,003 balance in 1973, and a major improvement for the GOP over the 5,100–2,385 post-Watergate balance in 1975.[14] Similarly, the 259–176 Democratic House advantage in 1987 is almost identical to the 255–180 ratio in 1972, just as the 1987 Senate division of 54–46 is identical to what it was in 1972. At one level, however, the GOP has made substantial gains beyond the pre-Watergate period: the governorships. In 1972, there were 30 Democratic governors and 20 Republicans, a Democratic edge that by 1987 had fallen to just 26–24.

■ ■ ■

These figures do not measure, however, what is perhaps the most important element of partisan politics: the political strength of the vision and message of each party. While Reagan has not succeeded in establishing a new, conservative consensus along the lines initially set out after the 1980 election, the power of the national consensus that underpinned the Democratic Party's liberal, post–New Deal coalition has been weakened, if not, to some degree, dissolved.

This collapse can be most readily seen in the range of options that has been available to the Republican Party when it has held the reins of government. In 1946, the GOP took over both branches of Congress and sent a broad array of measures substantially rescinding key portions of the New Deal to the White House, where they were vetoed by President Truman; two years later in the 1948 election, this decidedly conservative Republican Congress was turned out of office, as the GOP lost seventy-five House seats and nine Senate seats. The electorate, in effect, rose up in a major repudiation of conservatism in 1948. In 1952, when the Republican Party won both Congress and the presidency, no substantial challenge to the liberal state was made under Dwight D. Eisenhower, just as there was no overarching legislative drive from the right during the administrations of Richard M. Nixon.

What all these pre-Reagan Republican developments suggest is that Democratic hegemony—the continuing power of the center-left coalition of the 1930s—held sway over the electorate, a point reinforced by the landslide defeat of Barry Goldwater in 1964. The fact that a substantial majority of the electorate remained committed to the basic values of the Democratic Party and to the evolving New Deal approach to government acted as a powerful *brake* on conservatism, severely restricting the range of options available to conservative Congresses and Republican presidents.

The new political reality demonstrated by the success of Reagan's 1981 legislative program was that the Democratic-liberal consensus—the political force that had effectively defined the permissible range of issues available for serious consideration—no longer had the power to effectively obstruct the agenda of a conservative administration. The consequences of what had been a steady erosion of support for the Democratic Party for the prior decade began to emerge in policy.

Clear evidence of the weakness of the Democratic Party had surfaced in the elections of 1968 and 1972, first with the casting of 9.9 million votes for George C. Wallace in 1968, and then with Nixon's overwhelming defeat of George S. McGovern, 47.2 million votes to 29.2 million. However, the false comfort of the anti-Republican backlash in the 1974 election in the wake of Watergate allowed Democratic leaders the delusion of majority-party status, permitting party wounds to go untreated throughout the latter half of the 1970s. Among the major misjudgments of the Democratic Party were:

  • The economic abandonment of core working and
    lower-middle-class members of the Democratic coali-
    tion, by allowing the progressive marginal rates of
    the federal income tax to place a growing burden on
    these voters; at the same time, the regressive social
    security tax bite worked up the income ladder, in a

deadly combination that set back popular support for
a redistributive tax system by cutting too deeply into
the average workers' take-home pay.
- The failure through the 1970s and early 1980s to
build a party-based fund-raising structure, on the
mistaken assumption that as the majority party, incumbent Democratic candidates would always have
their own secure sources of contributions.
- The adoption of a system of presidential nomination
procedures that magnified the weight of upper-middle-class reform voters in primaries and in caucus
selection of party nominees, while simultaneously
neglecting to develop strategies and policies to mobilize voters in the bottom third of the income distribution.
- The continued neglect of racial and economic tensions between black and white constituents, tensions
glaringly apparent not only across the South, but
also in urban and often suburban centers of the
North.
- The unwillingness of the Democratic Party in the
1970s to take the modest step of enacting labor
legislation designed to slow the continued deterioration of the union movement, a vital Democratic constituency facing internal leadership problems and a
sustained challenge from corporate interests threatened by international competition.

These misjudgments were compounded by the political consequences of the abrupt halt in economic growth that began in
1973. Median family income, which grew from $12,539 (in 1981

dollars) in 1950, to $17,259 in 1960, to $23,111 in 1970, reached $24,663 in 1973, and then stagnated through the rest of the 1970s.[15] For a Democratic Party dependent on a continually expanding economic pie to provide ever larger benefits to each of its constituencies, economic stagnation had the effect of intensifying bitter conflicts between blacks and whites, between union members and upper-middle-class liberals, and between the recipients of federal welfare programs and those who pay the taxes to finance those programs. These were the kind of conflicts that provided political openings for an increasingly conservative Republican Party. Then by the late 1970s, at the post-Watergate height of Democratic strength, with the party in full control of Congress and the presidency, the economic picture disastrously worsened: not only had income and productivity growth come to a halt, but unemployment reached the then high rate of 7 percent, interest rates exceeded 20 percent, and inflation broke into double digits.

These pressures, combined with the most effective mobilization of conservative and business forces in at least two generations, cracked open the national Democratic-liberal consensus. The enactment of the 1981 Gramm-Latta budget cuts—a substantial reduction in programs targeted toward the poor and the working poor—and the enactment of the 1981 tax bill—reversing a Democratic tradition of using the tax system for progressive redistribution of income—served as evidence of the removal of the majority liberal coalition as a brake on conservative and Republican public policy. While poll data show significant restoration of public support for government spending on social programs by 1984, and a sharp reduction in the level of support for military spending,[16] Reagan's demonstration of the weakness of Democratic political dominance will have lasting consequences for the balance of power, and for the formulation of national economic strategies.

Although Reagan has not achieved a realignment of the electorate, his two victories have produced evidence of an emerging Republican-conservative electoral coalition fully equipped to compete with the depleted Democratic-liberal coalition. The emergence of this competing coalition has altered the relationship between the Democratic and Republican parties from what Samuel Lubell[17] described in 1955 as a battle between a dominant "sun"—the Democratic Party—and a subordinate "moon"—the GOP—into the sharply polarized competition of contemporary politics. In the elections of 1980 and 1984, Reagan has twice demonstrated the political muscle of a Republican coalition that capitalizes on divisions between those on the top of the income distribution and those on the bottom.

The changing composition of the Republican and Democratic parties in recent years can be seen by comparing the makeup of the supporters of each party in 1956 and in 1984. From 1956, when Dwight D. Eisenhower won a second term, to 1984, when Reagan won a second term, the two parties became increasingly polarized by income. In 1956, the Democratic partisan advantage was roughly the same across all income groups, ranging from a 22-to-13-point edge over the GOP, except among the most affluent top 10 percent of the population, who favored the Republican Party by a 22-point margin. By 1984, this pattern had shifted radically to produce a direct relationship between income and partisan allegiance, shown in the following table:

TABLE 1.

Party Allegiance by Income[18]

The Democratic Party's percentage advantage (+) or disadvantage (−) among different groups in 1956 and 1984:

	1956	1984
The affluent (91%–100%)	− 22	−33
The upper middle class (61%–90%)	+13	o
The middle class (31%–60%)	+17	+6
The working and lower middle classes (11%–30%)	+22	+29
The very poor (the bottom 10%)	+18	+36

The emergence of intensified voting on the basis of income began in the mid-1970s, but it was sharply accelerated by the Reagan candidacies and by Reagan economic policies, each of which encouraged the conversion of partisan conflict into an increasing, if modest by European standards, contest between the top and bottom of the income distribution.

In terms of altering the balance of power in this country, the most important aspect of the new Reagan-Republican coalition is that it can produce a winning combination of voters. It stands in direct contrast to the original Democratic Depression-era coalition, which took an almost identical division of the electorate by income to repeatedly defeat the Republican Party. The political strength in the 1980s of a economically top-heavy alliance has been demonstrated by Reagan's victories in 1984, and more importantly, by the fact that Republican gains at all levels—for state and federal offices, and not just the presidency—were highest when income polarization was most intense. Both the 1980 and 1984 elections, when the economic divisions between Republicans and Democrats were strongest, produced Republican gains at the grass-roots level of politics, in races for the House of Representatives (a 32-seat pickup in 1980, 16 seats in 1984) and in races for state legislative seats (a total gain of 188 in 1980 and 315 in 1984).

The fragility of the Republican coalition is reflected, however, in the election of 1986, when, according to data from the National Election Studies, there was a significant decline in voting and in partisan allegiance on the basis of income. The figures in Table 1 show that in 1984 the difference between the Democratic allegiance of the very poor and the affluent was a huge 69 percentage points (+36 for the poor, −33 for the affluent). By the 1986 election, the split between rich and poor fell to 51 points (+40 for the poor, −11 for the rich), according to the National Election Studies.[19] More important, the decline in income polarization coincided with Republican losses in the Senate (8 seats), the House (6 seats) and state legislatures (185 seats). The 51-point spread in 1986 was, however, significantly larger than the 40-point spread in 1956, and it is clear that this economic division remains an important element of the politics of the 1980s. In addition, the partisan spread between the bottom 30 percent of the income distribution and those in the upper middle class (the 61st through the 90th percentiles), which had grown from 6 points in 1956 to 31 points in 1984, remained as wide in 1986.

The GOP's advantage among the well-to-do has additional political significance because of the long-range trends in voter turnout. Since 1960 and 1964, the disparity in voter-turnout rates
between the top third of the income distribution and those in the
bottom third has grown from a roughly 25-point difference to a
40-point spread.[20] In other words, just those voters on whom the
Democratic Party has come increasingly to depend for large mar-
gins—those in the bottom third of the income distribution—are
those whose turnout rates have dropped the most, while the
affluent, who have become increasingly Republican, have continued to go to the polls at relatively high levels. A March 1987
national poll conducted by the *Washington Post* and ABC News,
showed, for example, that 45 percent of the voters who identify
with the Republican Party come from the high-turnout group
making thirty thousand dollars a year or more, while only 31
percent of the Democrats come from this group. In contrast, the
Democratic Party receives 42 percent of its support from the
income group that turns out at the lowest levels, those making less
than twenty thousand dollars a year, while the Republican Party
receives only 28 percent of its support from this group.

In describing the evolving shape of the two parties, the most
important trend is probably the intensification of income-based
partisan allegiance, because this kind of split points toward the
probability of the two parties adopting increasingly divergent
economic programs. At the same time, however, the composition
of the Republican and Democratic parties has been changing in
a number of other significant ways, including shifts in religious
and regional makeup.

■   ■   ■

Religion has provided the Republican Party with a vehicle to expand support into traditionally Democratic middle-and lower-middle-income constituencies, particularly in the South. Between 1980 and 1984, the partisan identification of born-again Christians shifted by 19 percentage points toward the GOP, reflecting what has been a realignment within this constituency. *New York Times* exit polls show that born-again Christians went from a 40–37 Democratic edge in 1980 (with 23 percent independent) to a 45–29 Republican edge in 1984. When measured in terms of actual votes cast in 1976 and 1984, the shift among these conservative white Christians is more extreme. In 1976, they supported Jimmy Carter, the Democratic nominee, by a 56–44 margin; in 1984, they backed Reagan by an 81–19 margin, a shift of about 8 million votes in eight years.

Just as the GOP has been making these huge gains, it is these same evangelical and fundamentalist churches that have experienced by far the largest increases in membership, across the nation. While all the mainline churches, including the United Presbyterians, the United Church of Christ, and the United Methodist Church, suffered losses of 8 to 21 percent in their memberships from 1970 to 1980, evangelical and fundamentalist churches flowered, Assemblies of God growing by 70 percent, Seventh-Day Adventists by 36 percent, and the Southern Baptist Convention by 16 percent.[21]

The Southern Baptist Convention, which in 1970 replaced the United Methodist Church as the single largest Protestant denomination in the United States, offers a case study in the growing institutionalization of the Republican Party within key religious denominations. For the past decade, conservative believers in what is called the "absolute inerrancy" of the Bible have conducted a bitter and successful fight to take over the denomination, winning the presidency of the Baptist convention with such committed leaders from the political right as Charles F. Stanley, Adrian Rogers, and James T. Draper, Jr. As the top leadership of the denomination has moved firmly into conservative hands, the allegiance of Southern Baptist ministers has shifted sharply toward the GOP. Surveys of the denomination's clergy by James L. Guth of Furman University in South Carolina found that the ministers went from a 41–29 Democratic edge in 1981 to a 66–26 Republican edge in 1984.[22]

Just as Republican strength is growing among both the leadership and the membership of the white evangelical and fundamentalist churches, a growing ideological split has emerged between the leadership of the more traditional, mainline churches and their members. In the elections of 1980 and 1984, Episcopalians, Lutherans, Methodists, and Presbyterians, for example, all cast stronger votes for Reagan than the public at large. During those same four years, however, the Washington office of the National Council of Churches, the principal lobbying arm of the mainline churches, conducted what A. James Reichley of the Brookings Institution described as "a steady barrage of opposition and criticism at most aspects of the administration's program. In May 1981, the governing board of the NCC issued a manifesto charging that the administration's policies represented 'a reversal of direction for this country as a whole, and [threatened] the vision of America as a model and embodiment of a just and humane society.' "[23]

Together these trends—the general shift to the right among the white evangelical churches and the splits within the mainline churches—have produced a new dividing line in the electorate: the "religiosity" of the voter. While a relatively unimportant factor in calculating the likelihood of Republican or Democratic allegiance from 1952 (when sophisticated polling began) through 1976, church attendance has over the last decade become an increasingly accurate measure of the probability of party allegiance. In a series of calculations, Frederick T. Steeper of the Republican polling firm Market Opinion Research and John R. Petrocik of UCLA found that by 1986, regular churchgoers, excluding blacks, were 22 percentage points more Republican than Democratic, while white nonchurchgoers were 13 points more Democratic than Republican.[24] Among white, Anglo-Saxon northern Protestants, for example, they found that among those who go to church once a week, the GOP enjoyed a 43-point edge, while among those who never go to church, the Democrats have a 9-point margin. Similarly, among Catholics, those who never go to church are Democratic by a margin of 42 points, while those who go regularly are Republican by a 10-point margin. The same patterns hold true for white southerners and, to a lesser extent, union members.

The affluent and the religious together form the fragile core of the new Reagan-Republican coalition, an alliance that a number of Republican strategists are seeking to institutionalize in order that it might act as a consistent counterbalance to what remains of the Democratic New Deal coalition: blacks; union members; those in the bottom third of the income distribution; Jews; urban voters in the North; and, in declining numbers, Catholics. The Republican coalition has, in addition, been strengthened—particularly in presidential contests—by the emergence of an increasingly muscular GOP in the South and the Mountain West.

Although far more attention has focused on the decline of the

Democratic Party in the South, it is in the Mountain West—
Arizona, Colorado, Utah, New Mexico, Nevada, Idaho, Montana,
and Wyoming—that, since the mid-1970s, a regional Republican
realignment has already taken place. Firmly Democratic during
the Depression, the Mountain West has now become the most
Republican section of the country. "Even though the Mountain
West has only about 5% of the national population, it elects 16
Senators, and change in the regional Senate delegation since
1974 can account entirely for creating the 1980–1986 Republican [Senate] majority," two experts on the region, Peter F. Galderisi and Michael S. Lyons, have written.[25] None of the eight
mountain states has voted for a Democratic presidential candidate
since 1964.

While these states have only 5 percent of the population, they
produce a solid block of 40 electoral votes. This means that the
Republican Party currently goes into any election with a base of
15 percent of the 270 electoral votes required to win the presidency. Without a major upheaval, these eight states have all the
earmarks of an impregnable Republican bastion in presidential
elections, a base that the Democratic Party can in no way match.

To this base of eight states, there are fifteen more that have
voted Republican in all five presidential elections since 1968, and
together these twenty-three states have 202 electoral votes. This
calculation, moreover, underestimates the GOP's electoral college
strength, because these twenty-three states exclude every southern state except Virginia, the only state below of the Mason-Dixon
line that did not support Jimmy Carter in 1976. "It can be argued
that the GOP holds a modern electoral college base of 202 electoral votes," Democratic pollster Patrick H. Caddell has written.
"The Democratic task is staggering. To win, we must win 4 of
every 5 remaining electoral votes, from among states like Texas,

Florida, Ohio, Michigan, Wisconsin, Connecticut, Maine and the entire South. If the Republican base held, the [Democratic] loss of Texas, Florida, Washington and Connecticut would result in [Democratic] defeat, even if Democrats carried every other state."26

In one respect, Caddell's assessment is overly pessimistic for the Democratic Party: many of the states that have voted consistently Republican in presidential contests from 1968 through 1984 are in fact showing signs of moving toward the Democratic Party in contests for lower offices, and are clearly legitimate targets for future Democratic presidential candidates. Such states as Iowa, Maine, and Vermont, once GOP bastions, have moved steadily away from the Republican Party, with the Democratic Party controlling each of these three state's legislatures in 1987. Other states that fall into Caddell's "[Republican] modern electoral college base" include Illinois, New Jersey, Oregon, and California, each of which has a strong Democratic voting base, and none of which is treated as automatically Republican by strategists for either party.

Conversely, Caddell's assessment downplays the deep shifts in partisan allegiance in the South, shifts that are making it increasingly difficult for a Democratic presidential candidate to win such key states as Florida or Texas, with 21 and 29 electoral votes respectively. As of 1987, white Southerners split their partisan allegiance right down the middle between the two parties, according to the Wirthlin Group.27 Registration figures downgrade Republican strength, although they reflect general trends, and in Florida from 1980 to 1984, GOP registration grew twice as fast as Democratic registration: 466,000 new GOP voters to 226,000 new Democrats. While most state legislatures were shifting toward the Democratic Party, the Florida State Senate shifted toward the GOP, as the Democratic majority fell from 30–10 to 25–15, enough to sustain a veto by the newly elected Republican governor, Robert Martinez. Similarly, the Texas House has gone from a 115–35 Democratic majority in 1983 to a 94–56 Democratic majority in 1987. In terms of partisan identification, what had been a consistent 60–10 advantage for the Texas Democratic Party from 1952 to 1972 had become a modest 4-point, 33–29, Democratic edge by the winter of 1987.[28]

These problems for the Democratic Party have been compounded by growing evidence of Republican Party strength in white working-class neighborhoods of northern cities, once the core of the New Deal coalition. Many of these communities have begun to vote regularly for Republican presidential candidates. The more threatening development to the Democratic Party, however, is the recent willingness of white voters in certain row-house, gritty city neighborhoods to elect Republicans to the state legislature and city council, a phenomenon unheard of a decade ago. In 1987, almost all local offices in northeast Philadelphia—a community of policemen, carpenters, retired union members, firemen, and teachers—are Republican, and the GOP tide has moved down to the city's far tougher and poorer river wards, where the representative in the State House is a Republican. In the white working-class neighborhoods of west Chicago, both the 24th Senate District and the 7th Senate District are represented by Republicans, Robert Raica and Walter Dudycz, respectively. In Dearborn and other white working-class suburbs of Detroit, the local Republican Party has begun to win offices that were conceded without serious challenge to the Democrats in the early 1970s.

In all three of these cities, momentum behind the GOP in such white neighborhoods is being driven in part by the election of black Democratic mayors. "You can't tell people in these river wards how to vote. They go in and pull white, white, white," a Democratic organizer and bartender in the Kensington section of Philadelphia, commented.[29] Stanley B. Greenberg, president of the Analysis Group, a Democratic polling organization that conducted a series of focus groups in 1985 in the white blue-collar suburbs of Detroit, wrote: "For these white suburban residents, the term 'blacks' and Detroit are interchangeable: Detroit is just 'one big ghetto.' For them, blacks mean 'crime,' above all, but also 'dirty' and 'corrupt.' . . . In each of the focus groups, we read out a statement from Robert Kennedy that called on Americans to honor special obligations to black citizens who lived through the slave experience and racial discrimination. The participants rejected the concept without qualification and without hesitation: 'That's bull—.' 'No wonder they killed him.' 'I can't go along with that.' . . . The race question has been deeply assimilated, as it defines attitudes toward their neighborhood, Detroit, the Democratic Party, Democratic themes and the government. These Democratic defectors believe government has personally intervened to block their opportunities. Appeals to fairness, opportunity, etc. are now defined in racial terms that have been stripped of any progressive content."[30] The depth of such ugly and destructive racism is a fact of life for Democratic organizers attempting to rebuild a winning coalition.

It is in just these kinds of communities that the power of one of the mainstays of the Democratic Party, organized labor, is declining. The erosion of the union movement, particularly the private-sector union movement, began well before Reagan took office, but during his tenure union membership has nose-dived. In 1954, organized labor represented 34.7 percent of the wage and salary work force, a percentage that has been declining steadily. By the start of the Carter administration, the percentage had dropped to 23.8, where it held with modest fluctuation through 1980. Since then, the downward spiral has accelerated, with union membership dropping to 17.5 percent of the work force by 1986, the lowest level in 50 years.[31] Union losses were highest from 1980 to 1985 in manufacturing, mining, and construction, where organized labor lost 2.2 million jobs, along with an estimated loss of 400,000 union jobs in airlines and trucking, as government deregulation encouraged the growth of nonunion competition.

Just as importantly, the composition of the unionized workforce is shifting from the industrialized private sector to the public and service sectors. From 1975 to 1985, the United Steelworkers lost 490,000 members, a 46 percent drop; for the International Ladies' Garment Workers Union, the 42 percent decline of 152,000 workers was almost as extreme; membership in the International Association of Machinists and Aerospace Workers dropped by 260,000, and the United Automobile Workers fell by 176,000. The labor organizations showing growing membership are generally limited to the government and service sectors: the American Federation of State, County, and Municipal Employees; the Service Employees; the American Federation of Teachers; and the Communications Workers.[32]

For the Democratic Party, these shifts within the union movement mean the loss of an institutionalized base of support within white working-class communities. From 1983 to 1985, the union movement as a whole lost 721,000 members, all of whom were white. For a party attempting to reestablish a national coalition, these losses are very damaging. Just as the Democratic Party has lost the once reliable South while the GOP has established a firm beachhead in the Mountain West, the Republican Party has been gaining an institutionalized avenue to certain white voters through the fundamentalist and evangelical churches while the Democratic Party has been losing a prime mechanism, the union hall, to reach its white constituents. For those in the midst of political campaigns, the availability of sure bases of support can be critical: at moments when the campaign is in trouble, there are resources and committed workers who will stay the course; when the campaign is moving successfully, there are reliable pillars on which to construct a broader coalition. In this respect, the long-range trends are problematic for the Democratic Party.

The acceleration of the decline of the union movement is one of the major political successes of the Reagan administration, as the administration has used the power of the presidency and of the federal regulatory apparatus to chop away at organized labor. The tenor of the antiunion drive was set by Reagan himself when he fired 11,345 striking air-traffic controllers in 1981, setting an example that would be widely followed in the private sector, where employer-ordered lockouts, challenges to union collective-bargaining rights, and the hiring of nonunion workers during labor disputes proliferated during his administration. The under-mining of labor was then intensified by deregulation, and by decisions of regulatory boards and agencies as diverse as the Federal Maritime Commission and the National Labor Relations Board, although the NLRB has played perhaps the key role. During the Reagan administration, the NLRB has issued rulings that allow employers to hire temporary nonunion workers during lockouts, that facilitate the relocation of unionized plants to nonunion facilities while the union contract remains in effect, that restrict the power of unions to penalize members who resign during strikes, and that increase the latitude of employers to refuse to take back workers accused of misconduct during strikes. The effect of all these rulings has been to weaken severely the collective-bargaining leverage of unions.[33]

The Reagan administration's calculated efforts to weaken labor are a prime example of a comprehensive drive to use the powers of the federal government to achieve what can best be called a *forced realignment.* On other fronts with the same objective, there have been a series of continuing legal fights over, for example, the repeated efforts of the Office of Management and Budget to exclude from the beneficiaries of the $120 million Combined Federal Campaign charity collection such Democratic-leaning or left-of-center organizations as the NAACP Legal Defense Fund and the Planned Parenthood Federation, and to add such GOP-leaning organizations as the National Right to Work Committee and the National Rifle Association. A small sampling of the use of the government to encourage the development of the political right includes awards and grants by the Justice Department, the National Endowment for the Humanities, and the State Department to such conservative groups as the Shavano Institute for National Leadership, a division of Hillsdale College; the evangelical Protestant Institute on Religion and Democracy, and to the dean of Jerry Falwell's Liberty University for the development of a set of volumes for a course on the Constitution.[34]

While the political and substantive consequences are far harder to measure than in the case of organized labor, the administration has conducted a series of attacks on the traditional legal remedies in civil rights and affirmative-action cases that appear designed to strengthen Republican support among whites, while weakening mechanisms blacks have used to gain economic power. In both Indianapolis and Buffalo, the Justice Department has filed suit seeking to end the use of hiring goals to correct for past discrimination. In federal lawsuits filed against the cities of Washington and Birmingham, the department charged that the two cities discriminated against white men by setting hiring goals for blacks and women.

These lawsuits parallel the political tactic of using "wedge" issues to split the Democratic coalition, one of the best examples of which is a battle over symbols in South Carolina. "Nothing reflects better the problems of white Democrats than the Confederate flag flying over the State House," said John Courson, a state senator from Columbia, South Carolina, and member of the Republican National Committee. Republicans, he said, watch with delight as black state legislators in South Carolina attempt to force roll-call votes on legislation removing the flag, while the white Democratic leadership pulls out the stops to prevent a tally in which members would have a public record on the issue. For white Democrats in South Carolina, voting to keep the flag flying threatens black support in primary elections, while voting to prohibit the flag threatens white support in the general election. "There is no way for a white Democrat to come out ahead on the issue," Courson noted.

While many of the larger forces in society are working to the benefit of the GOP—the long-term deterioration of unions; the shift from traditional manufacturing to technology and service jobs; continued racial tensions within the Democratic coalition;

the emergence of bedrock Republicanism in the Mountain States; the inherent Republican advantage as the core of campaigning shifts from traditional organization to fund-raising; the sustained economic expansion and growth in the number of jobs after 1982—there are also a number of factors working to sustain the competitiveness of the Democratic Party. Perhaps the most important of these are the fissures that have emerged in the Republican coalition, schisms that are functioning to place the Democratic Party on roughly equal footing in terms of the divisive campaigning designed to undermine the opposition's support that dominates politics when neither party has a clear majority.

The sharpest of these divisions is between Republican Party regulars and newly mobilized white Christians, whose votes are critical to future GOP candidates. The angry and bitter contests in 1987 and 1988 between supporters of Vice President George Bush and the charismatic and evangelical Christians backing the Reverend Marion G. (Pat) Robertson during the primary duels in such states as South Carolina, Michigan, and Iowa point toward an internal Republican split that may well get tougher and tougher to patch over without a Ronald Reagan at the top of the ticket.

At a more subtle level, there has been a substantial deterioration of the coalition that in 1980 and 1981 gave vitality to the candidacies of Ronald Reagan and other Republicans, and then to the Reagan administration during its first year in office. The business community, united in the late 1970s and early 1980s to a degree unprecedented in generations, has since been split by the trade issue between exporters and importers, and by the tax bill of 1986, with conflicts occurring between manufacturing corporations that pay low rates of taxation and a wide range of service, high-tech, wholesale, and retail industries that pay relatively high tax rates. Not only did business shift its campaign-contribution pattern in 1980 sharply in favor of the Republican Party, but the larger political mobilization of stockholders and mid-level management provided a powerful lobbying force in behalf of the 1981 budget and tax bills, flooding congressional offices with pro-Reagan mail and swamping the phone lines to Capitol Hill on the eve of key votes. The more recent legislative agenda has, however, divided the business community, ending almost ten years of what had been a near-monolithic force in Washington. "The leadership of the [Business] Roundtable really split on the [1986] tax issue. . . . When business speaks with two voices, it tends not to be heard," said Irving Shapiro, a former head of the organization of Fortune 500 companies and former chairman of Du Pont. "We've entered a period where economic forces are producing tremendous strains on business," said Lawrence O'Brien, a key lobbyist for the network of high-tax corporations supporting the 1986 tax bill. "You can no longer come up with an effective consensus."[35]

Furthermore, the collapse of the domestic oil industry has meant the drying up of a major source of campaign money for conservative Republicans seeking to challenge incumbent liberal Democrats, and for the network of right-wing PACs and foundations that had provided cash and intellectual support to the conservative movement. In the 1980 Republican takeover of the Senate, a vital ingredient of some of the razor-thin GOP victories was the willingness of the independent oil community to provide large contributions early in the race. This early money was a key factor in the defeat of such Democrats as Senators Frank Church of Idaho, George McGovern of South Dakota, Birch Bayh of Indiana, and Gaylord Nelson of Wisconsin.[36] In the years since then, the combination of the decline of the oil industry's ability to make contributions and splits within the larger business community have resulted in a significant lessening of the commitment of business to the Republican Party, at least in terms of campaign contributions. During 1979–80, corporate PACs gave nearly twice as much money to Republicans as Democrats, $12.29 million to $6.87 million; by 1985–86, the GOP advantage had declined, approaching just 3–2, or $30.2 million to $19.2 million,[37] as the total level of contributions from these PACs has nearly tripled.

Just as business is no longer a united political force, the network of conservative PACs—the cutting edge of the political drive to the right—has been unable to generate new agendas, and its financial base of support has been collapsing. The National Conservative Political Action Committee (NCPAC) has been in a tailspin—after gaining a reputation as a killer of liberal giants in 1980, when its negative ads were credited with contributing to the defeat of a host of Democratic senators. After raising a total of $19.5 million in 1983–84, NCPAC revenues fell to $9.3 million in 1985–86, and, for the first six months of 1987, just $1.1 million. At the same time, NCPAC has been unable to dent a massive, $3.9 million debt, over $1 million of which is owed to Richard A. Viguerie, the conservative specialist in direct mail. Viguerie, in turn, has put his Virginia offices up for sale and has sold off his magazine, *Conservative Digest,* in order to stay afloat. From 1985 through 1987, there have been at least eight suits and countersuits filed in the Alexandria, Virginia, Federal Court between conservative organizations, their vendors and their fundraisers, accusing each other of failing to pay bills or to live up to contractual agreements. The Christian Voice Moral Government Fund by 1987 had ceased to actively raise money; Howard Phillips, head of the Conservative Caucus, cut back sharply on raising money for his PAC in order to maintain adequate funds for his lobbying and educational wings; the Fund for a Conservative Majority was in court fighting commercial fund-raisers.

The financial problems of the right wing in 1987 were, in part, replicated by a sharp downturn in financial support flowing to the major Republican Party organizations, the Republican National Committee (RNC) and the Republican National Senatorial and Congressional committees. At these three committees, contributions fell to $33.9 million during the first six months of 1987, compared to $55.1 million for the comparable period in 1985, a 39 percent drop. At the RNC, the cash shortfall in 1987 forced the firing of forty staffers and the termination of contracts with ten politically influential consultants.[38]

Conservative and Republican financial difficulties point to a much larger problem: the political right has experienced major difficulties in maintaining a broad-based political agenda that both encourages continuing participation by hard-core activists, particularly donors, and functions to broaden and strengthen the larger coalition of prospective supporters in the electorate at large. The issues driving the antitax movement have for the time being largely run out of gas, although advocacy of new or higher taxes remains a high-risk political gamble. The right-to-life movement is torn by internal dissension, and it has become clear that Congress will not enact legislation or a constitutional amendment barring abortion. Public opinion in the years 1984 through 1987 took a left turn from the trends in 1980–81, as support for military spending has dropped sharply, while support for federal spending on such domestic programs as welfare, education, and minority assistance has moved back up to the levels of the mid and early 1970s.[39]

After running into a series of roadblocks in Congress starting in 1982, the Reagan administration by 1987 was looking for long-lasting institutionalization of its conservative agenda through the creation of a conservative majority on the Supreme Court, a step that would give additional strength to Reagan's success in appointing conservative jurists at all levels of the federal judiciary. This tactic, however, raises the danger of a long-term hazard to conservatism. One of the major problems of the liberal agenda in the 1960s and early 1970s was that significant elements of the agenda were initiated and enforced through the courts, often lacking the critically important endorsement that only a vote by the elected Congress can provide. Busing, the prohibition on capital punishment from 1972 to 1976, the continuing prohibition on school prayer, the *Roe* v. *Wade* abortion decision, were all major social policies adopted outside of traditional democratic procedures, that is, without a vote by the public's elected representatives. It can be argued that these decisions contributed mightily to the explosion of support for conservative causes in the 1970s. As the Reagan administration sought in the 1980s to achieve such goals as a reversal of *Roe* v. *Wade* and an end to affirmative-action remedies in discrimination cases, through the same judicial mechanism used by liberals in the past—judicial appointments— without legislative action by Congress, it provoked the kind of reaction from the left, in the case of the Bork nomination, for example, that at least temporarily breathed new life into the Democratic Party. Such reactions are likely to be all the more severe if a court-imposed set of conservative policies is not accompanied by at least a partial revival of Republican strength in the House and Senate.

. . .

In the long run, however, the most important factor determining
the outcome of the struggle between the two parties is likely to
be the economy. There is no doubt in my mind that if the enactment of the 1981 budget and tax bills had not been followed by
a recession, but instead by the sustained economic growth that
extended from the end of 1982 to at least late 1987, there would
have been a genuine realignment. Taken alone, the first four of
those recovery years—data is not yet available for 1987 and
1988—produced a 9.6 million increase in the number of jobs;
growth in the median family income from $26,116 to $28,906 (in
1985 dollars); a lowering of the rate of inflation from 13.3 percent
at the end of the Carter administration to an average of 3.3
percent from 1982 to 1986; an expansion of the gross national
product from $3.17 trillion to $3.68 trillion (in 1982 dollars); and
productivity growth of 1.9 percent annually.[40] Without the recession, these kinds of economic trends would have served as a
powerful locomotive pulling the GOP over the top to majority
status.

In fact, however, these boom years cannot be treated in isolation, nor can they be kept distinct from some highly complex
economic developments over the course of the entire Reagan
administration. One of the strongest trends through both the
1981–82 recession and the subsequent recovery has been a sharp
increase in income inequality, a development that appears to have
been exacerbated by changes in the tax system. The following two
tables based on annual surveys conducted by the Bureau of the
Census trace patterns in the distribution of income in 1980 and
1985 for all households, before taxes:

TABLE **2.**

Shares of Pretax Income[41]

Shares of *pretax* income for each quintile (blocks of 20 percent of the population) and for the top 5 percent in 1980 and 1985:

	1980	1985
The top 5 percent	16.5%	17.6%
The top fifth	44.2%	45.7%
The fourth fifth	24.8%	24.4%
The third fifth	16.8%	16.3%
The second fifth	10.2%	9.7%
The bottom fifth	4.1%	3.9%

While the shift in the percentages may seem small, in fact the shift from 16.5% to 17.6% of total income going to the top 5 percent of the income distribution is a shift of $30.3 billion. From another angle, the top 20 percent of the population received roughly $44 billion more in 1985 than it would have if the income distribution had remained what it was in 1980, while the bottom 80 percent of the income distribution received roughly $44 billion less than if the distribution of pretax income had remained the same.

There is an extensive, conflicting and unresolved debate over the causes of this growing pretax income disparity.[43] Recessions in-

TABLE 3.

Changes in Pretax Income[42]

Changes in median household *pretax* income for various segments of the population from 1980 to 1985, all in 1985 dollars:

	1980	1985	% Change	$ Change
The top 10% (the well-to-do)	$66,462	$72,183	+8.6%	+$5,721
The top 40% (the upper middle class and the rich)	$41,163	$72,183	+6.1%	+$2,525
The 41st through 80th percentiles (the middle and upper middle classes)	$28,075	$28,973	+3.2%	+$898
The 21st through 60th percentiles (the working and middle classes)	$18,446	$18,811	+2.0%	+$365
The bottom 40% (the poor and the working class)	$9,768	$9,954	+1.9%	+$186

crease income inequality by putting a disproportionate number of those in the lower 40 percent of the income distribution out of work, while recoveries tend to reduce inequality by putting those same people back to work and raising their incomes. The baby boom has in recent years resulted in larger numbers of young workers, whose income tends to be lower than average, therefore increasing the number of households with low incomes. At the top end, household income has increased sharply with the growing number of wives entering the work force. Conversely, divorce tends to sharply lower women's income, and the growing incidence of female-headed households has increased the number of families living on small incomes. The shift from manufacturing to service-industry jobs has altered the structure of salaries, although those who peruse the literature will see that scholars have come to very different conclusions using the same data.

While there is a substantial debate over the causes of growing pretax inequality, the census data provides strong evidence that tax changes enacted during the Reagan administration have significantly added to this growing inequality. Tables 4 and 5 describe patterns of income inequality in much the same way as in Tables 2 and 3, but in this case, instead of pretax income of households, the subject is after-tax income. What these tables show is that inequality is significantly larger when measured in terms of after-tax income rather than pretax income. For those in the bottom 40 percent, 1980 to 1985 were years of income stagnation. In contrast, for those in the top 40 percent, there was a significant $2,262, or 7.2 percent, increase in real, after-tax income—enough, in effect, to be able to pay $188 more a month in mortgage payments. For those in the top 5 percent, the $5,418, or 11.5 percent, increase in spendable income is the equivalent of an additional $451 a month.

These income patterns are part of a highly complex—and politically inconclusive—economic picture which, in the long run, will

TABLE 4.

Changes in Shares of After-Tax Income[44]

Changes in the shares of *after-tax* income from the five quintiles of the income distribution and for the top 5 percent in 1980 and 1985:

	1980	1985
The top 5 percent	14.1%	15.5%
The top fifth	40.6%	42.6%
The fourth fifth	25.1%	24.7%
The third fifth	17.9%	17.2%
The second fifth	11.6%	11.0%
The bottom fifth	4.9%	4.6%

decisively influence which party will edge ahead of the other, and which will have the best shot at achieving majority status. It is possible to construct scenarios that work to the advantage of either party.

Under a Democratic scenario, for example, the failure of those in the bottom half of the income distribution to share fully in economic success, and the growing difficulty of middle- and lower-middle-class families in achieving what has come to be thought of as a traditional middle-class standard of living, will result in a restoration of support for government intervention to ensure both expanded availability of housing and vastly improved education and training to provide access to better jobs. The likelihood of such a restoration may sharply increase if the stock market

TABLE 5.

Changes in After-Tax Income[45]

Changes in median household *after-tax* income for different segments of the population from 1980 to 1985, all in 1985 dollars:

	1980	1985	% Change	$ Change
The top 10% (the most affluent)	$47,122	$52,540	+11.5%	+$5,418
The top 40% (the upper middle class and the rich)	$31,334	$33,596	+7.2%	+$2,262
The 41st through 80th percentiles (the middle and upper middle classes)	$22,417	$23,258	+3.8%	+$841
The 21st throught 60th percentiles (the working and middle classes)	$15,599	$15,868	+1.7%	+$269
The bottom 40% (the poor and the working class)	$8,960	$8,925	−0.4%	−$35

crisis of late 1987 turns out to be a precursor to a recession. The years from 1982 to 1986 produced a significant increase in median family income, but this is a gain from a recession base; 1986 family income was below what it was in 1973, 1978, and 1979. "In the decades prior to the 1970s, children expected early on

to live better than their parents. Such is not now the case," Frank
S. Levy and Richard C. Michel have written.[46] "[Consider] a
young man who was 30 in 1949. On average he was earning
$11,924 per year (in 1984 dollars), an apparently modest figure.
But with the housing prices and interest rates of the time, he
could carry the median-priced home for about 14 percent of his
gross monthly pay. And his wages were far from their peak. Over
the next ten years, his annual salary would rise by 63 percent in
real terms. . . . For a 30-year-old man in 1973, carrying charges
for the median-priced home would have absorbed 21 percent of
monthly pay (up from 14 percent). More important, over the next
decade his annual salary (adjusted for inflation) did not rise at all.
. . . Last year [1984], a typical 30-year-old man who purchased
a median-priced home would have had to devote 44 percent of his
gross income to carrying charges." At the same time, the income
of young heads of families—a key target group for the GOP—has
been falling during the Reagan years, a process that has resulted
in a significant decline in home-ownership among couples between the ages of 25 and 35 from 1980 through 1986.[47]

These kinds of findings have been used by Democratic leaders
and policy analysts to argue that the growing economic pressures
on those in middle- and lower-income categories have the potential to result in an economically driven reunification of the poor
and the middle class, in a coalition providing a strong base of
support for the Democratic Party. This kind of argument works
best, however, when a national recession or significant slowdown
functions to drive home the common interest of the poor and the
working and lower middle class in a government that provides
services and programs for those thrown out of work or threatened
by unemployment.

There is an equally strong, if not stronger, argument to be made that income-distribution trends will lead toward a strengthened coalition on the right. According to this scenario, changing patterns in the distribution of after-tax income have clearly served to solidify the Republican Party's base of support in the top 40 percent of the income distribution, just those voters who turn out in the highest numbers on Election Day. While the gains for those in the middle of the income distribution have not been as large as for those at the top, those in the middle have seen a modest increase in household income, which is more than can be claimed for them during the Carter years.

Just as importantly, the economic trends within the economic groups most likely to vote Democratic—the poor and those with incomes just above the poverty line—all point toward growing difficulties in the attempt to mobilize these forces politically. The population falling into the ranks of the poor and near poor has become increasingly filled with female-headed households,[48] just the families facing the greatest difficulties on a day-to-day basis, and least accessible to a political party seeking to build an expanded base of popular support. The feminization of poverty, for the present at least, effectively serves to intensify the political isolation of those who are poor.

At the same time, long-term projections for the shape of the job market through the year 2000 point toward growing difficulties for poor young blacks and Hispanics seeking work, difficulties likely to further isolate both economically and politically the two Democratic-leaning groups from the mainstream. Noting that "blacks and Hispanics are disproportionately represented among those with less education," a Department of Labor analysis of the changing job market through the rest of this century pointed out that "those with less than a high school education face increasing difficulty in their job search and less opportunity for good pay and advancement."[49]

Clearly, under both Republican and Democratic scenarios, the balance of power belongs to the middle class. The middle class forms the fulcrum of what has increasingly become, during the Reagan years, an intensified contest between the parties to shape a winning coalition. Within the range of acceptable options in American politics, these competing coalitions, in turn, represent alliances that would set national agendas with, in many ways, diametrically opposed emphases on economic policy and, to a lesser extent, on social policy. The Reagan administration has contributed significantly to the process of setting up this confrontation—and through the creation of a national debt exceeding $2 trillion, a Republican White House has severely restricted the ability of the Democratic opposition to restore action and vitality to its own agenda. The Reagan years have failed, however, at least for the present, to carry the battle to the kind of conclusion that leads both to a realignment of the partisan structure and to a full majority conversion of the voting electorate.

THE POLITICAL LEGACY
OF THE REAGAN YEARS

WILLIAM SCHNEIDER

What difference has Ronald Reagan made in American politics? Not much, according to the polls. Public opinion hasn't shifted to the right. If anything, the voters have moved to the left since Reagan took office—there is less support for military spending; more support for domestic social programs; increased concern about arms control, hunger, and poverty. It has long been the conventional wisdom that the president's personal popularity does not translate into public support for his policies. But it does translate into something.

"There has been a profound change in the agenda," said Senator Daniel Patrick Moynihan. "The Stockman strategy of disabling the finances of the federal government worked. It worked disastrously," the New York Democrat hastened to add, "but it worked."

Moynihan reached into his desk. "I have a wonderful document here from Senator [Daniel J.] Evans of Washington. He has a bill he calls 'the Federalism Act of 1986—FACT.' It would expand the coverage of Medicaid and work-training programs to poor pregnant women and to poor children whether they're on welfare or not.

"It's the kind of thing we should have done twenty years ago," the senator added. "It's incremental, sensible, and sane. First you establish Medicaid for indigent, dependent families on welfare. Then you come along and say, 'What about families that are poor but not on welfare? Can't we give a pregnant mother Medicaid attention? Can't we give poor children Medicaid attention?'

"*But,*" the senator rejoined, finger in the air, "Senator Evans says we will have to pay for this by abolishing the Economic Development Administration, the Appalachian Regional Commission, community services block grants, urban development action grants, community development block grants, mass transit operating assistance, mass transit research, waste water treatment grants, rural waste water disposal grants, federal impact aid, social services block grants, new low-income housing, and vocational education.

"I know something about those programs," Moynihan continued. "They aren't just the social agenda of the last twenty years. Vocational education was begun by the federal government in 1917. You would be abolishing the first entry of the United States government into education. But those are the terms. In order to go forward, you have to go back."

■ ■ ■

The Long Run: Institutional Changes

Democrats and Republicans agree that Reagan has transformed the agenda, but in a peculiar way. We want to do the same things as before—fight drug abuse, stabilize the economy, protect the poor and the elderly—only with less government. The impact of the Reagan revolution is more likely to be felt in the long run than in the short run. The president did not, after all, dismantle the New Deal welfare state. As Hugh Heclo has written, "Much as F.D.R. and the New Deal had the effect of conserving capitalism, so Reaganism will eventually be seen to have helped conserve a predominantly status-quo, middle-class welfare state."

Fair enough, but in the same volume on the Reagan legacy, Jack A. Meyer offered what he called "a long-term perspective." "The Administration seems to highlight its *social philosophy* toward federal programs, an area where most of its accomplishments seem rather marginal. By contrast, it downplays and is defensive about its *fiscal policies* which, while incomplete, herald a major accomplishment for the Administration." That accomplishment was to "pull the revenue plug" on the federal government. First came the 1981 tax cut, then year after year of record budget deficits. Now and for the foreseeable future, everything the federal government does must accommodate to one central fact: there is less money.

"I suggest that the United States is entering a new phase of expenditure control policy," Meyer wrote, "in which it is recognized that the safety net for the poor cannot be cut much further; that the social insurance and retirement functions must at least be on the table for discussion . . . ; and that there will not be too much room in the future for all other federal government social expenditures." That, in sum and substance, is the Reagan revolution.

The country bought the administration's economic program as a short-run response to a national calamity. Just before Reagan took office, he was being urged by some of his advisers to declare a national economic emergency. He didn't have to. Everyone knew the country was in an economic crisis. The president sold his tax and budget policies as a means to an end, which was to curb inflation and restore the nation's economic stability. In the public's view, the policies worked. But tax cuts, budget deficits, and tax reform are no longer passing items on the political agenda. They are the basis of a new institutional order, one that will set the terms of political debate far beyond the Reagan years.

Five long-term changes can be identified:

1. The federal budget *deficit* makes it impossible for Democrats to talk about any major new domestic spending programs unless they also talk about raising taxes. Which is exactly what the Republicans want them to talk about. For instance, having taken control of both houses of Congress after the 1986 midterm election, the Democrats proposed "a new agenda for social progress." But they had to face the challenge of financing their new agenda without resorting to a general tax increase. Hence the pressure for "new ideas" in the Democratic Party.

2. *Tax reform* did more than simplify the nation's tax code and curb the influence of special interests. It also weakened the principle of progressive taxation and challenged the notion that the tax system

should be used as an instrument of social policy. By reverting to the old idea of "taxes for purposes of revenue only," tax reform has made it harder for the Democrats to legislate through tax policy. And that, President Reagan has said, is exactly what he set out to achieve.

3. A significantly higher level of *defense spending* has become the norm. While there is little public support for the sharp increases President Reagan requests from Congress every year, most Americans still do not want to make substantial cuts in the military budget. Cutting defense has come to mean going back to the perceived military weakness of the 1970s. Thus, as defense spending has risen year after year, the public's response has essentially been, "This far, but no farther." Moreover, arms control does not undermine the president's military program; it helps to institutionalize it. An arms-control agreement represents the long-awaited payoff for the Reagan administration's defense buildup.

4. By the time he leaves office, President Reagan will have appointed about half of the nation's federal judges. While not all of those appointees can be described as ideologues, the administration paid special attention to their views on key social issues such as affirmative action, abortion, and criminal rights. Throughout the Reagan presidency, the religious right has complained that the administration has done little to fight for its social agenda in the

legislative arena. That is correct, and the explanation is that it would have been politically unwise. Instead, President Reagan is relying on the federal *courts* to reverse the judicial activism of the last three decades. Which they may well do—after he leaves office, when he will not have to suffer the political consequences.

5. Finally, the Reagan administration has changed the *political consensus* in both parties. The withdrawal of Howard H. Baker, Jr., from the 1988 presidential race removed the only prospective candidate who represented the traditional moderate Republican establishment. Instead, Baker chose to become White House chief of staff and shore up his Reaganite credentials. All the candidates in the GOP race were conservatives of one sort or another. Representative Jack Kemp was an aggressive leader of the New Right. The Reverend Marion G. (Pat) Robertson tried to muster a Christian army to fight for the religious right. Former Delaware Governor Pierre S. du Pont, despite his high establishment origins, was a born-again populist and supply-sider. Vice President George Bush shed his moderate skin in 1980 and converted to Reaganism. Senate Minority Leader Bob Dole assiduously courted the right during his two years as Senate majority leader. Although he differed with the right on some important issues, Dole established his credentials as someone who could deliver. Dole's message to the right was, "I may not be one of you, but I can deal for you."

Compare the situation in the Democratic Party. With Senator Edward M. Kennedy out of the race and Governor Mario M. Cuomo stepping back, there seemed to be no one to fight for the Old Politics—free-spending, high-taxing, big-government liberalism. To traditional Democrats, the 1988 field looked like Jesse Jackson and a crowd of yuppies (at least until they took a good look at Senator Paul Simon and projected him as a substitute for Cuomo). All the other Democrats were "pragmatists" who wanted to try "new ideas." In the Democratic Party, pragmatism means giving up the burden of defending big government. Government cannot be the solution to every social problem, pragmatists say; instead, it should be the source of new ideas. Thus, the primary role of government is not to redistribute income but to stimulate economic growth. Most Democrats remain committed to the principles of sharing, compassion, mutuality, and help for the disadvantaged. But these days, that message sounds too much like the old politics. It is a message many Democrats fear they can't sell anymore.

The Reagan revolution changed the coalition structure of American politics. Reagan brought together a variety of interests united by a distaste for big government. That coalition is larger than the traditional Republican Party. Consequently, it is more diverse. It includes business interests and middle-class voters who dislike taxes and regulation. It includes racial and religious conservatives who dislike the federal government's reformist social agenda. It includes neoconservatives who want a tougher and more assertive foreign policy. These interests disagree on many things, but they will stick together as long as they see a common enemy, namely, the liberal establishment with its interventionist domestic policies and its noninterventionist foreign policies.

Benjamin Ginsberg and Martin Shefter have analyzed how the

Reagan administration "reconstituted" American politics. For example, some groups have changed their political identity. Middle- and upper-income suburban voters who used to see themselves as beneficiaries of government programs now identify themselves as "taxpayers, individuals whose chief concern is the cost of federal programs." Groups that used to share a common interest have been divided by the Reagan program—public-sector and private-sector professionals, for instance, or business and labor in deregulated industries. In still other cases, the Reagan revolution has created new political forces by uniting disparate interests: Catholic and Protestant religious conservatives, upper-income managers and professionals, big business and small business. "The result of these efforts is a new constellation of forces in American politics, one that is more consonant with the President's programmatic and partisan goals and that increases the probability of the Reagan regime enduring."

What keeps the Reagan coalition together is not mutual affection or agreement, but the perception of a common threat. The threat is that liberals will regain control of the federal government and use it, as they did in the past, as the instrument for carrying out their "redistributionist" or "reformist" or "antimilitary" program. The threat will not disappear when Reagan leaves office, and neither will the Reagan coalition.

Not even if it loses the 1988 election. The fact that a coalition is defeated does not mean it has been destroyed. In the short run, the Republicans are likely to lose many elections, as they did the Senate elections in 1986, just as the Democrats lost many elections over the fifty-year history of their New Deal coalition. The short-term fate of the Republican Party depends on factors like the condition of the economy, the fallout from the Iran-contra scandal, and the state of U.S.-Soviet relations. But the Reagan coalition would come to an end only if the various groups that comprise it no longer feel they have a mutual interest in limited government.

Above all, the political agenda has changed. Looming over everything is the federal budget deficit. The antigovernment revolt that brought Reagan and the GOP to power in 1980 is over. But we have come out of it with a new institutional order, one based on low taxes and limited government. That new order does not lack for defenders.

The Short Run: Unintended Consequences

What surprises many observers is the lack of evidence of any ideological change, at least in the short run. As Thomas Ferguson and Joel Rogers found in 1986, "poll after poll demonstrates that the basic structure of public opinion in the United States has remained relatively stable in recent years." Hugh Heclo took note of "the amount of effort that must be exerted to find even modest movement in the public's mind toward ideas favored by Reaganism." Both analyses were published before the Iran-contra scandal had its debilitating effect on President Reagan's image.

Basically, Reagan has been a victim of the Law of Unintended Consequences, a law that initially helped him get elected president. What the Law of Unintended Consequences says is this: by solving one problem, you usually create another. You may even make the situation worse instead of better. That point was made over and over again during the 1960s and 1970s by neoconservative intellectuals—former liberals who argued that liberal social programs were creating more problems than they were solving.

The classic case, cited again and again by neoconservatives, was Aid to Families with Dependent Children (AFDC), the federal welfare program. The program provided assistance to low-income families, but only if the father was absent. So, in effect, the program gave fathers an incentive to abandon their families.

Such arguments, made by respectable intellectuals, gave conservatives like Reagan the evidence they needed to support what they had been saying for years: that government spending is bad. That the federal government makes things worse. And that most of what the government does to help people is wasteful and counterproductive.

The voters did not buy conservatism because it became intellectually respectable, however. They bought it because, over a twenty-year period, public confidence in government collapsed. A decade of social conflict—racial violence, the war in Vietnam, student protest, Watergate—was followed by a decade of economic decline—the energy crisis, recession, the Great Inflation of the 1970s. Not only was government unable to solve these problems; it was government that created them in the first place.

Runaway inflation was the final straw. The public placed the blame squarely on out-of-control government spending. The result was a tax revolt that spread across the country like wildfire in 1978. Then, two years later, the Republicans swept the presidency and the Senate. The revolt against government came about because of good timing: a conservative movement armed with new and powerful arguments against government, and an electorate that, as a result of inflation, was finally receptive to what the conservatives were saying.

A remarkable thing happened next. Reagan got credit for solving the two problems he was elected to solve. During his first term in office, inflation was subdued and the nation's sense of military security was restored. Then the Law of Unintended Consequences took over.

Reagan's success in curbing inflation had the unintended consequence of ending the revolt against government. Beginning in 1983, when the inflation rate reached zero for the first time in thirty years, attitudes toward government began to improve. Polls showed rising support for government regulation and for government spending on domestic social programs like education, health care, and poverty. Tax resentment declined. And trust in government increased. Fewer people said that public officials were wasteful, crooked, and incompetent, and more people felt they could count on the government to do what is right. Thus, the ultimate irony of Reagan's presidency: he restored people's faith in government, which is certainly not what he set out to do.

Reagan's success in improving the nation's sense of military security had the unintended consequence of reducing support for his defense policies. By 1987, polls showed that less than 20 percent of the public believe the Russians are now stronger than the United States. That view was held by a majority in the late 1970s. Consequently, fewer than 20 percent favored higher defense spending. The polls showed increasing support for an arms-control treaty and for improving relations with the Soviet Union. Thus, another irony of the Reagan presidency: by making Americans feel more secure, Reagan laid the groundwork for renewed détente, which is certainly not what he set out to do.

President Reagan came to power by seizing the moment, and in 1980 the moment was ripe for conservative leadership. He also managed to sustain his political power even as the Law of Unintended Consequences began to work against him. In a system without strong political parties, like that of the United States, public opinion is the president's principal source of power. An American president must be constantly preoccupied with managing public opinion, even to the point of delegating important policy responsibilities to others. Since managing public opinion was one of Reagan's greatest strengths, delegating authority became his most serious vulnerability.

A high approval rating gives a president clout with the press, the bureaucracy, and Congress. If a president's approval rating declines significantly—as Reagan's did in 1982 at the time of the recession, and as it did again at the end of 1986 as a result of the Iran-contra scandal—the president literally loses power, even over his own party. In a system of independent political entrepreneurs, there is little advantage for a politician to remain loyal to an unpopular president. In 1982, Reagan used his considerable personal appeal, as well as his skill at media management, to rally the American public to "stay the course" in the face of the deepest recession since the 1930s. In 1986, he was not so lucky. The Iran arms deal caused the president's approval rating to go down almost twenty points in one month, the sharpest drop on record. While his ratings subsequently stabilized at about 50 percent, the president suffered a serious loss of credibility. Few were afraid of him anymore. Moreover, the polls showed that the electorate was in a mood for change. Even before the stock market crash of October 1987, a slim majority of voters were saying they would prefer a Democrat to a Republican as the next president.

The simple truth is that once the Reagan administration did what it was elected to do—resolve the nation's economic crisis and restore the country's sense of military security—the public lost interest in the Reagan agenda. The Law of Unintended Consequences took over, and its effects were heightened by the administration's grievous mismanagement of foreign policy. The president lost power. The 1988 election suddenly looked winnable for the Democrats.

While the short-run outlook may not be good for the administration or for the Republican Party, the Reagan revolution is not an evanescent phenomenon. It is strongly rooted in the institutional changes outlined above. It will not disappear as easily as Ronald Reagan's personal "magic." There have been lasting changes in the American electorate. These changes started long before the Reagan revolution. In fact, they go back twenty-five years, to the social and foreign-policy conflicts of the 1960s. Ronald Reagan himself is a creature of the 1960s. He first gained prominence as a result of a speech supporting Barry Goldwater for president in 1964, and he was elected governor of California in 1966 in reaction to the social turmoil in Watts and Berkeley. The Iran-contra scandal and the Oliver North phenomenon can be understood only in terms of the legacy of the Vietnam War. The conflicts surrounding the Supreme Court and the nominations of Judges Robert Bork and Douglas Ginsburg derive from several decades of controversy over judicial activism.

The quarter century from 1964 through 1988 was a distinctive cycle in American politics, an era of ideological change and party realignment. The Reagan revolution was as much a consequence as a cause of those developments. Thus, the changes now visible in American politics have deep roots and cannot be destroyed by the shortcomings of one presidency.

The New Politics

Two things happened. The first was the rise of the New Politics, which brought about the ideological realignment of the Democratic and Republican parties. Beginning in the 1960s, the Republicans moved to the right and began to attract a new conservative coalition. At the same time, the Democrats started moving to the left, with the result that the party gained a new liberal constituency and alienated its old-line conservative wing. These changes occurred mostly at the elite level, among political activists coming out of the New Right and the New Politics left. These activists eventually gained influence over, if not total control of, the two major parties.

The second change, the rise of antiestablishment populism, occurred at the mass level and had little to do with ideology. It was stimulated by two decades of failure and frustration. Populism is neither liberal nor conservative, but antielitist. The last two presidents, one a Democrat and the other a Republican, were both anti-Washington candidates who appealed to this neopopulist sentiment. As a result of the Great Inflation of the 1970s, antiestablishment populism turned into a revolt against government, the ultimate symbol of the establishment and the status quo. The first stirrings were visible in the tax revolt of 1978, two years before Ronald Reagan won the presidency. It was the antigovernment revolt that brought the conservative coalition, and the Reagan revolution, to power.

The year 1964 marks the dividing line between the old politics and the New Politics. The Republican nomination of Barry Goldwater defined a new style of conservatism and occasioned a sharp break with the past. The Democrats, under the leadership of John

F. Kennedy, Lyndon Johnson, and Hubert Humphrey, also broke
with their past by making the courageous, and ultimately costly,
decision to embrace the civil rights movement. For the next two
decades, the parties continued to move apart ideologically. This
transformation is symbolized by the two principal third-party
movements of the last twenty-five years. Conservative Democrats,
mostly southern whites, felt homeless in 1968 and rallied behind
the independent candidacy of George Wallace. They could not
stay in a party committed to civil rights. Liberal Republicans felt
homeless in 1980 and rallied behind the independent candidacy
of John Anderson. They could not stay in a party that had become
completely Reaganized.

Nowhere did this realignment have a greater impact than in the
South. What was once the most solidly Democratic region of the
country is now predominantly Republican in presidential elec-
tions. Since 1964, the South has given majority support to the
Democratic ticket only once, in 1976, and even then Jimmy
Carter failed to carry white southerners. The South and the
West—the Sunbelt—are the base for what has become a normal
Republican presidential majority.

In the 1950s, it was possible to talk about a Democratic Party
establishment and a Republican Party establishment who were
more or less in control of their parties' policies and organizations.
While divided on economic issues—the Democrats were the big
spenders, the Republicans the party of austerity—neither social
issues nor foreign policy entered the partisan debate. Both sides
endorsed the bipartisan Cold War consensus. And the most pressing social issue, race, was confused. The Democrats still had a
large contingent of southern white racists, while it was a Republican chief justice who wrote the 1954 Supreme Court decision

mandating school integration and a Republican president who sent troops to Little Rock to enforce it.

In the 1960s and 1970s, both party establishments were the targets of protest movements. The first challenge came from the right, in 1964, when the Goldwater movement mobilized conservative activists to wrest control of the Republican Party from the eastern establishment. The protest from the left emerged with the antiwar candidacy of Eugene McCarthy in 1968. Four years later, liberal activists mobilized in the Democratic primaries and caucuses to nominate George McGovern and defeat the party establishment that they felt had stolen the nomination from them four years earlier. The presidential nominations of Barry Goldwater in 1964 and George McGovern in 1972 signaled the initial victories of these protest movements. Although both candidates were defeated in the ensuing general elections, their followers moved into positions of prominence in the two parties, either displacing the party regulars or forcing them to accommodate.

The protest movements introduced new ideological issues into party politics. The New Right conservatives attacked the Republican establishment for making too many compromises with big government—including acceptance of civil rights legislation— and for being too willing to accept peaceful coexistence with communism. The Democrats had already taken a giant step to the left when the party establishment supported civil rights. The New Politics movement went one step further and challenged the party leadership's commitment to the Truman Doctrine, the principle of anticommunist intervention that led the United States into Vietnam. Beginning in the 1960s, social issues and foreign policy became partisan issues, alongside enduring party differences over taxes, spending, and regulation.

Party leaders like to say that a political party is a big tent, with room inside for all kinds of people. That certainly used to be true. Democrats ran the gamut from southern white racists to blacks and northern liberals. The old GOP included right-wingers like Barry Goldwater and left-wingers like John Lindsay. In recent years, however, the tents have gotten smaller. Racists and right-wingers are no longer welcome in the Democratic tent. Liberal Republicans face a choice of either losing (like Jacob Javits and Clifford Case) or leaving (like John Lindsay and John Anderson).

The parties have been trading supporters as a result of the new politics. While the suburban vote in the South has become solidly Republican, Democrats have made substantial inroads among affluent upper-middle-class voters outside the South. These New Politics voters, many of whom, like John Anderson, were traditionally Republican, cannot abide the reactionary social conservatism of the new Republican Party. They are attracted to New Politics liberals like George McGovern, Morris Udall, and Michael Dukakis, not to old-fashioned Democrats like Walter Mondale or moderates like Jimmy Carter.

On the other hand, the Democratic Party has been losing much of its traditional support among white southerners, conservative Catholics, and blue-collar voters who feel threatened by social and cultural change. Conservative Democrats are not attracted to moderate Republicans like Gerald Ford but to right-wing Republicans like Ronald Reagan, Strom Thurmond, Jesse Helms, John Connally, and Phil Gramm—all of whom used to be Democrats. All of them, as conservatives, found themselves out of place in the Democratic Party. They "realigned" and took many of their supporters with them.

This realignment occurred in two stages. First came the social realignment of 1968 and 1972. In 1968, the Democrats lost the support of racial conservatives, mostly southern whites. Then in 1972, they lost a smaller but influential group of foreign-policy conservatives, or neoconservatives. The party was still competitive, however, as demonstrated by its comeback in the 1974 and 1976 elections. All the Democrats needed was a bad economy and a good scandal.

The second stage of realignment, 1980–84, was more damaging because the Democrats were in danger of losing their economic base. What held the Democratic Party together for fifty years was economic populism—the belief that the party would protect people against economic adversity. That belief kept the party going during the years when it was tearing itself apart over civil rights and Vietnam. Under Jimmy Carter, however, the Democrats failed to offer economic protection. Under Reagan, the Republicans succeeded. Without the economic issue, the Democrats risk becoming a liberal party rather than a populist party, that is, a party of upper-middle-class liberals and minority groups who share the same social philosophy.

The realignment has been in the direction of ideological consistency, with the Republican party becoming socially as well as economically conservative and the Democratic party endorsing social as well as economic liberalism. Lower-status voters tend to be liberal on economic issues and conservative on social issues, while higher-status voters are just the reverse. Thus, the typical voter is ideologically inconsistent. Many working-class voters look to the Democratic Party for economic protection but do not trust its social liberalism. Middle-class suburbanites favor Reagan's fiscal conservatism but are disturbed by the messages of religious fundamentalism, antienvironmentalism, and foreign interventionism that sometimes emanate from the White House.

That is one reason why several moderate Republican senators refused to support Robert Bork's nomination to the U.S. Supreme Court. A conservativized Supreme Court threatened to reopen the agenda on abortion and religious issues, thereby exacerbating class tensions in the Republican Party. These days, religion is to the Republican Party as race is to the Democratic Party: whenever the issue comes up, it tears the party apart. In many ways, the New Deal party system with its ideologically inconsistent parties fit the electorate better. As Walter Dean Burnham has argued, realignment has narrowed the parties' bases and left many voters with no comfortable home.

The Issue of Government

Most of American history has been a complex interplay between economic and social conflict. The role of government is the eternal issue. An economically activist federal government is one that manages, guides, and regulates the economy. Is that liberal or conservative? In the nineteenth century, when government was regarded as the bastion of privilege, the out-groups in society favored a laissez-faire state. Jacksonian Democrats, as the party of the "left," resolutely opposed all forms of government economic intervention—currency controls, a national bank, incorporation through legislative charter, protective tariffs, even government-sponsored internal improvements. The Federalists, Whigs, and later the Radical Republicans were more comfortable with statism and government intervention, which they defended in the name of nationalism (for instance, Henry Clay's "American System").

Even more divisive was the view that the federal government

should endorse or mandate certain social values, such as aboli-
tionism, temperance, racial equality, sexual freedom, or religious
rights. Those who favor a socially activist federal government
usually do so in the name of universal moral values or human
rights. Those who resist say they are defending pluralism: we are
a country with no official religion, ideology, or culture, and so the
state must be scrupulously neutral in such matters. In the nineteenth century, the conservative parties were the parties of the
cultural establishment, usually the Protestant elite who wanted to
use government to reform and control society. The Jeffersonian
Democrats were the party of the out-groups and the disestab-
lished. Consequently, it was the Democrats who supported religious freedom, states' rights, and cultural laissez-faire.

These historic party positions were reversed in the twentieth
century for a simple reason: the role of government changed.
Capitalism is revolutionary. It creates rapid and large-scale social
change through what Joseph Schumpeter called the process of
"creative destruction." Those who are threatened by change, the
losers in the process, gravitate toward government for protection—not just impoverished farmers and workers, but also victims of discrimination and those whose values are endangered by
cultural change.

Historically, in the United States as well as Europe, government power had been allied with economic power and social
privilege. Out-groups distrusted and opposed the state. The
Progressives were the first to use the power of the state to attack
private concentrations of power. Eventually, the New Dealers
extended this fundamentally new role of government. They saw
the state as an agency to protect people against economic adversity. Government became the enemy of economic privilege, or

what Franklin D. Roosevelt called "the economic royalists." Economic out-groups began to look to the federal government for protection—for jobs, relief, unemployment compensation, old-age pensions, and the safeguarding of labor rights. Government power became associated with the economic left.

The second change occurred in the 1950s and 1960s. The civil rights movement redefined the role of the federal government in social relations. Government was again used to reform society, only this time it was to benefit the victims of discrimination. The Democrats in the 1930s used the power of the federal government to promote economic justice. In the 1960s, they used the power of the federal government to promote social justice. The sociology of the Democratic Party remained consistent. It was still the party of the underprivileged and the out-groups (the party of "losers," as Republicans sometimes say at intemperate moments like party conventions).

What changed was the party's ideology. From the 1930s through the 1970s, the Democrats became firmly identified with activist government. They became statist in social as well as economic affairs. Antistatist Democrats—which include both economic conservatives and racists, both of whom claim continuity with the party's states'-rights and laissez-faire tradition—have been made to feel distinctly unwelcome. The Republican Party retained its traditional economic conservatism but added to it a vigorous and muscular social conservatism. The latter materialized as a backlash against federal interference, especially judicial interference, in racial and religious matters.

Government, which was once seen as a bastion of social and economic privilege, came to be viewed in this century as a force for social and economic egalitarianism. That would seem to give the Democrats a populist appeal. It did exactly that, for about fifty years. But then something happened in the 1960s and 1970s to undermine that appeal. What happened was a revolt against government—and against the party of government.

The antigovernment revolt was the culmination of twenty years of crisis and decline. First came "the sixties" (1964–74), a sequence of events that seemed to expose the underlying corruption of our institutions: the Vietnam War; racial violence; the rise of feminism, environmentalism, consumerism, and campus protest; and the final paroxysm, Watergate. In "the seventies" (1974–84), the news was just as bad, only now most of it concerned the economy: the energy crisis, surging interest rates, and a Great Inflation sandwiched between two major recessions.

The failures of the 1960s and 1970s were failures of government. Over those decades, the nation experienced four failed presidencies in a row. In fact, the country had gone through a comparable experience earlier in this century. A decade of depression (the 1930s) was followed by a decade of world war (the 1940s). The difference was, those crises were resolved by the vigorous and innovative use of government. Franklin D. Roosevelt's four-term presidency, which spanned most of those two decades, was a monumental success. To the Depression generation, government meant the New Deal, World War II, and the prosperity of the 1950s. Government was the solution. To the generation that came of age in the 1960s and 1970s, government was the problem.

It was inflation that brought the antigovernment revolt out into the open, starting with the passage of Proposition 13 in California in 1978. In repeated tests of public sentiment across the 1970s, big government was the institution most consistently blamed for inflation. Distrust of government was strongly related to support for Proposition 13 in California and for similar measures elsewhere—more strongly related than partisanship, ideology, or income. As it happens, most of those who favored tax cuts did not feel that they were voting to reduce public services. According to a poll taken in 1978 by the *Los Angeles Times,* only 5 percent of Proposition 13 supporters thought government services would be cut back permanently as a result of the measure. Twenty-six percent felt other taxes would have to be raised. The prevailing view, held by 45 percent, was that the revenue loss would be closed "by cutting out waste and inefficiency."

The single most prominent characteristic of public opinion during the 1970s was widespread disillusionment with government. The public did not reverse its position on the legitimacy of most government functions, such as helping the poor and regulating business. But the feeling grew that government had become excessively wasteful and ineffective in carrying out those functions. Something had to be done.

The antigovernment revolt had been brewing for many years. Polls taken by the University of Michigan showed steadily rising antigovernment feeling after 1964. The percentage of Americans who believed they could trust the government in Washington "to do what is right" went from 76 percent in 1964 to 54 percent in 1970, 33 percent in 1976 and 25 percent in 1980. The number who felt that the government was run "by a few big interests looking out for themselves" was 29 percent in 1964, 50 percent in 1970, and 69 percent in 1980. Less than half of the public thought the government wasted a lot of tax money in 1964; the figure was two-thirds in 1970, and over three-quarters by 1980.

Reagan's conservative regime is less a cause than a consequence of this trend. When he took office in 1981, the polls showed that the public strongly supported his new economic program of spending cuts and tax cuts. People supported it in spite of many doubts and reservations. What got the program through was the overwhelming mandate for change. When Reagan took office, inflation completely dominated all other issues on the national agenda. The chairman of the House Budget Committee observed, "The elections of 1978 and 1980 demonstrated dramatically that inflation had become the dominant issue and, in most [congressional] districts, your attitude on inflation is measured by your attitude on government spending."

To the administration, however, the economic crisis provided the opportunity to accomplish what Republicans had been talking about for fifty years, namely, reducing the size and power of the federal government. The cuts in government spending at the heart of Reagan's economic plan were not the means toward the end of economic recovery. They were ends in themselves.

The American public was quite aware at the outset that the administration's program would cause special hardship for the poor. Just after Reagan's first budget speech in 1981, the public was asked by ABC News and the *Washington Post* who they thought would be hurt the most by Reagan's proposed budget. Forty-two percent said poor people, 22 percent said middle-income people, and 2 percent said the rich. Only 30 percent felt that everyone would be affected the same. The cross section was then asked, "Regardless of who might be hurt, would you say you generally approve or disapprove of the spending cuts Reagan has proposed?" The margin of approval was overwhelming, 72 to 21 percent, despite the perceived unfairness of the program. The reason: by 64 to 28 percent, the public felt that President Reagan's program would help bring an end to inflation.

Even in 1981, however, it was difficult to find majority support for specific spending cuts. The ABC/*Post* poll asked people how they felt about spending cuts for fourteen specific programs, including child care, synthetic fuels, unemployment insurance, aid to the arts, food stamps, Medicaid, student loans, public television, and the postal service. The answers ranged from 4 percent who favored a decrease in spending for Medicaid to 49 percent who supported cuts in food stamps. In other words, a majority of Americans did not favor spending cuts in any specific program. They supported Reagan's program as a whole, however, including the spending cuts, because they wanted strong, decisive action to end the nation's economic crisis. The administration's mandate was to "do something—anything" to get the economy back on track, even if that entailed specific cuts that were not popular.

In his 1981 budget speech, President Reagan said, "Spending by government must be limited to those functions which are the proper province of government." The president may have been surprised to find out what the public thought the proper province of government was. In the ABC/*Post* survey, the same national cross section that approved the president's proposed spending cuts by more than three to one was asked whether they agreed with the following proposition: "The government should work to substantially reduce the income gap between rich and poor." They very definitely agreed, by a margin of 64 to 31 percent.

Polls like that reassure Democrats that Americans never intended to dismantle the welfare state. The antigovernment revolt was more of a populist than a conservative phenomenon. But that does not mean it was any less real, or any less damaging, to the Democratic Party. The party became identified with the status quo and the vested interests who had been running things in Washington for fifty years. To most Americans, the federal government had become the establishment, and defending it meant defending statism and interest-group liberalism. Democrats tended to forget that their heroes, the Progressives and the New Deal liberals, used government power to attack the vested interests and the status quo. In the Reagan era, it was strange to reflect that the federal government had once been seen as an antiestablishment force.

Hidden-Agenda Politics

The crowning domestic achievement of the Reagan presidency— the one likely to have the most lasting impact—was tax reform. The most serious failure of the Reagan presidency—the one likely to have the most lasting impact—was the deficit. Both are examples of hidden-agenda politics.

Senator Howard Baker, who was Senate majority leader when the Reagan economic program was set in place, offered a pointed observation in 1986 about President Reagan's priorities. "I think he would really like to get his fiscal house in order," Baker said. "But those who say that is last on his agenda are probably right. He wants tax reform and he wants a strong defense. And *then* he wants to balance the budget." Representative Kemp made the same point. "I remember very clearly Reagan being asked, 'What about the deficit?' He said, 'I would take a deficit if by a deficit I were able to implement my tax cut and my defense build-up.' I am sure Reagan talked about a balanced budget as a theoretical point. But the defense build-up and the tax cuts were sacrosanct."

Reducing the deficit was important to the president, at least as a rhetorical point. But keeping taxes down and defense spending up were more important. Reagan was not alone in this judgment. Throughout the Reagan administration, everybody—Congress, the president, Democrats, Republicans, and the American public—believed the deficit was a serious problem. But at the same time, everybody believed that something else—cutting entitlements, raising taxes, slashing defense spending—would create a worse problem. That is how the country got into the deficit mess in the first place.

There is not much evidence that Congress, the president, the Democrats, or the Republicans have changed their minds. As for the public, a *Time* magazine poll taken in October 1987, after the stock market crash, found the public opposed to raising taxes or reducing spending for social programs and split on reducing military spending. In fact, the public failed to accept the view that the stock market crash was a crisis. Most Americans said they were unaffected by the troubles on Wall Street. They continued to express confidence in the economy and did not foresee a serious economic downturn. A survey taken by the Conference Board found that consumer confidence dropped by only 5 percent after the stock market plunge. By comparison, consumer confidence dropped 33 percent after the 1973 surge in oil prices.

What did people think would happen as a result of high deficits? When CBS News and the *New York Times* asked this question in 1986, almost half of the public had no idea, and an additional 10 percent said it would not affect them at all. The consequences people thought of most readily were higher interest rates, higher taxes, and more inflation. But inflation remained low, taxes were cut, and interest rates seemed reasonably stable. So what was the problem?

What people were afraid of was not the deficit, but what government might have to do to reduce the deficit. It was difficult to
find majority support for any of the available options—cutting
defense spending, reducing spending on social programs, cutting
back on entitlements like Social Security and Medicare or, least
popular of all, raising taxes. In early 1986, when Congress was
wrestling with the Gramm-Rudman-Hollings Balanced Budget
and Emergency Deficit Control Act, the *Los Angeles Times* asked
people to assess four options for dealing with the deficit. Two were
soundly rejected: allowing the Gramm-Rudman sequesters to go
into effect ("deep across-the-board budget cuts in defense and
domestic programs") and passing what was identified as President
Reagan's budget proposal ("no new taxes, an eight percent increase in defense spending and sharp reductions in domestic
programs").

In 1986, two options were found to be acceptable. By far the
most popular was the "grand compromise"—smaller cuts in defense and domestic programs but also some tax increases in order
to meet the goals of the Gramm-Rudman-Hollings bill. The problem was that, at that time, neither the administration nor the
Democrats in Congress would support a tax increase. The other
acceptable option? "Suspend the Gramm-Rudman Act; vote for
some relatively small reductions in defense spending and domestic programs and only minor cuts in the federal budget deficit."
Which is what Congress and the president eventually agreed to.
In effect, the deficit institutionalized the Reagan revolution. It
paralyzed the welfare state while avoiding a frontal assault on
social programs.

Democrats learned two big lessons from the Reagan era. One
was that the only social programs that are politically secure are

those that benefit everybody. Medicare, for example, is the principal enduring legacy of Lyndon Johnson's Great Society. Like Social Security, Medicare helps everybody, not just those in greatest financial need. The Democrats found it impossible to sustain support for LBJ's War on Poverty, however, precisely because it was not a universal "entitlement." It was targeted at the poor.

The other lesson: don't raise taxes that hurt everybody. Democrats saw what happened to Walter Mondale in 1984 when he proposed a general tax increase. The safest way to raise taxes is to target the increases. Make the beneficiaries pay the taxes (user fees). Earmark specific tax increases for specific programs (designated revenues). Or, best of all, shift the burden of paying for social programs from individual taxpayers to business (mandated benefits).

That is the language of "new ideas," and one heard it often from Democratic presidential candidates and congressional leaders who talked about "a new agenda for social progress." The objective was to get away from the old politics of taxing and spending, or more precisely, taxing us and spending on them.

There are two problems with this approach. It does very little to reduce the federal budget deficit; and it is inherently regressive. A great deal of money goes to people who don't really need it, essentially as a bribe for their political support, and people are taxed without regard to their ability to pay. Neither of these problems is a serious political liability, however. To the voters, a system that helps the many and taxes the few seems eminently fair.

Polls taken since 1983 show that the public is more and more willing to pay higher taxes for a wide variety of social needs, such as improving the nation's educational system, repairing bridges and highways, protecting the environment and aiding the homeless and the hungry. The one thing people will still not pay higher taxes for is reducing the deficit. The public does not seem to mind taxes that are spent on legitimate social needs, but they draw the line at a deficit tax. That sounds too much like subsidizing big government.

And so Congress hit upon the notion of designated revenues. Raise a particular tax and make sure people can see what it is being used for. That was the principle behind the highway bill passed in 1987 over President Reagan's veto. The bill designated revenues from the Highway Trust Fund to pay for road and bridge construction. Congress proudly pointed to the fact that the bill did not do anything to increase the federal deficit. But it did not do anything to reduce the deficit either.

A related principle is that of "toll road" or "pay as you go" taxation. Make the people who use the service pay for it, so they feel they are getting something for their money. That is how the House of Representatives proposed financing the expansion of Medicare coverage to include catastrophic illnesses. The added benefits would be paid for by the elderly themselves. The higher payments were to be thought of as "premiums." The premiums would be mandatory, however, which means they are really a tax.

An even more ingenious solution to the revenue problem is not to raise taxes or spend government money at all. Just mandate that employers pay higher benefits to their workers. Thus, Congress considered bills to raise the minimum wage and to require employers to pay mandatory health insurance and grant parental and medical leave. The idea was to expand "workers' rights" and "family rights"—that is, entitlements—by making business, not government, pay for them.

Such proposals elicit few complaints from taxpayers. According to a 1987 poll taken by the Service Employees International Union, the public supports legislation requiring employers to provide parental and medical leave by a margin of 77 to 15 percent. Raising the minimum wage is endorsed by 71 to 20 percent. By 62 to 29 percent, the public favors requiring employers to provide a basic minimum health-insurance package to employees and their dependents.

These proposals elicit a great many complaints from business, particularly small business, which bears most of the burden. Most big business firms have the resources and flexibility to meet or surpass the mandated standards. According to John Sloan, Jr., president of the National Federation of Independent Business, "Congress is notorious for trotting out social programs which sound wonderful to everyone but must be paid for by the private sector. The private sector then has no choice but to pass along those costs in the forms of higher prices, . . . reduced wage increases, lower dividends, delayed capital investment and fewer jobs." What it adds up to, Sloan feels, is "a sure-fire recipe for reducing a nation's competitiveness."

Congress has been forced to be devious because Americans want more government than they are willing to pay for. Uwe E. Reinhardt has pointed out that in 1984 the total tax burden in the United States was lower than that of any industrialized country except Japan. And of those taxes we do collect, a higher proportion goes to defense.

Tax reform, like the deficit, also entailed a hidden agenda. In fact, it was the same agenda, namely, reducing the size and power of the federal government.

The tax issue today bears a striking resemblance to the tariff issue in nineteenth-century American politics. Before the income tax, the tariff was a major source of revenue for the federal government ("external" as opposed to "internal" revenue). Republicans supported a high tariff, not only because they wanted to protect American industry, but also because they favored a strong, activist federal government. The Democrats of that era tended to be antigovernment; they were still the party of states' rights and laissez-faire. Consequently, every Democratic platform included a call for tariff reduction. The formula used was "a tariff for purposes of revenue only." Compare the basic philosophy of taxation Reagan revealed in his 1981 budget message to Congress, when he said, "The taxing power of government must be used to provide revenues for legitimate government purposes. It must not be used to regulate the economy or bring about social change." The issue now is the same as it was then, namely, shall we make the federal government less active and less powerful by starving it of funds?

In fact, taxes are used all the time for purposes other than raising revenue. One is to redistribute income from the rich to the poor. That is the purpose of progressivity in the tax code. President Reagan called this principle into question in 1985, when he said his tax-reform proposal would make the tax system less progressive. "We believe that there's nothing progressive about tax rates that discourage people from climbing up the ladder of success," the president said. Unlike Reagan, Americans do believe in a progressive income tax. In a Roper Organization survey taken in 1986, a three-to-one majority rejected the idea of lowering the top tax rate to 35 percent for people with the highest incomes. The public wanted to see taxes raised for the wealthy and lowered or eliminated for the poor. As Howard Baker put it in 1986, "It is the most remarkable political paradox in my time, this support for the repeal of progressivity. Liberal Democrats, conservative Republicans—the abdication of progressivity as a public policy has near universal support. For the life of me, I don't know how that happened."

The use of taxes as an instrument of social policy is another principle that used to be firmly established. The government has three means at its disposal to carry out a social objective. It can start a government-operated program, it can make transfer payments to individuals, or it can offer tax incentives. To alleviate unemployment, for example, the government can create jobs, give money to the unemployed, or offer tax incentives to induce businesses to hire the unemployed. In order to help poor people find housing, the government can build low-income housing projects, it can give poor people rent subsidies, or it can give real-estate developers tax incentives to build low-cost housing.

In these and similar cases, the tax system is arguably the best way to achieve a policy objective. And the public has agreed. A 1986 Roper poll explained, "Aside from raising money, the taxing system in our country has come to be used for a variety of purposes—to redistribute the wealth, or to encourage or discourage certain types of behavior, or to stimulate segments of the economy, etc." People were then asked whether they thought the tax system should be used just to raise revenues or for other purposes as well, "bearing in mind that these other purposes can be ones that you disapprove of as well as purposes you approve of." A 51 to 38 percent majority said yes, taxes should be used for purposes other than raising revenues.

There is no question that using taxes as an instrument of social policy often led to inefficiency, inequity, and abuse. Businesses and real-estate developers piled up tax advantages. Some industries were favored over others. Pointless research was done, unproductive workers were hired, and uneconomic housing and office space got built. In too many cases, tax preferences were granted because of the political power of a well-organized special interest, and not in response to a legitimate social need. Both Republicans and Democrats saw tax reform as an irresistibly populist issue. Republicans could use it to shed their elitist image as the party of wealth and big business. Democrats could shake off the charge that their party was a captive of special interests.

The administration liked to claim that, in the tax-reform battle, President Reagan rallied public opinion against a hostile Congress. But that is not the way it happened. From beginning to end, the American public was wary of tax reform. What really happened was that Reagan rallied Congress against a hostile public. In the end, tax reform was a bipartisan effort supported by the president and by Democratic leaders in Congress, each side for its own reasons.

In July 1987, Reagan announced a drive for budget reform, hoping to duplicate his 1986 experience with tax reform. The American public was as skeptical of budget reform as it was of tax reform. The budget issue was different from tax reform, however, because there was almost no compatibility of interests between the president and Congress. It took an extraordinary presidential-congressional committee to come up with a budget compromise in November 1987, and that happened only because of pressure from the stock market and because of the impending deadline for automatic spending cuts.

Presidential candidates of both parties were extremely cautious in their response to the stock market crisis of October 1987. Insofar as the leading candidates were willing to link the market plunge to the national debt, they endorsed the idea of handing the deficit issue over to a bipartisan, legislative-executive committee—in other words, treating the issue as if it were "above politics" (and keeping it out of the campaign). Senate Minority Leader Robert Dole, for example, seconded New York Governor Mario Cuomo's call for a "National Economic Commission" to produce a detailed blueprint for balancing the budget—after the 1988 election. Only two candidates, Democrat Bruce Babbitt and Republican Pete du Pont, offered any interesting new ideas for dealing with the deficit. But they were at the back of their respective packs, and their budget ideas were quickly labeled bold and unrealistic.

President Reagan's solution to the budget impasse was to demand procedural reforms—a balanced budget amendment to the Constitution and the power to veto individual items in spending bills. Congress's solution was to pass the Gramm-Rudman-Hollings bill mandating across-the-board budget cuts to meet deficit-reduction targets. In effect, what Congress and the president wanted were *weapons* to use against each other. The president wanted new powers to veto or outlaw congressional spending, while Congress threatened to hold the president's military budget hostage in order to force him to accept higher taxes. What the public wants is a *process* whereby both sides work together to keep the deficit under control. Eight years of confrontation may lead the public to conclude that they will never get such a process as long as there is a Republican in the White House. In which case, Reagan's confrontational strategy on the budget will turn out to have been a serious political blunder.

A Covert Foreign Policy

In future biographies of Ronald Reagan, the week between February 26 and March 4, 1987, will be called "The Revenge of the Establishment." First the establishment passed judgment on the Reagan administration and found its behavior unacceptable. Then reliable agents of the establishment were called in to repair the damage. This was quite a reversal for a president who made his career by running against establishments—first the eastern establishment that controlled the Republican Party and then the liberal establishment that ran the federal government.

The Tower Commission, acting as the executive committee of the Washington power elite, reproached the administration using the strongest terms of disapproval in the establishment's vocabulary: it called the Iran arms initiative "a very unprofessional operation." Recoiling from this harsh invective, the president fired his chief of staff, Donald T. Regan, and replaced him with a consummate professional who had the total confidence of the power elite, former Senate Majority Leader Howard Baker. The appointment of Baker, along with Frank C. Carlucci as national security adviser and William H. Webster as director of the Central Intelligence Agency, were acts of penance designed to "restore credibility" with the Washington power elite.

The Iran arms deal and the diversion of funds to the contras in Nicaragua were motivated by ideology. They were carried out by zealots who had contempt for foreign-policy professionals. Ideology is alien to the Washington power elite. Washington insiders prefer to deal with pragmatists and consensus-builders, moderates who are skilled at the art of compromise. Exactly like Howard Baker.

The administration gave up its true believers, John M. Poindexter, Robert C. McFarlane, and Oliver L. North, who saw the world in black and white. In their place came Baker, Carlucci, and Webster, men with exemplary establishment credentials—a former congressional leader and presidential candidate, a career foreign-service officer and former ambassador, an FBI director and former federal judge. More to the point, Baker, Carlucci, and Webster made their reputations long before Reagan became president. Unlike their predecessors, they did not depend on Reagan for their legitimacy.

At the congressional hearings on the Iran-contra affair, North offered an elaborate and compelling justification for covert operations. "I think it is very important for the American people to understand that this is a dangerous world . . . and they ought not to be led to believe, as a consequence of these hearings, that this nation cannot or should not conduct covert operations." There was one big flaw in North's argument, however. What North was talking about was not a covert operation; it was a covert foreign policy.

A covert foreign policy is one that pursues secret objectives. Why did the Reagan administration pursue a covert foreign policy? Because it could not get political support for the objectives it wanted to pursue. If the Congress or the American public knew that we were trading arms for hostages—thereby violating our explicit commitment never to negotiate with terrorists—there would have been a political explosion. As for sending military aid to the contras in Nicaragua, Congress, with demonstrable public support, had already placed severe restrictions on such a policy. The National Security Council, under the operational leadership of Colonel North, was not "executing" American foreign policy.

It was making American foreign policy—and hiding that policy from the Congress, the American public, and the world.

At one point, North explained, "I want to go back to the whole intent of a covert operation. Part of a covert operation is to offer plausible deniability of the association of the government of the United States with the activity. Part of it is to deceive our adversaries. Part of it is to ensure that those people who are at great peril carrying out those activities are not further endangered. All of those are good and sufficient reasons."

Those are indeed good and sufficient reasons for a covert operation. But in this case, it was the objectives and not just the operations that were being kept secret. North claimed that the Iranian arms deal had to be kept secret in order to combat terrorism and save lives. "I put great value on the lives of the American hostages," he explained. "We got three Americans back. . . . For almost eighteen months there was no action against Americans." The assumption was that the goal—trading arms for hostages—was obvious and unobjectionable. Yet President Reagan himself refused to admit that that was what he was doing until the Tower Commission forced him to accept that conclusion.

The smoking gun did not turn up at the hearings, but President Reagan's credibility was severely damaged nonetheless. According to the polls, most Americans continued to believe Reagan lied about how much he knew. Two-thirds believed Poindexter's testimony that Reagan had signed a document authorizing a direct arms-for-hostages trade with Iran, and of that number, over 60 percent thought Reagan was lying when he said he could not recall signing the document. In other words, in the public's view, North and Poindexter did not get Reagan off the hook. Their testimony implicated the president and other high administration officials in the cover-up. Most Democrats wanted to see Reagan damaged but not destroyed by the scandal. That is exactly what happened.

Hence another puzzle: Reagan's approval rating was hardly affected by the Iran-contra hearings. It stayed at about 50 percent through all the tumultuous events of 1987. The big drop-off in public support had already come in late 1986. As soon as the public learned of the arms deal with Iran, they docked twenty points from the president's approval rating. When the *Los Angeles Times* asked people in July 1987 what upset them the most about the affair, the leading answer was the arms deal with Iran (27 percent). The cover-up, which the public suspected all along, came in second (20 percent). Only 4 percent were most upset by the diversion of funds to the contras. Even though the contra diversion was the smoking gun that could have led to impeachment proceedings, the public was far more disturbed by the spectacle of the president of the United States selling arms to Iran.

Coalition Government and "The Vision Gap"

The final report of the congressional committees investigating the Iran-contra affair, released in November 1987, did not mince words. It said that the president "created or at least tolerated an environment" in which people believed they could go above the law. It also said that President Reagan "abdicated his moral and legal responsibility" to "take care that the laws be faithfully executed."

The public's response appeared to be "So what?" The president's job-approval ratings remained stable at around 50 percent. Nothing that happened during 1987—the Tower Commission report, the congressional hearings, the stock market crash—had a noticeable effect on the president's support. He neither gained nor lost popularity. About half of the public appeared to like Reagan no matter what happened—which suggested, not that the president's position was secure, but that by the end of his administration, he was becoming irrelevant. Events did not undo Reagan because he was not perceived to be in control of events.

The problem can be traced back to the 1984 election, when the president ran an essentially substanceless campaign. As noted, once inflation was subdued and the nation's sense of military security was restored, the public lost interest in the Reagan agenda. Reagan won a smashing reelection victory in 1984, but without an agenda and without Republican gains to support him. As a conservative activist observed, "I wish the President had proposed a serious program in that campaign. He might have ended up carrying 42 instead of 49 states, but at least he would have had a mandate."

The loss of the Senate in 1986, followed immediately by the Iran-contra scandal, further weakened the president's position. The Republicans lost the Senate despite a vigorous campaign by a president who was near the peak of his popularity. The 1986 results demonstrated that Reagan could be opposed with impunity. He had lost his power to rally the electorate. The Iran-contra scandal destroyed the president's remaining credibility. The president said at the outset that he was responsible for selling arms to Iran, but he argued that the policy was not a mistake. The public, horrified at this revelation, chose to disagree. The president also said at the outset that the diversion of profits to the contras was a mistake but that he was not responsible for it. The public refused to believe this either.

The end result was a coalition government. Whatever the president has accomplished during his second term, like tax reform, has required the support and collaboration of Congress. This meant, in effect, the support and collaboration of the Democrats. In his speech to the nation on August 12, 1987, the president listed four items on his agenda for the remainder of his administration.

The first was the confirmation of Judge Robert Bork to the U.S. Supreme Court. Reagan lost that battle and, after being embarrassed by his second choice, he gave in and nominated someone more acceptable to Congress.

The president's second agenda item was his so-called economic bill of rights, including line-item veto power and a balanced budget amendment to the Constitution. In the face of determined congressional opposition, both requests evaporated. Instead, Reagan had to endorse a budget compromise with Congress that involved $9 billion in tax increases and $5 billion in defense cuts.

Third, President Reagan endorsed a bipartisan peace plan for Nicaragua. Within days, however, the initiative passed to Central American leaders, who proposed a peace plan of their own. The administration failed to become engaged in the diplomatic process, so the congressional leadership stepped into the void, with House Speaker Jim Wright taking the initiative.

Finally, the president called for "a comprehensive and verifiable agreement with the Soviet Union on reducing nuclear arms." Here, too, the president had to share power with Congress. The Senate promised to be unusually conscientious in examining the treaty. Conservatives were suspicious of any deal with the Soviet

Union, while many Democrats had been offended by the administration's effort to reinterpret the 1972 Antiballistic Missile Treaty
in such a way as to allow testing of the Strategic Defense Initiative.

In 1987, President Reagan was forced to accept the fact that
he could govern only in coalition with the Democrats. Contemporary politics requires the two political parties to learn equally
difficult lessons. The Republicans will learn that Reaganism is a
spent political force. They will gain little by promising bold new
policies aimed at continuing the Reagan revolution. The Democrats will learn that Reagan has established a new institutional
order. They will gain little by promising to undo that order. The
mandate of the 1988 election will most likely be a weak one, more
revisionist than visionary. It will be a mandate to correct the
mistakes and excesses of the Reagan revolution, not to extend the
revolution or destroy it.

For the party out of power, a political campaign is an exercise
in market research. First, the opposition party has to find out
what the voters want that they are not getting. Then it has to
figure out how to sell it to them.

Look at the marketing strategies that have worked over the
past thirty-five years:

- In 1952, after Harry Truman, the voters wanted a
  leader who was "above politics"—Eisenhower.
- After eight years of Ike, Americans wanted youth,
  vigor, and dynamism—Kennedy.
- In 1968, when the country was being torn apart by
  racial violence, protest and the Vietnam War, the
  public wanted order. And so Nixon promised to
  "bring us together."

- After Watergate, what the country wanted was morality. Carter shrewdly read the national mood in
1976 and promised, "I will never lie to you."
- After four years of Carter, the country yearned for
leadership. Which is exactly what Ronald Reagan
had to sell.

The candidates who were doing well in the early stages of the
1988 campaign—Democrat Michael Dukakis and Republicans
George Bush and Bob Dole—were all selling more or less the
same thing: management, competence, and experience. That
seemed to be what the country was looking for, according to a
Gallup poll taken in September 1987 for the Times Mirror Company. Respondents were asked which one of three qualities they
considered most important when judging a candidate for president. The top-ranked quality, chosen by about half, was the
"ability to accomplish things." About a third said, "his stand on
the issues," while only one in seven considered "character" most
important. When asked what kind of experience better prepares
someone to be president, "serving as a U.S. Senator or Congressman and gaining experience in Washington and in foreign policy"
was preferred to "serving as a state's governor and gaining experience as the head of an administration" by a margin of three to
one.

Why were competence and management so important? Because
that was what people were not getting from Ronald Reagan. The
Iran-contra scandal drove the point home that President Reagan
was a poor manager who often did not know what was going on
inside his own government. Reagan's less-than-reassuring response to the stock market crash created the impression that
economic policy was out of control. The president even had dif-

ficulty getting a Supreme Court nominee confirmed. The Reagan experience clearly damaged the image of the Republicans as the party of good management. But the Democrats have been unable to claim much of an advantage on that issue either. When a 1987 Times Mirror poll asked people which party was better able to manage the federal government, the result was almost a dead heat—24 percent said the Republicans and 25 percent said the Democrats, while a plurality, 28 percent, volunteered the response that neither could manage the government very well.

In 1980, the Democrats, who were then the incumbents, tried to argue that the presidential election was about the future. In his acceptance speech at the Democratic National Convention, President Jimmy Carter depicted the election as "a stark choice between two men, two parties, two sharply different pictures of America and the world. . . . It is a choice between two futures." The out-party tried to keep attention focused on the present. "Are you better off than you were four years ago?" asked Republican candidate Ronald Reagan in his closing statement at the final campaign debate.

In 1988, the same kind of choices are being posed. Only this time, the position of the in-party and the out-party are reversed. The incumbent Republicans must argue that the election is a referendum on the present: are things better now they they were when the Democrats were in office? The Democrats, now the challengers, must try to make the election a referendum on the future: if we don't change direction, won't the country be headed for some kind of disaster? The public's inclination is to answer yes to both questions. The outcome depends on which party makes the more compelling case—whether the present or the future counts more in the voters' minds.

The partisan trends seem to favor the Democrats. The third-quarter 1987 party identification figures from the Gallup poll show the Democrats regaining a 42 to 29 percent lead over the Republicans. Two years earlier, following Reagan's reelection victory, the parties were nearly equal in strength. By about the same margin (41 to 28 percent), respondents to an October 1987 *Time* magazine poll said it would be better for the country to have a Democrat rather than a Republican as the next president.

But the margin was much closer in a CBS News/*New York Times* survey taken after the stock market crash; 36 percent of registered voters said they expected to vote Democratic and 33 percent said they expected to vote Republican. There appears to be some disparity between wanting to see the Democrats win and being willing to vote for a Democratic candidate. At least part of the explanation lies in the fact that a majority of those polled said the Republicans had better presidential candidates.

According to the Gallup poll, economic problems—particularly unemployment and the federal budget deficit—have dominated the nation's concerns for several years, with international problems, including the arms race and the threat of war, running second. Gallup asks people which party they feel will do a better job of handling whatever problem most concerns them. The results of this question have closely predicted presidential election outcomes going back to 1956. The results for April 1987: 37 percent said the Democrats would do a better job and 29 percent said the Republicans.

Presidential-election outcomes tend to be sensitive to two conditions—the popularity of the incumbent president and the condition of the economy. In 1983, political scientists Richard A. Brody and Lee Sigelman demonstrated that 50 percent is the break-even point for a president's job-approval rating. Below 50 percent, a president is unlikely to be reelected or succeeded by another president of the same party. Similarly, if the "misery index"—the sum of the nation's inflation and unemployment rates—rises above 10 percent, that means trouble for the incumbent party. Throughout 1987, President Reagan's popularity figures were running just below 50 percent in the Gallup poll. The misery index was in the 11-to-12 percent range. Both indicators signal the likelihood of a change in control of the White House, but not necessarily, and not necessarily by a decisive margin.

That would be consistent with the notion that there is a normal eight-year cycle in American politics. After a two-term administration, the "out" party takes control of the White House, usually as a result of a close election with no elected incumbent on the ballot (1952, 1960, 1968, 1976). Two years into his term, the president's party suffers modest losses in the midterm congressional election (1954, 1962, 1970, 1978). At the four-year mark, presidents typically win reelection by a landslide (1956, 1964, 1972). Then comes the disastrous six-year midterm when the president's party suffers a severe setback (1958, 1966, 1974). That sets the stage for Year 1, a close election with no incumbent on the ballot and a change of party control.

Like most historical models, this one works except when it doesn't work. It certainly didn't work for Jimmy Carter in 1980, when he failed to win reelection at all, let alone by a landslide. So far, however, the model has held up pretty well for the Reagan presidency: a modest Republican setback in 1982, a landslide reelection in 1984, a major setback in 1986. If the model holds up, 1988 will be a close election with a slight advantage for the Democrats. A close election like those of 1960, 1968, and 1976

usually means a centrist campaign in which the candidates minimize their ideological differences.

By the end of 1987, political commentators were beginning to
complain about a "vision gap" in the 1988 campaign. The two
leading Republican candidates, Bush and Dole, had roots in the
moderate wing of the GOP. Neither offered much by way of a
vision of the country's future. All of the Democratic candidates
except Jackson were pragmatists who espoused relatively conservative fiscal policies. In other words, they had learned to live with
the Reagan revolution.

Of course, there is still a market for visionary politics in both
political parties. Candidates like Pat Robertson on the Republican side and Jesse Jackson and Paul Simon on the Democratic
side—not to mention the Democrats' leading noncandidate,
Mario Cuomo—tried to exploit their parties' dissatisfaction with
a campaign obsessed with character and competence. In short,
there are plenty of candidates out there with visions to sell. The
problem is, after eight years of Ronald Reagan, the country seems
to feel it has had enough vision for a while.

What the voters seem to want is change, but not too much
change. A *Time* magazine survey taken just after the October
1987 stock market crash showed that 58 percent of those polled
shared the opinion that things are going fairly well or very well
in the country—down only slightly from the 60 to 62 percent who
felt that way at various times earlier in the year. Only 36 percent
were worried about their own financial future. But 46 percent
were worried about the country's economic future. And 65 percent wanted to see the next president follow different policies
from those of the Reagan administration.

The polls also reveal a disparity between people's positive

evaluations of their own personal well-being and their negative assessments of the national condition. A September 1987 Gallup poll showed 43 percent who felt financially better off than they were a year ago, compared to 29 percent who felt worse off. Eighty-three percent said they were satisfied with the way things were going in their personal life. When attention shifted from the personal to the national, however, confidence dropped significantly. By 49 to 45 percent, people said they were dissatisfied with the way things were going in the country, the most negative result in four years.

What the voters seem to want is a new administration that can go in and correct the mistakes of the old administration. The Republicans may be just as capable of doing that as the Democrats, depending on whom they nominate and what kind of campaign they run. The voters are not likely to support a full-scale assault on Reaganism, however, unless the economy goes into a deep recession or there is a foreign-policy disaster. If neither of those things happens, the new institutional order created during Reagan's first term and confirmed by the 1984 election is likely to persist. Why? Not because Reagan converted Americans to his beliefs or persuaded them to join his party, but because he did what all successful political innovators do—he created new facts.

REAGANISM, LIBERALISM, AND THE DEMOCRATS

ROBERT KUTTNER

I

In 1926, three years before the Great Crash and a decade before publication of his own grand synthesis, John Maynard Keynes wrote a prophetic essay titled "The End of Laissez-Faire." "Some coordinated act of intelligent judgement is required," he wrote, "as to the scale on which it is desirable that the community as a whole should save, the scale on which these savings should go abroad in the form of foreign investments, and whether the present organisation of the investment market distributes savings along the most nationally productive channels. I do not think these matters should be left entirely to the chances of private judgement and private profits as they are at present."

Over the course of the 1930s, that lesson was learned at great cost. The major democracies came out of World War II persuaded that the capitalist system itself could not withstand the instabilities of pure laissez-faire, either economically or politically. The postwar Keynesian era enlisted the nation-state to make the "coordinated act of intelligent judgement"—to regulate demand, to channel investment, to broker social contracts between industry and labor, and to prevent speculative excess from wrecking the market itself. Yet, in the shelter of a mixed economy and a social peace, a peculiar reversion happened; "Keynesianism" was captured by moderate conservatives, while pure, brute capitalism abruptly made a phoenixlike recovery, both as institution and as ideology. By the late 1970s, the globalization of commerce resurrected the reality of laissez-faire and blurred the memory of its multiple hazards.

The global integration of the economy and the abrupt decline of the United States as hegemon have created a series of interlocking political and economic problems, exacerbated by the second stock market crash. They add up to a political economy in which the available instruments of the Keynesian compromise have lost much of their potency. Almost by definition, the policies of regulation, stabilization, redistribution, the recognition of trade unions, and the other tricks in the postwar Keynesian kit operate within the nation-state. Social contracts between industry and labor, public-purpose strictures on private financial institutions, and policies of fiscal stimulus can only work when the polity has a boundary. But in a porous economy, national governments have far fewer devices to tame the brute energy of the market. François Mitterrand discovered that this constrained French socialism in 1981, and Ronald Reagan belatedly discovered that it equally constrained the American supply-side experiment, on a Monday in October 1987.

In effect, the nation-state has lost a good measure of its sovereignty, both to other nations and to private-market forces. Moreover, the few, relatively modest transnational public institutions invented after World War II to stabilize the private global economy—the World Bank, the International Monetary Fund, the Bretton Woods system of currency stabilization, and the GATT—have also lost substantial influence to private-market forces. Reinventing a stable mixed economy at a global level will prove far more difficult than devising one within a nation-state.

Both the economic and political implications of these developments are profound. At the most general political level, the resurrection of laissez-faire institutions and the resurrection of laissez-faire ideology have gone hand in hand. Conservative governments have cheered on the deregulation, the privatization, and the internationalization of global markets. And as the resurrection of laissez-faire has proceeded, it has put democratic-left parties in a predictable quandary. It has left them far less able to deliver economic well-being to their constituencies, and therefore necessarily weaker politically. This has been especially true in the United States, where our "left" party, the Democrats, have always been ideologically squeamish about challenging the primacy of the market.

If wages are in global competition, social contracts between industry and labor quickly come unstuck and unions are less believable as defenders of workers' living standards. If a policy of demand stimulus "leaks out" to buy imports, then a government can put the nation further into deficit and get nothing for its pains but a cheapened currency. If the worldwide producer with the cheapest price gets to dominate the market, then comparative advantage merely means which nation pays the lowest wage. Against a context of global laissez-faire, the necessary tools of domestic planning lose their potency. The justifiably celebrated program of farm stabilization, or the regulation of special-purpose financial institutions, or attempts to rebuild uncompetitive industries, are both ideologically illegitimate and economically ineffective.

All of these dilemmas were gathering force throughout the 1980s. The United States, for a time, was able to defy the Mitterrand dilemma only because the dollar is still the dominant reserve currency of international commerce. As a result, America could run a growing trade deficit and a large budget deficit, which would normally lead to a run on one's currency (as befell the French franc in 1981). But in the American case, the government could compensate for the weak fiscal picture by keeping U.S. interest rates relatively high and the dollar artificially strong. This induced foreign investors, in a newly deregulated global money market, to invest in dollars, in U.S. Treasury bonds, and in the New York Stock Exchange. In the long run, of course, a high dollar only deepened the competitiveness problem and widened the trade deficit, because it made U.S.-made goods dear and foreign ones cheap. But the maneuver bought time.

In September 1985, however, the finance ministers of the major industrial nations agreed that the dollar was too high, that the growing trade imbalance threatened the very viability of the trading system, and that floating exchange rates cost more in instability than they gained in textbook "efficiency." This bit of almost Keynesian heresy was devised by the most conservative of officials, representing the conservative administrations of Yasuhiro Nakasone, Helmut Kohl, Margaret Thatcher, and Ronald Reagan. It was a necessary concession to reality—and it bought two more years. Although foreign private investors holding dollars or dollar investments could expect to lose something when the dollar began falling, foreign central banks, who were pledged to support the deal, stepped in where foreign private investors got off. Foreign capital continued financing the twin U.S. deficits, and interest rates stayed moderate. As a result, the U.S. stock market kept climbing and foreign investors stayed in, hoping to gain more from stock appreciation than they lost from dollar depreciation. It was also hoped that the cheaper dollar would lead market forces to purchase more U.S. goods, and thereby eventually shrink the U.S. trade deficit. This scenario was optimistically termed "the soft landing."

But by early fall 1987, it was clear that a cheaper dollar wasn't solving the U.S. trade deficit. On the contrary, it meant that it took more U.S. exports to buy the same quantity of foreign imports. And foreign producers—who managed their production and collaborated with their governments far more than the laissez-faire ideology acknowledged—proved very adroit at shaving their prices and maintaining their market share. The dollar could drop 60 percent against the yen, and the U.S. retail price of a Toyota did not move. By the fall of 1987, the available policy levers had ceased to work. Fear of U.S. inflation led the Federal Reserve to tighten the money supply, pushing interest rates above 10 percent and spooking the stock market. The dollar nonetheless seemed primed for a further drop, making both domestic and foreign investors nervous. The spirit of the Plaza Accord was turning frosty; the Germans were unilaterally raising their own interest rates and U.S. Treasury Secretary James Baker was publicly sniping at Bonn. That spooked the market, too. Any of these events might have provided the spark, because it was all too clear that the system was out of running room. Failing to raise taxes and widening the twin deficits only meant crawling farther out on an unsustainable limb. But belatedly acting to raise taxes, once the damage had been done, would contract demand and only increased the likelihood of recession. When the stock market crashed, commentators argued whether the proximate cause had been talk of a tax increase—or failure to enact one. In a sense, both views were correct.

At this writing (early November 1987), a lot of laissez-faire shibboleths have been rapidly abandoned. It was not only the stock market that crashed in October; the credibility of an entire generation of neo–free-market intellectuals was questioned. A mixed economy has never looked better. After resisting for six years, President Reagan at last blinked and accepted a modest tax increase (in exchange for more spending cuts). When he announced his capitulation, Reagan, significantly, declared that "everything is on the table but Social Security." He exempted our most socialistic (and expensive) domestic program not out of love for socialized retirement, but because Social Security is simply too well entrenched to oppose. There may also be a lesson here for some of the more fainthearted Democrats.

The disgrace of laissez-faire is further evidenced by the fact that the Great Powers have been attempting a far greater degree of international economic management than the invisible hand would otherwise condone. Monetarist dogma has been discarded in the interest of supplying the system with liquidity. The monetary spigot, for the moment, is the one device that seems available. Reportedly, Federal Reserve Chairman Alan Greenspan kept the crash from worsening only by reportedly pumping billions of extra liquidity into the economy, pushing down interest rates and keeping investors from deserting stock markets altogether.

In early 1988, confidence was restored, and the market seemed to be probing for a bottom that represented a bearable drop of 30 to 40 percent rather than the thud that finally marked bottom in 1933—a drop to one-tenth of the market's 1929 peak, accompanied by a 50 percent loss in the output of the real economy. But in the original Great Crash, that result took four years. It was not until 1931 that the Great Depression really hit, after President Hoover had acted to balance the federal budget, after the Fed acted to tighten credit, after unprotected banks began failing, and after a trade war broke out internationally. We are, of course, less than a year into the Crash of '87, and the long term is fraught with peril, both economically and politically.

Economically, the risk is that the stock market crash finally got Ronald Reagan's attention—but too late, and only to substitute the depressive economics of Hoover for the giddy and unsustainable economics of Laffer. Politically, the risk is that the Democrats won't be able to think up anything better. There is now a dreadful, dismal bipartisan consensus that a day of reckoning is at hand, that the bill for the credit binge of the 1980s, as predicted, has finally come due; and that whatever we may want politically, there is simply no technical alternative to a period of austerity and lower living standards. Peter G. Peterson, a traditional Republican Wall Street conservative (and one-time Nixon commerce secretary), is the grand apostle of this view. Peterson, in what seemed to be a masterstroke of prophetic timing, was on the cover of the October *Atlantic* with a gloomy jeremiad ("The Morning After"), warning that it would be better to tighten belts moderately now than disastrously later. The need to impose fiscal discipline serves as a handy stalking horse for the broader ideological and partisan agenda of continuing to dismantle the welfare state and the mixed economy. Peterson's Democratic counterpart, Lester Thurow, had argued in his 1985 book *The Zero-Sum Solution* that rebuilding the American economy would require increased savings rates, shrunken deficits, and "sacrifices," albeit sacrifices more equitably shared. Just as French socialists circa 1982 made grim jokes about "austerity with a human face," the 1987 stock market crash seemed to confirm the inevitability of some form of austerity in the United States. And thanks to the integrated global economy, even the virtuous nations with high rates of savings and productivity seemed likely to be dragged down into a general cycle of recession.

In the partisan maneuvering over the Reagan budget deficit, the Democrats got themselves painted into a fiscal and ideological corner. Increasingly, the only domestic issue came to be the budget deficit. In their new role as champions of fiscal responsibility, Democrats found themselves accepting the premise that any new taxes had to be used to reduce the budget deficit, rather than for new spending. This meant that even as Democrats began to recover some ideological self-confidence after 1986, and began proposing neglected public needs such as health insurance or lifetime education, the impulse to spend was nicely short-circuited by the fiscal legacy of Reaganism.

Astonishingly, in September 1987, it was the Democrats who voted to tighten the fiscal noose when they devised and sold to a reluctant White House a surprise resurrection of the Gramm-Rudman-Hollings bill, whose "trigger" had been declared unconstitutional by the courts in 1986. This unlikely outcome both symbolized and prolonged the disastrously misplaced fiscal politics of the Democratic response to Reaganism, which in turn prolongs the ideological paralysis. It dramatized the short-term, purely tactical nature of Democratic thinking, and the way that the internal legislative preoccupations of the Congress obscured broader strategic imperatives of liberalism. It was the culmination of several years of Democrats' frustration in the effort to make President Reagan share responsibility for a tax increase that virtually everybody else in Washington considered both inevitable and already dangerously delayed.

In late 1987, Gramm-Rudman provided the framework for the long awaited compromise in which the President reluctantly accepted a token tax increase and Congressional Democrats accepted further spending cuts. Another round of deficit reduction is scheduled for 1988, and at this writing, no prominent Democrat seems inclined to propose that taxes should be increased not just to clean up Reagan's bookkeeping mess, but to address public needs that benefit the constituents of the Democratic party.

The stated views of prominent Democratic presidential candidates and semicandidates serve to illustrate the depth of the fiscal paralysis and the ideological paralysis that it engendered. Paul Simon, the avowed New Deal/Fair Deal Democrat in the early field for 1988, proposed a liberal version of Ronald Reagan's own "voodoo economics"—spending increases (social, not military), no new taxes, and a balanced budget. The program seemed appealing, but the plain arithmetic had no more plausibility than Reagan's version circa 1980. Michael Dukakis advocated minimal spending increases, but proposed mainly deficit reduction, to be financed primarily by hoped-for windfall improvements in IRS compliance. Bruce Babbitt did call for higher taxes, but regressive consumption taxes, with the proceeds to be dedicated mainly to deficit reduction, and not for new public spending. Even Mario Cuomo, the most New Deal–oriented of the prominent Democrats, could be found in late 1987 squiring Peter G. Peterson around Washington, embracing Peterson's call for a bipartisan commission to install fiscal orthodoxy as the sequel to Reaganomics. Cuomo's own fairly bold advocacy of government as champion of the oppressed and instrument of democracy's common purpose was thus effectively short-circuited by his embrace of budget balance as the main concern of public policy.

In short, no Democrat, other than Jesse Jackson, has seemed able to transcend the fiscal and philosophical legacy of Reaganism, despite the fact that the Reagan presidency was largely discredited. In Congress, the main task continues to be budget-cutting. In exchange for Republicans agreeing to trim military spending, Democrats got to cut social programs and raise taxes—not a very populist or electorally attractive program.

Though the political pendulum seems primed for one of its epochal swings, the fiscal deadlock prevents it from swinging to progressive policies and ideas. As the more eccentric conservatives—supply-siders and monetarists—were discredited by events and by the arithmetic of the twin deficits, the mantle of legitimacy has fallen back upon ordinary conservatives. There could be no better metaphor for that reality than the odd alliance between Peter G. Peterson and Mario Cuomo.

II

American liberalism had stumbled into the 1980s, unsure about its principles and substantially immobilized in its means. The Reagan presidency only intensified both problems. It deepened the liberal confusion about core beliefs, and deprived liberals of necessary policy levers.

Since the 1930s, liberalism has been the prevailing ideology of Democrats, and Democrats the instrument of liberalism. Modern liberalism has been politically ascendant whenever Democrats have been successful at building bonds with ordinary voters, usually based on a kind of rough economic populism that tempered the extremes of the marketplace and delivered security and opportunity to the nonwealthy majority. Philosophically, Democrats still tend to identify partly with the older liberal tradition of individualism. Yet practically, the one notion that reliably unites the party is the idea that government ought to be deployed to benefit common people. When the formula works, the voters reciprocate; but when government seems paralyzed and Adam Smith seems the only available salvation, voters are more inclined to support Republicans.

At the level of stated ideology, Democrats begin at a slight disadvantage, because they are the party that more or less believes in government, in a society that is, by reflex, antistatist. But they more than compensate for this liability when they manage to deliver concrete benefits.

This is the partisan implication of the famous observation made two decades ago by the political scientists Lloyd Free and Hadley Cantril, who noted the seemingly anomalous public-opinion finding that Americans are "philosophical conservatives, but operational liberals." In practice, post–New Deal Democrats are really operational social democrats. In practice, though seldom in theory, the implicit liberal ideology is that the market generates unacceptable instability and injustice, for which the polity must compensate. In this respect, the American voter is the opposite of his French cousin, who is said to carry his heart on the left but his wallet on the right. Americans carry their libertarian hearts somewhere on the right. But they are quite willing to enjoy the

benefits of activist government, as long as nobody puts too fine
a philosophical point on it. That is why implicitly socialistic
programs like Medicare, Social Security, and public education
enjoy overwhelming support, despite wide professed voter skepticism of "big government." And this, of course, is the essence of
the Democratic electoral strategy otherwise known as tax-and-
spend. The original version of that line, incidentally, was uttered
by Harry Hopkins in 1934, and it went, "Tax and tax, spend and
spend, *elect and elect.*"

Democrats got into trouble in the 1970s for several reasons; the
world economy faltered into a bout of stagflation, which justly or
unjustly exposed the Democrats as poor economic managers. The
Vietnam War and the "social issues" left legacies that split the
New Deal coalition along its latent fault lines, where once economic populism had bridged them. Working-class Democrats
began deserting the party, or simply staying home, based on a
number of mutually reinforcing factors. The party's social conscience suddenly seemed directed only at minorities and the dependent poor; the war generated an antiwar movement that was
culturally alien to the white working class; the good years turned
into hard times and the abrupt globalization of the world economy
weakened the labor movement and left blue-collar workers doubting that traditional liberal approaches any longer protected their
interests. The failure of consecutive presidents to grasp the populist aspect of tax policy left inflation to mix poisonously with the
tax code, pushing working-class voters into high tax brackets and
inviting a tax revolt, depriving government of the taxes to finance
the spending.

The New Deal formula, in short, hit stall speed. The welfare
state and the activism of government became something for

"them"—for ethnic and cultural minorities and the certified poor. In the liberal heyday, 1933–68, activist government was something for "us." A generation ago, the link between citizen, polity, and party was nicely bonded by things like FHA starter homes, and Social Security, and GI college loans, and two decades of useful, visible public works, ranging from the interstate highway system to local junior colleges. But today, when a youngish voter wonders what government has done for him lately, he is more likely to think of the IRS. Without public strategies that address contemporary needs, there is little prospect of extending these necessary links to a generation too young to remember the New Deal, and for whom Social Security signals not safe retirement but annoying payroll taxes. Not since the Medicare legislation of 1965, a generation ago, has legislation been enacted giving the broad electorate tangible, solidarity-enhancing benefits from government.

And finally, toward the end of the decade, the Democratic incumbency of 1977–81 was presided over by a president with weak party loyalties who was skeptical of the traditional liberal formula. When the economy went into a tailspin, Jimmy Carter abandoned the constituency politics of "tax and spend," bowed to the free market, and reverted to traditional fiscal conservatism.

So Democrats entered the 1980s doubting their principles, as well as lacking practical resources. The election and subsequent presidency of Ronald Reagan compounded both problems. Thus, while the Iran-contra scandal and the recapture of the Senate in 1986 served to embolden liberalism somewhat, the continuing straightjacket imposed by Reagan's fiscal legacy short-circuited the progressive impulse whenever Democrats began imagining affirmative uses of government that might address needs, appeal to voters, and restore the Democrats' role as political guardian of a functioning social contract between citizen, economy, and polity.

In this respect, Reaganism is the full-blown manifestation of trends that were already weakening the liberal camp a decade ago. Fiscal Reaganism and ideological Reaganism reinforce each other, and moot the liberal impulse. That is the practical legacy of Reaganism as it affects liberalism. It leaves liberals with a choice: either they must embrace neoliberalism, forswear taxing and spending, and compete as better managers, more attractive faces, and more cogent wielders of symbols in a polity that increasingly addresses only the upper middle class; or they can blast out of the immobilizing assumptions of Reaganism, much as the necessary activism of wartime government in the third Roosevelt term finally achieved the full-blown form of Keynesianism that eluded FDR throughout the New Deal. In the economy of the 1990s, which is likely to be stagnant, grossly unequal, but not cataclysmic, this will be no easy task, either philosophically or fiscally.

For almost a decade, the necessary link between practical government and Democratic electoral success has been severed, first by the budget crunch, then by a misreading of Ronald Reagan's popularity and Walter Mondale's defeat, and finally by a politics of permanent fiscal paralysis that Democrats ironically helped impose. It was widely held that Mondale's worst single mistake was his call for a tax increase, when in fact his tax proposal was only the most visible nail in an ornate political coffin. Moreover, public-opinion polls suggest, as they have throughout his presidency, that Reagan won voter support for everything *but* his ideology, and that his extreme negative view of government actually cost him voter approval. But the prevailing view was that

Mondale lost because he was "too liberal" and that successful Democrats must move toward the center.

The political success of Reaganism seemed to validate the neoliberal critique of Democratic progressivism. Neoliberals embraced Republican-style critiques of special-interest politics, excluding from this category, however, bankers, brokers, and the Fortune 500. This became a ritual critique of Democrats, mindlessly repeated by commentators, as if general-interest policies could be accomplished on the cheap!

Neoliberals shared the Republican view of "entitlements" and of trade unions. They saw broad, embracing programs like Social Security and Medicare not as coalition-building enterprises in social citizenship that had the further virtue of locking in support for affirmative government and its natural custodian, the Democrats, but as budget-busting monstrosities that subsidized the middle class instead of targeting money to the "truly needy." What this critique overlooked was the most fundamental principle in the political economy of social spending: programs that only serve the poor are poor programs. Poor people, when isolated as a distinct category, are monumentally unpopular. Means-tested programs such as Medicaid and Aid to Families with Dependent Children are chronically underfunded, while citizen entitlements like Social Security and Medicare are nicely bolstered against conservative attack. Labor unions, instead of being seen as a core constituency of working-class political mobilization and the necessary glue of the nation's left-of-center party, were excoriated as just another narrow interest group. The AFL-CIO executive board contributed to that view when it brought the teamsters' union back into the federation without exacting any reforms in return.

In this climate, a new party faction, the Democratic Leadership

Council, became the institutional embodiment of the current wisdom that Democrats were too liberal; that they had to move away from taxing and spending, and recapture the hearts of white southern voters in particular by demonstrating toughness on defense and disdain of trade unions, minorities, and poor people. The DLC appropriated earlier critiques of the party's "New Politics" wing, without understanding that the one serious fault of the New Politics was its abandonment of the lunch-bucket voter. The DLC failed to indicate how macho foreign policy and little else would repair the links to alienated working-class white voters.

The DLC represented the latest phase in the stormy, shotgun marriage between the national Democratic Party and its once-solid southern wing. Prior to 1968, many Dixiecrats had been racist, but surprisingly populist on economic issues; their populism simply excluded blacks. After the civil rights revolution, most elected southern Democrats became racial moderates; but as they moved cautiously left on civil rights, they moved right on economics, embracing "modern" regional business elites. Thus, the southern wing of the party became less a force for racial conservatism than for economic conservatism.

The signal difference between the Reagan era and the one that began fading after 1968 was that during the middle third of the century, Democrats and liberals defined the public agenda: How to keep the economy at full employment. How to tame and domesticate the brute energy of laissez-faire capitalism, via regulation and redistribution. How to care for society's unfortunates. Republican responses during the Democratic ascendancy were typically weak imitations of Democratic proposals: "Eldercare"—a circa-1964 voluntary substitute for Medicare; Nixon's Family Assistance Plan, a stripped-down version of the left's call for a guaranteed annual income; as well as probusiness variants on antitrust, health, safety, and environmental regulation. After about 1978, Republicans defined the issues—tax-cutting, privatization, deregulation, budget balance, celebration of the entrepreneur—and Democrats responded with their own weak tea.

Many of the "new ideas" offered by ostensible Democrats in the Reagan era reflected the vain effort to compete on Republican terms, and underscored the Democrats' distance from both their historical identity and electoral logic. One proposal widely embraced by neoliberals was Professor Martin Weitzman's blueprint for a "share economy"; Weitzman hypothesized that unemployment persisted because workers were paid in wages, which were rigid, rather than in shares of company earnings, which could fluctuate with the economy and allow firms to keep hiring more workers (though presumably at lower pay). Professor Weitzman's plan invited workers to share the risks of entrepreneurship, but conferred none of the perquisites of shareholding. Nor did it deal with the role (or nonrole) of trade unions. It was splendidly indifferent to the power relationships within a corporation. Though hailed by no less than the *New York Times* as the best idea since Keynes, the Weitzman proposal was more accurately the best idea since Adam Smith. It was a pure variant on the invisible hand, simply replacing a worn-out gear with a more efficient one, to keep the automatic clockwork economy running smoothly.

In the 1980s, the Democrats' own economic advisers were very like Republican economists in their new romance with Adam Smith, whether the issue was international trade, exchange rates, industrial policy, or trade unionism. Keynes had taught that economies periodically slip into inflationary booms or depressive busts unless government intervenes to manage aggregate demand. "Macroeconomics" mattered. A generation of progressive presidents and prime ministers, some of them slightly anticipating

Keynes, acted on this prescription. While Keynes the man had a lot more to say about the limits of laissez-faire, the socialization of savings, etc., by the time Keynes was canonized and fossilized by the economics establishment as a fixture of the "neoclassical synthesis," his teachings had been constricted into the view that *only* macroeconomics matters, and that attempts at regulation or industrial planning are impermissible distortions of natural price mechanisms, which are best left to the free market. By the advent of the Reagan era, the Democrats' own economic advisers were quick to short-circuit any impulse that perhaps the new economics of global interdependence required a more full-blooded form of Keynesianism and a more interventionist use of government. Thus, any impulse to be venturesome met censure from the party's own experts as scientifically unsound.

III

Because of these twin constraints—the ideological confusion and the fiscal straightjacket—any Democrat elected to Congress since about 1978 has been denied the experience of spending public funds to address public needs, or intervening to civilize the private economy. Rather, the exercise has been primarily a debate about what to cut, how to deregulate, how to undermine the mixed economy on which Democratic bonds with voters depends. To the extent that Democrats indulged the thought of raising taxes at all, this has usually been directed at fiscal responsibility and not at delivering benefits to citizens. But of course that approach really does risk repeating Mondale's fatal mistake of offering the tax without the "spend" (and hence without the "elect").

After their narrow recapture of the Senate in 1986, in which several relatively populist candidates won Republican seats, Democrats began to recover a measure of philosophical self-confidence. The copycat, antigovernment rhetoric from the party's center-right subsided. It began to dawn on the Democratic presidential field that the deferred problems left by the departing Reagan administration will all require substantial public expenditure. Other than such fiscally neutral ventures as a more enlightened foreign policy, and perhaps some selective reregulation, all the themes Democratic candidates have sounded carry a price tag. Welfare reform costs money. Public works cost money. Rebuilding the educational system and upgrading the quality of the work force for the sake of competitivenness cost a lot of money. So do day care, starter homes for young families, and targeted research and development, to say nothing of national health insurance and a cure for AIDS. To put a very crude, back-of-the-envelope estimate on the cost of all these needs, something like $40 billion is necessary to put money where the Democrats' mouth is.

But on both sides of the political aisle, as the 1988 presidential election approached, the only seeming domestic issue of consequence was the budget deficit. Democrats remained paralyzed by the same assumption that immobilized Walter Mondale's hapless campaign—that they had to be more fiscally responsible than the Republicans. That meant embracing the awkward politics of a tax increase, but only to balance the government's books, not to address citizen needs. In fact, in the bizarre fiscal politics of 1987 and 1988, the business community actually outflanked both Republicans and Democrats, proposing a national value-added tax as the remedy for the deficit (from Charls Walker's antitax American Council for Capital Formation!), as well as an $11 billion increase in aid to education (from the mainline Committee for Economic Development). Meanwhile, the Democrats were reviving the Gramm-Rudman-Hollings bill, whose "trigger" had been declared unconstitutional by the courts in 1986.

From the perspective of most Democrats, the original 1985 law was a desperation measure, with one big flaw and one big appeal. The flaw was that its schedule of mandatory deficit reductions was unrealistically stringent, and was depressive fiscal policy. The original formula, requiring the deficit to be cut to $108 billion by Fiscal Year 1989 and zero by 1991, would have required spending cuts of such draconian proportions that the economy would be thrown into a depression, and what remained of discretionary social spending would be all but wiped out. On the other hand, the very stringency of the Gramm-Rudman formula would, as the saying went, "put the gun to Reagan's head" and force him to take either a tax increase or cuts in military spending, or both. On that basis, several liberal Democrats led by Massachusetts Senators Ted Kennedy and John Kerry put aside their misgivings and reluctantly voted for the original bill.

In retrospect, Kennedy and Kerry were onto something. However, before the issue could be forced, the Supreme Court disarmed Gramm-Rudman's mandatory trigger. The court held that the law breached the constitutional separation of powers by directing a congressional employee, the comptroller general, to carry out the mandatory cuts in the event that Congress missed the budget targets. That left Gramm-Rudman as a series of goals and timetables, but without teeth. If Congress failed to meet the targets, there would be no worse consequence than another spate of embarrassing headlines and the knowledge that the fiscal fuse was continuing to burn while the legislators fiddled.

In the meantime, the moral suasion imposed by even a tooth-less Gramm-Rudman law did not work out so badly for the Democrats, either in terms of budget priorities or as fiscal policy. From a liberal viewpoint, the budget of fiscal 1987 was by far the best of the Reagan budgets. Military spending was held virtually level at about $289 billion, which was about a 3 percent real cut over 1986 when adjusted for inflation. Domestic social spending was protected from further cuts, and a few programs such as Head Start and Aid to Education actually got modest increases. For the first time since 1981, the reductions in health outlays were achieved by reducing payments to providers rather than limiting services to consumers. The year 1987 also saw token increases in taxes. And the deficit was actually cut from $222 billion in 1986 to an estimated $155 billion in 1987. Economically, this sort of glide path toward a soft landing also made sense as fiscal policy. With unemployment still above 6 percent and inflation still low, it described a sensible, sustainable form of Keynesianism.

But 1987 was a fortuitous fiscal year in several respects, which could not be repeated. Congress benefited from the architecture of the 1986 tax-reform act, which was written to be "revenue neutral" on the whole but to surreptitiously increase revenues in its first year to buy politically painless, one-time deficit reduction. Because of the "structural" nature of the real deficit—the fact that projected tax revenues simply fell short of projected spending—the deficit was expected to head back toward the $200 billion range in 1988 and 1989. In the 1987 fiscal year, Congress also saved money from slightly higher-than-projected growth, from a one-time cash-in of capital gains, from sales of federal assets that will not be repeated, and from an unexpected drop in interest rates, which are now on the rise again. FY 1987 was the year of the free lunch.

Throughout 1987, there were off-and-on negotiations to put a new trigger back into Gramm-Rudman. This was easy enough to accomplish technically; it simply involved giving authority to the Office of Management and Budget, in the executive branch, to carry out the mandatory cuts, rather than the comptroller. But as a political matter, fixing Gramm-Rudman proved very difficult—and very illuminating. Until the deal was struck, in September 1987, every time Democrats and Republicans got close to a formula, the White House stepped in, imploring congressional Republicans to back off, for precisely the reason that Senators Kerry and Kennedy foresaw: a Gramm-Rudman formula with teeth would indeed require a hefty tax increase or stiff defense cuts, and probably both.

In the yearlong jousting about what sort of deficit-reduction formula to reinvent, timing became the key issue. Republicans generally and White House loyalists in particular pressed Democrats to "rear-load" the formula—impose very modest cuts in the final two Reagan budgets, and make sure that very stiff ones occur during the next administration. If the Democrats won the White House in 1988, this would make them take responsibility for the inevitable tax increase and would force them to cut programs serving Democratic constituencies, quite possibly in the midst of a recession, when Democratic constituencies would be needing increased public outlays. In this jousting, Senator Gramm, of all people, emerged as apologist for big deficits, arguing for only token cuts in fiscal 1988 and 1989. On the other hand, liberal Democrats (once tarred as big spenders) held out for much tougher deficit reduction in the short run, both as necessary fiscal policy and to get the present administration to share the political pain with the next one.

Finally, in mid-September 1987, the Republican bluffing worked; Democrats caved in, as the price of winning a common deficit-reduction program. Those Democrats in Congress who grasped the long-term, paralytic logic of Gramm-Rudman were in the minority. The new house speaker, Jim Wright, who had advocated scrapping Gramm-Rudman and raising taxes, could not deliver support. His archrival in the Democratic leadership, Ways and Means Committee Chairman Dan Rostenkowski, offered a formula letting the White House off with quite modest and flexible cuts in the two final Reagan years, leaving the draconian cuts for after the 1988 election. Rather than imposing specific year-by-year deficit *targets* for the remaining two Reagan budgets (as the original Gramm-Rudman law did), the new formula merely required annual reductions. The deficit had to be cut by $23 billion from 1987 to 1988, and another $36 billion in 1989.

The difference in the two approaches seems arcane, but it is crucial. Not only are the 1988 and 1989 cuts relatively modest; the approach is far more flexible (and sensible), because it pegs the cuts to changes in the real economy. If the economy goes into a slump, and the actual 1988 deficit is higher than anticipated, Gramm-Rudman II provides only that the required cut will be a reduction from the actual deficit, and not a number mandated according to a predetermined schedule. In a recession, this could mean the difference between having to cut $23 billion and having to cut $70 billion or $80 billion. Ironically, Reagan himself was so obsessed with avoiding a tax increase that he threatened a veto until the very last minute, despite the evident partisan windfall to the Republican side.

The 1988 and 1989 cuts mandated by Gramm-Rudman II were sufficiently moderate that any tax increase would be very mild. The mandatory sequestering of funds, which would go into effect if Congress failed to meet the target, indeed forced Reagan to swallow some higher taxes and some defense cuts, but only token ones. The Democrats won their symbolic victory of forcing Reagan to take some taxes, but the "gun to Reagan's head" was a popgun. The real headache is saved for the next administration. Beginning in Fiscal 1990, the first budget of the new administration, the formula reverts to a much more rigid approach: a deficit of no more than $100 billion in FY 1990, $64 billion in 1991, $28 billion in 1992, and zero in 1993.

Not only will this put the next administration under excruciating pressure either to enact exorbitant and unpopular tax increases or further slash social programs, or both, but unless Reaganomics has repealed the business cycle, this will very likely happen in a recession when demands for unemployment compensation, emergency jobs, urban aid, etc., are rising and revenues are falling. Although there is a waiver suspending the formula in the event of a serious recession, as soon as the recession ends, the formula springs back, and this will have the effect of aborting a recovery as soon as it begins. Fiscally, Gramm-Rudman is improbable Democratic politics, since it essentially endorses Hooverian economic logic. In a normal economy, a reasonable and sustainable deficit is 1.5 to 2 percent of GNP, or about $100 billion, not zero. It is a mark of how far they strayed from both their political compass and their economic common sense that a majority of Democrats in both houses voted to write into law a mandatory balanced budget.

By all accounts, the Democratic leadership went along with this scheme for three reasons. First, they had been waiting for more than five years to make the Republicans share responsibility for raising taxes, and they got caught up in the exhilaration of finally seeming to do it. Second, in the Rostenkowski compromise, Democrats were able to get Republicans to give up several other odious budget "reforms," such as a proposal to let the president sign or veto appropriation bills one at a time, which would have given him free rein to cut social programs without giving up any defense spending in return. But Republicans did not have the votes to enact this scheme in any case.

Third, the House leadership got dazzled by the prospect of a short-term "win," and convinced itself that it should be easy to go back and revise the formula in 1989, should a Democrat be elected president. But that may turn out to be a disastrous miscalculation. In January 1989, if a Democrat is in the White House, Congress will be laboring to produce a FY 1990 budget against a mandatory deficit target of $100 billion. According to current projections, that means finding new taxes or program cuts of $50 billion to $70 billion (and more if the economy is in recession). Republican legislators will hardly be eager to let the Democrats off that delicious hook.

The most obvious "hopeful" scenario is the usual one that plagues Democrats: seemingly, they are left with no strategy more imaginative than rooting for a recession. In a recession, all fiscal bets are off. Assuming that Democrats are lucky enough that the next recession hits the Republicans rather than them, there is still a very tricky balancing act to consider. They would need to raise taxes enough to reduce the deficit somewhat, but not so much that the fiscal contraction causes the recession to deepen; and they also need to overcome their aversion to "tax-and-spend" jeers, and reap enough revenues to spend some public money.

Without some new resources to spend on long-neglected problems, the Democrats have little prospect of restoring the crucial link between voter, party, and constructive government, which is their time-honored recipe for electoral success. Democrats, one way or another, have to bite this bullet or they might as well join the Republican Party.

IV

A few illustrations of recent policy paralysis make the point. The needs of today's wage-earning voters are obviously different from those of the New Deal or Great Society eras, but the political logic—of connecting citizen to polity to party—persists. This is evident in the several issues that invariably end up on the short list of Democratic platforms: "competitiveness," job opportunity, education, health care, housing, family policies.

Welfare reform is a particularly poignant case because it dramatically illustrates just how Democrats have finally developed an approach that makes very good sense both as social policy and as coalition-building politics—and how fiscal Reaganism has rendered that approach moot. For nearly twenty years, a consensus has been emerging among both experts and politicians that the Aid to Families with Dependent Children program is disastrously self-defeating. From the recipient's perspective, it stigmatizes, demeans, and subsidizes squalor. From society's viewpoint, it promotes dependency. The "safety net" metaphor is all too apt: it is a net in which one stays entangled.

The overwhelming consensus of experts is that there is a straightforward way out of this conundrum. The basic problem is that the means-tested welfare state leaves the welfare mother substantially worse off if she chooses to quit welfare and take a job. A single mother with a young child gets about five hundred dollars a month in AFDC benefits; as a welfare recipient she gets Medicaid, and often subsidized housing, and food stamps, and she is doing her own child care. Taking a job reduces these ancillary benefits. It requires a job that pays seven to eight dollars an hour just to break even. Some of the better Democratic-sponsored state "workfare" programs have wrestled with this dilemma. It turns out, for example, that the much-acclaimed Massachusetts Employment/Training (ET) program actually spends most of its money on child care and on health-insurance subsidies, not on training, for those are the key elements that make it possible for single mothers to get off welfare.

In the federal efforts to reform welfare, Senator Daniel Patrick Moynihan grasped these conundrums, and drafted an imaginative bill to set a general child-support floor; to require all welfare recipients to train for jobs, or work; and to finance transitional benefits so that their income would be held harmless, at least for a few months. But Moynihan quickly bumped up against the reality that doing the job right—with day care and health insurance and meaningful job-training as well as decent child-support levels—would cost $2 billion to $4 billion a year in new money: something unthinkable in the Gramm-Rudman era.

Note also that workfare, done humanely, turns a "wedge" issue back into a "bridge" issue. It puts working-class voters and welfare recipients back on the same side by making it possible for AFDC mothers to go back to work; the Republican version of workfare is mainly society extracting a pound of flesh from people unfortunate enough to be on public assistance. But the Democratic version can't work without public money.

The same logic holds with regard to getting back to a one-class health system, or recognizing that the average American family today is a working family and that the absence of a national child-care policy is a major policy default, or defining competitiveness as having a first-class work force, with access to ongoing education and retraining throughout working life. Polling and focus-group research—and common sense—identify these as winning issues for liberals and Democrats; the themes turn up in one party document after another. But the perceived scarcity of resources intimidates Democrats and cramps the work of spelling out a program.

By the same token, Democrats and moderate Republicans, bolstered by support from mayors of both parties and emboldened by the Democrats' recapture of the Senate, worked throughout 1987 to write the first housing bill in seven years. Housing, while not a highly emotional issue, has taken steeper cuts under Reagan than any other program, with annual appropriations dropping from just over $30 billion before the Reagan era to under $10 billion in 1987. Since most of this money goes to subsidize mortgages or rentals on preexisting contracts, the effect has been to dry up the supply of federally aided new housing to almost zero. The homelessness problem, though partly the reflection of the state's shedding responsibility for the mentally ill, also reflects the fact that housing costs have been outstripping incomes for a decade. Some of the homeless are people of sound mind who simply can no longer afford homes.

The bipartisan bill proposed restorations of community-development block grants, to be used with wide discretion by mayors for housing programs, as well as a new program to build affordable housing using proven community groups. Reagan, of course, threatened a veto of the bill as budget-busting. That proved unnecessary. Under Gramm-Rudman, it was only necessary to raise a point of order that the program busted the budget targets. This budgetary pincer, in the absence of substantial new taxes, is likely to keep the normal shift to the out-party, or the out-philosophy, from being consummated, regardless of who leads the next administration.

In fact, the resources required to begin initiatives in all of these policy areas are not astronomical. About 1 percent of GNP, or $40 billion to $45 billion, which is just about the amount President Reagan cut social spending, could make a dramatic start. There are many available ways to find tax dollars without kindling a new taxpayer revolt, but that requires acknowledging that the purpose of the exercise is to spend new money as well as to reduce the deficit, and to look beyond the conventional sources of "revenue enhancement."

For example, the two-year debate about tax reform gave birth to a new concept—"revenue neutrality" that can be usefully flipped on its side. In the tax-reform process, the idea was that any reduction in tax rates had to be paid for by closing a loophole. However, it is also possible to use something of the same logic to close loopholes in order to redirect tax expenditures. Consider one of the most enormous tax expenditures in the revenue code, the unlimited deduction for home-mortgage interest. This has three seriously negative effects. It provides subsidies regressively (the bigger the house and the higher the tax bracket, the more valuable the tax break); it makes housing too lucrative an investment and hence bids up the cost of housing for young homebuyers; and it costs the Treasury over $30 billion a year.

If the mortgage-interest deduction were capped at, say, 100

percent of the cost of a median-priced house in the local housing market, this would give everybody tax-subsidized basic shelter, but people who wanted luxury shelter would pay the full cost of the increment. That would save the Treasury $10 billion to $15 billion, which could be redirected to where it is needed—starter homes for first-time buyers. Would that be good politics? It certainly would be good for the tens of millions of voters in their twenties and thirties camped out in their parents' houses. Even their parents might be prepared to give up a little tax subsidy to get their adult children out of their spare room.

This approach retargets tax expenditures to more defensible uses within the same general policy purpose. Another example: payroll taxes, which finance Social Security, unemployment compensation, and Medicare, are the most regressive form of tax. What makes them explicitly regressive, as opposed to merely nonprogressive, is the fact that the amount of earnings on which you pay tax is capped. Under current law, if you are fortunate enough to earn more than $43,800 a year, you pay no Social Security tax on the excess, and your rate of payroll tax begins dropping. At incomes of $43,800 or less, it is a flat 14.3 percent (half of which is ostensibly paid by your employer). But if you earn, say $100,000, your effective payroll tax rate is just 6.2 percent.

This system is also perverse in other respects. Not only is it regressive, but its downward bias makes it more expensive for employers to take on new workers, since total payroll taxes increase labor costs by over 15 percent. But policy could reverse that bias by removing the cap at the top, to add some relief at the bottom by exempting the first four thousand dollars of earnings. That would not only make the payroll tax a progressive tax rather than a regressive one and cheapen the cost of adding new workers; it would also produce billions of dollars' worth of additional net revenue to use on payroll-related social costs, such as retraining and lifetime learning.

And this suggests a second new concept, which is really a new wrinkle on a very old idea, namely the idea that specific sources of revenue should be tied to particular uses. We already do this to some extent. Public education is substantially financed by local property taxes; Social Security and Medicare are financed largely by payroll taxes; highways are paid for out of trust funds funded by taxes on fuel. This approach is currently out of fashion in modern public-finance theory, for two reasons. First, it is said to be inflexible. In flush periods, more money comes in than the system needs; in slack periods, needs go unmet. Ideally, in theory, government should raise its revenues from the most appropriate general sources, and decide its spending priorities according to current needs, unconstrained by artificial trust funds. Second, trust funds and single-purpose taxes are in bad odor because they are said to create insatiable constituencies—"iron triangles" of bureaucrats, providers, and consumers.

However, this view leaves out the quite valid political purpose of protecting defensible programs from periodic right-wing wrecking crews. When partisan conservatives are at work destroying programs and severing that necessary link between public program, voter, and the Democratic Party, a little iron is just what is indicated. One of the reasons why airports are such a mess is that President Reagan has refused to spend funds dedicated to airport maintenance and construction. The highway program has been relatively immune to Republican wrecking mainly because it is financed by a more ironclad trust fund. Social Security has escaped largely unscathed because people feel they have earned it with their payroll taxes. In this approach, there is admittedly a danger of excess—programs that outlive their usefulness—but at present the danger is the opposite one that genuine public needs (and Democratic Party purpose) are being starved.

Franklin Roosevelt may have been the last Democratic president who fully grasped this logic. The fiscal experts around Roosevelt who proposed the design for Social Security in 1935 thought he was being a bit silly when he insisted that the entire system be financed out of payroll taxes. They also questioned the device of trust funds as a bit disingenuous, since in practice tax revenues flowed in and benefits flowed out, as in any other public program. But Roosevelt, according to then Labor Secretary Frances Perkins' memoir, presciently explained, "We put those payroll contributions there so as to give the contributors a legal, moral, and political right to collect their pensions and their unemployment benefits. With those taxes in there, no damned politician can ever scrap my social security program."

Modern public-finance theory aside, Democrats may well find that they have to reinvent this approach of tying visible taxes to visible benefits, for good sound political reasons. For example: value-added taxes to finance a modernized labor market, and education and training system; higher estate taxes on the wealthy to pay for college tuition of kids without rich grandfathers; some new progressive luxury-consumption tax to finance necessary social overhead such as day care and health insurance; and maybe a tax on Smith's real-estate windfall to pay for Jones's starter home. This, by the way, should be good populist electoral politics. When the voters are getting something for their taxes, Republicans can scream "Tax and spend!" all they want, and it rolls off.

Unfortunately, the ongoing debate about appropriate fiscal policy has been narrowed by the obsession with the deficit and by the conviction that the voters would be hostile to new taxes. Even the menu of tax options, as illustrated by the encyclopedia published in 1987 by Dan Rostenkowski's House Ways and Means Committee *(Description of Possible Options to Increase Revenues)* reflected the prevailing timidity. It did cost out dozens of possible tax increases, several of which make good political sense, including a capital-gains tax on inherited stock ($5.3 billion in 1988), and a lower limit on the tax deductibility of home-equity loans ($1.8 billion). But Rostenkowski directed his staff not to include such big-ticket and more populist items as a cap on home-mortages loans, or a tax on stock transfers, or a higher top bracket on the personal income tax. Real populist tax reform was just beyond the imagination of most established Democratic politicians.

This was compounded by the infighting between Rostenkowski and House Speaker Jim Wright. In late 1986, Rostenkowski told a conference on tax policy that if taxes should be raised we should begin with a higher top rate on the personal income tax, which is scheduled to drop to 28 percent in 1988. But when Speaker Wright made that proposal his own, Rostenkowski backed away from it.

Holding the top rate at its current level of 38.5 percent for people earning over $75,000 a year would avert up to $22 billion in revenue losses. A stock-transfer tax, which was once on the books in the United States and is still public policy in such booming economies as Japan and Germany (and even in supply-side Britain) would save another $10 billion. Instead, many Democrats have looked timidly to a plague of small and regressive excise taxes.

A populist program of tax increases would be good politics; the top bracket on the income tax would hit only a small fraction of voters, most of them Republicans. Taxing inherited capital gains would not pinch the overwhelming majority of Democrats. A further $20 billion to $30 billion a year can indeed be obtained by tighter tax enforcement, of the sort pioneered by such popular Democratic state tax commissioners as North Dakota's Byron Dorgan (now a congressman), and Massachusetts's Ira Jackson. But tighter tax enforcement to secure budget balance has one political meaning, while increased revenue collection to address deferred public needs has a very different one. The money is not so hard to come by; the political will is.

V

As the Reagan era ends, several interlocking forces isolate the liberal opposition from its New Deal roots: the politics of campaign finance, in which the Wall Street primary matters more than the one on Main Street; the globalization of the economy, which makes it harder for minimalist government intervention to deliver for Democratic voters; and the perverse discipline of the deficit, ironically created by an administration that campaigned on balanced budgets. Reagan managed both to use Keynesian economics to save his own administration and to spoil it for liberals.

Today a basic philosophical divide separates neoliberal Democrats from Democratic progressive populists. For the neoliberals, the Democrats' involvement with interest-group politics and an activist public sector was a mistake; it invited demands that the polity was incapable of satisfying and splintered the coalition. For progressives, the affirmative use of government is the essence of the modern Democratic Party; the only mistake was a failure to continue the momentum of the New Deal/Great Society period; a failure to continue serving broad majorities of wage- and salary-earning voters, who live paycheck to paycheck, and who require the economic opportunity and security that only a mixed economy and an activist government can provide.

Liberalism will remain in the political desert until it regains that essence. It remains to be seen whether that will require an economic depression, or an intellectual revolution, or both. Whether or not Reaganism succeeded in its professed policy goals only history can judge. But it has already been remarkably successful at paralyzing the liberal impulse. If history is any guide, that paralysis is painful but still reversible.

CONSERVATISM AND
THE PRICE OF SUCCESS

JOHN B. JUDIS

> When a way of thinking is deeply rooted in the
> soil, and embodies the instincts or even the
> characteristics of the people, it has a value
> quite independent of its truth.

—George Santayana, *Character and Opinion*
in the United States

Some conservatives believe that when Ronald Reagan leaves office in 1988, he will take the conservative movement with him into retirement. Kevin Phillips, the author of *Post-Conservative America,* writes, "The tides that began launching the conservative era twenty years ago are old and beginning to ebb." New Right activist Paul Weyrich complains that "the 'Reagan Revolution' turned out to be not a revolution at all, but rather a temporary bloodless coup." But others believe that the Reagan years laid the foundation for a conservative America. A future historian, neoconservative Irving Kristol writes, could define the Reagan years "as the first critical stage in the evolution of a conservative majority in American politics." According to Heritage Foundation Vice President Burton Yale Pines, Reagan's "ideas, policies, and principles will continue to dominate U.S.

politics for years after he leaves office, just as the policies and philosophies of Andrew Jackson and Franklin Roosevelt long dominated."

Who is right here? Will the Reagan years have the same impact on the politics of the next decade as did Roosevelt's years in office? Or will Reagan's influence and that of conservatives disappear, as Reagan's right-wing critics claim they did in California after Reagan left the governor's mansion in 1974? It could be that both sides are right. If one looks at conservatism as a rising movement that formed in the mid-fifties, won the Republican nomination for Senator Barry Goldwater in 1964 and then the presidency for Reagan in 1980, its moment may have passed. In 1988, Republican conservatism is very much like the Democratic liberalism of the late forties. It has lost its political majority. Its immediate legislative agenda has been exhausted. Its older leadership is tired. But like the liberalism of the forties, American conservatism has neither expended all its internal resources nor its ability to influence American politics. The Reagan years saw both growth and decay in the movement. While some conservative organizations endured a kind of boom-bust cycle, overinvesting in the hope of political prosperity, the conservatives succeeded in strengthening and consolidating a political infrastructure—in Sidney Blumenthal's words a "counterestablishment"—that will survive the twists and turns of electoral fortune.

Conservative Republicans will undoubtedly suffer from divisions in their ranks, but short of being identified with a losing war or an economic depression, they may remain within striking distance of national and state majorities. And conservative opposition to "big government," Third World nationalism, and affirmative action for minorities will continue to resonate among a significant minority of voters.

I

The existence of an infrastructure is the key to conservatives' political survival. This infrastructure consists of both institutions and trained individuals—what the conservatives, following the Leninist left, call "cadres."

In 1964, when Goldwater unexpectedly won the Republican presidential nomination, the conservative movement had a cause and about thirty thousand grass-roots activists, but few if any political consultants, policy experts, and political scientists. The only conservative organizations were the Young Americans for Freedom and the disreputable John Birch Society. Goldwater had few conservatives experienced at practical politics to run his campaign. Had he miraculously won the presidency, he would not have had been able to fill cabinet or major staff posts with conservatives.

By 1968, the situation had not changed. When Anthony Dolan, a Yale undergraduate and future Reagan speechwriter, met William F. Buckley, Jr. at the Republican Convention in Miami, Dolan predicted that Reagan would win the nomination and lead a Roosevelt-like political revolution in the country. But Buckley, aware of the conservatives' lack of trained leaders, replied, "Where are the assistant professors?"

Over the last two decades, conservatives have developed a political and governing elite capable of sustaining the movement. During the mid and late seventies, lobbying groups, think tanks, and political action organizations were created; during the Reagan years, conservatives have been able to get on-the-job training in running the country. As a result, a new generation of conservative leaders has emerged, capable of filling high Cabinet and White House posts in a future administration.

William Bennett, Reagan's secretary of education, is a case in point. In 1978, he was an assistant to Boston University President John Silber, and under Silber's influence was transformed from an antiwar liberal into a conservative Democrat. He also met neoconservative godfather Irving Kristol, and Kristol's wife, the historian Gertrude Himmelfarb. In 1978, on Himmelfarb's recommendation, Bennett was appointed assistant director of the National Humanities Center in Research Triangle Park, North Carolina. When the director was murdered in 1979, Bennett replaced him. Then in 1981, the neoconservatives waged a successful and acrimonious campaign to win Bennett's appointment as chairman of the National Endowment for the Humanities. In 1985, Bennett succeeded Terrel Bell as Secretary of Education. Bennett not only became one of the administration's principal spokesmen, but brought into the department many young conservatives, including Kristol's son William.

Gary Bauer, Reagan's domestic-policy chief in his second term, enjoyed an even more meteoric rise. In 1980, he was a lobbyist for Direct Marketing Association. His prior political experience had been in the early seventies as a low-level staffer on the Republican National Committee while attending Georgetown Law School. He joined the Reagan campaign in the summer of 1980, and after the election was hired in the Office of Policy Development, where he came to the attention of Attorney General Edwin Meese III. In 1982, Bauer moved to the Department of Education as an assistant secretary. By 1985, he had become Bennett's chief deputy. In 1987, at Meese's urging, he returned to the White House to head the Office of Policy Development. At this post, he advanced the conservative agenda, superintending the administration's stand on abortion, AIDS, and welfare. And he brought in as many young conservatives as he could.

Another cadre, Daniel Oliver, began his political career as a college volunteer on James Buckley's 1970 Senate campaign. From 1973 to 1976, he served as executive editor of *National Review* before rejoining a New York law firm. In 1981, with William Buckley's support, Oliver was appointed general counsel of the Department of Education. After clashing with moderate Terrel Bell, however, he moved to the Agriculture Department in 1983. There, as general counsel, he challenged government aid to farmers. In 1985, again with Buckley's support, he became chairman of the Federal Trade Commission. *Business Week* described him as "the last Reagan revolutionary." He was what was formerly a contradiction in terms: an experienced conservative bureaucrat.

The conservative think tanks were crucial in extending the influence of such cadres. The American Enterprise Institute (AEI), the Hoover Institution, and the Heritage Foundation helped fill many of the administration's mid-level positions and federal judiciary vacancies. AEI, which contributed such luminaries as former U.N. Ambassador Jeane Kirkpatrick, former White House Director of Communications David Gergen, and World Bank President Barber Conable, was a shoestring operation in 1964, when it served as Goldwater's tiny brain trust. By the early eighties, its budget was over $10 million. Heritage, begun in 1973 with a $250,000 grant from right-wing brewer Joseph Coors, moved in 1983 from a set of modest row houses to an $11 million edifice overlooking Capitol Hill. Heritage's staff of more than a hundred published four or five position papers every week. Its computerized personnel office, manned by Louis Cordia, former deputy director of the Environmental Protection Agency, funneled conservative professionals into government jobs.

With the think tanks' help, the Reagan administration reshaped the federal judiciary into an outpost of the conservative movement that will survive immediate changes in government. Before Reagan's term is over, he will have appointed about half the country's 573 federal district judges and 156 appeals court judges and filled as many as three of nine Supreme Court seats. The path from the think tanks to the bench was well worn. For instance, in 1977 Antonin Scalia and Robert Bork, both of whom Reagan nominated to the court of appeals and then the Supreme Court, and Laurence Silberman, whom Reagan appointed to the court of appeals, were AEI fellows—members of a regular discussion group with Kirkpatrick, Kristol, and James C. Miller III, who later became the director of the Office of Management and Budget. Another judge, Danny Boggs, a former Young Republican and disciple of Milton Friedman, was recruited by the Heritage Foundation to help write its massive policy agenda for the incoming Reagan administration, *Mandate for Change.* Heritage then championed his ascent through the federal government, from White House assistant to deputy secretary of energy, and then to the Sixth Circuit U.S. Court of Appeals.

AEI, Heritage, and Hoover are the best-known conservative institutions, but dozens of others have sprung up over the last decade, from the Mountain States Legal Foundation, which contributed James Watt and Anne Gorsuch to the Interior Department, to the Federalist Society, which is incubating a generation of cadres for combat in the legal profession. Founded in 1981, the society by 1987 boasted a membership of over two thousand lawyers and law students. According to Justice Department official Stephen Calabresi, one of its founders, all twelve assistant attorney generals and at least half of the 153 Justice Department officials that Reagan appointed participated in the society.

Across the country, local and regional conservative think tanks have sprung up to supplement the work of Heritage, AEI, and Hoover. Colorado boasts the Shavano Institute for National Leadership, founded by Hillsdale College, and the Independence Institute; Chicago has the Heartland Institute; Seattle, the Washington Institute for Policy Studies; New York, the Manhattan Institute for Policy Research; Dallas, the National Center for Policy Analysis; and San Francisco, the Pacific Research Institute for Public Policy. These think tanks begat others. Heartland, founded in April 1984 by a group of Chicago businessmen, established spinoffs in Cleveland and Detroit.

Conservative publications and other media supplemented the work of the think tanks. During the Reagan years, both *Human Events* and *National Review* reached circulations of over one hundred thousand, and *National Review* served as a training ground for the president's and vice president's speech-writing staffs. Publications like *American Spectator* and the Heritage Foundation's *Policy Review* gained circulation. Conservatives also gained a foothold in the national media. Conservatives controlled the *Wall Street Journal*'s editorial pages. The *Washington Post*'s editorial pages featured conservative columnists George Will, William F. Buckley, Jr., Rowland Evans and Robert Novak, and Charles Krauthammer. And the *New Republic,* once the flagship of modern liberalism, veered rightward, as conservative Fred Barnes joined Krauthammer and neoconservative Morton Kondracke on the masthead. Conservatives also gained some influence in national television. Will became a commentator for ABC-TV. And *National Review* Washington editor John McLaughlin hosted his own weekly talk show, "The McLaughlin Group," funded by the conservative Edison Institute. New publications were launched: *This World Magazine, The National Interest,* and the *Washington Times.* The John M. Olin, Smith Richardson, Lehrman, and Bradley foundations funded publications like Charles Murray's *Losing Ground* and established university chairs to be filled by conservatives. Certain universities and university departments—the Claremont Colleges, the University of Dallas, the University of Chicago Law School and Economics Department, Hillsdale and Rockford colleges—became conservative preserves. And within major universities, conservatives, with the help of the Washington-based Institute for Educational Affairs and wealthy right-wing donors, set up a network of student newspapers. According to IEA director Leslie Lenkowsky (a Kristol protégé), IEA funded thirty-four conservative newspapers, including the *Dartmouth Review,* notorious for publishing articles ridiculing blacks and gays.

Young conservatives were apprenticed on the movement's publications. Two former editors of the *Dartmouth Review,* Ben Hart and Dinesh D'Souza, joined Heritage and a third, Greg Fossedal, arrived at Hoover by way of the *Wall Street Journal* editorial page. In June 1987, D'Souza was hired to work in the White House as an assistant by Gary Bauer. After graduating from the University of Chicago, David Brooks, another pure cadre, was hired by *National Review;* he subsequently went to the *Washington Times,* and from there to the *Wall Street Journal* as book-review editor.

Through this institutional framework of think tanks, organizations, universities, and publications, conservatives have produced a governing class capable of running a Republican administration or constituting itself as a shadow government if the Democrats recapture the White House.

During the Reagan years, the conservatives have also strengthened their hand in the Republican Party. In the forties and fifties, eastern bankers and corporate executives dominated Republican presidential politics, while the midwestern "Old Guard," anti–New Deal and isolationist, reigned supreme in Congress. In 1960, Richard Nixon had to demonstrate his loyalty to the party's eastern wing by pledging to back New York Governor Nelson Rockefeller's platform planks. But in 1964, a coalition of new conservatives from the South and the West and Old Guard midwestern Republicans won the nomination for Goldwater. Reagan's nomination in 1980—along with conservative Alfonse D'Amato's defeat of incumbent Jacob Javits in the New York senate primary—signaled the final defeat of the liberal eastern establishment of John Hay Whitney, John Lindsay, and Nelson Rockefeller. During the Reagan administration, the party was dominated by conservatives and Old Guard Republicans.

There was friction between the Old Guard Republicans and conservatives like Senator Jesse Helms, but the two groups worked together to secure passage of the bulk of the original Reagan economic program. Still suffering from a dearth of experienced officials, conservatives turned to the Old Guard for practical leadership in the Senate and in Republican national committees, but the Old Guard increasingly deferred to the conservatives' ideological leadership. This ideological dominance was most evident in the presidential primaries.

In 1980, the presidential field contained only two acknowledged conservatives, Reagan and Illinois Congressman Phil Crane. George Bush, John Anderson, and Dole positioned themselves in the Republican center, and former Democrat John Connally tried to carve out a niche of his own. By 1988, all the major GOP candidates tried to appeal to the conservative wing. Dole hired conservatives David Keene and Donald Devine for his campaign, wrote an article deploring abortion for the *Human Life Review,* and threatened an invasion of Nicaragua. Pierre S. du Pont IV, who had been a moderate as a congressman and as governor of Delaware, battled Representative Jack Kemp and televangelist Pat Robertson on the far right, advocating breaking relations with Nicaragua, "scrapping" the welfare system, and random drug-testing of teenagers. And every candidate except Vice President Bush, and, after initial hesitation, Senator Dole, opposed the Reagan administration's INF Treaty.

The conservative influence over Republican politics was exercised through a network of national and state political action committees and lobbies that expanded in number during the Reagan years. Many of these groups, like Howard Phillips' Conservative Caucus or Helms' Congressional Club, dated from the late seventies, but others, like Citizens for America, an ambitious "grass-roots" lobby headquartered at the Heritage Foundation, and the Young Conservative Alliance, which tried to rescue a Soviet defector on the Mississippi River, originated during the Reagan years. These groups howled every time a Republican strayed. For instance, in 1986, when Gray & Co., the public-relations firm founded by the cochairman of the 1980 Reagan inauguration, Robert K. Gray, signed up Angola as a client, the Young Conservatives staged a sit-in at the firm's offices. Even the president was not immune. When the administration in 1987 gave half-hearted support to the Central American peace plan proposed by Nobel Peace Prize winner Oscar Arias, president of Costa Rica, conservatives circulated buttons: SUPPORT THE CONTRAS, IMPEACH REAGAN.

The growth of the religious right also reinforced conservative strength in the Republican Party. Before the 1980 election, the

religious right had been principally organized by the Reverend
Jerry Falwell's Moral Majority, by Ed McAteer's Religious
Roundtable, and by conservative leaders of the Southern Baptist
Convention, the rapidly growing Assembly of God churches, and
other evangelical groups. By 1986, the strength of the religious
right was apparent in state and local elections, and in Republican
Party factional fights. In Indiana in 1986, two religious-right
candidates won congressional primaries against party moderates.
In the 1986 Oregon Senate primary, fundamentalist minister Joe
Lutz almost upset powerful incumbent Robert Packwood—in
spite of being outspent fifty to one. In Texas, Iowa, Minnesota,
and Michigan, Bible conservatives won party leadership posts. In
Texas, for instance, a group calling itself the Grassroots Coalition
demanded that every Republican running for public office sign a
nine-point "covenant." In 1988 primaries, Reverend Pat Robertson's campaign galvanized evangelicals.

The religious right built public support for conservative politics
in the South, as it tried to take over not only the Republican Party
but also church organizations. In June 1986, the Reverend
Adrian Rogers, an ally of Robertson's, became president of the
14.5-million-member Southern Baptist Convention—part of the
highly organized campaign to take over that religious denomination. The success of the right was evident in a political shift
among white southern evangelicals. According to a survey of
Southern Baptist ministers, party identification went from 41
percent Democratic and 29 percent Republican in 1981 to 66
percent Republican and 26 percent Democratic by 1984—a clear
indication of the conservative movement's impact. According to
another survey, white southern evangelicals voted Democratic by
56 to 44 percent in 1976 and Republican by 81 to 19 percent
in 1984.

During the Reagan years, conservatives established a formidable political apparatus capable of winning elections and pressuring legislators throughout the country. Hundreds of young conservatives set up shop in Washington as political consultants, pollsters, and media specialists. For instance, Charles Black, Paul Manafort, and Roger Stone, who worked for the Reagan campaigns in 1980 and 1984, set up a consulting and lobbying firm. For sizable fees, the firm advised both international clients, like Jonas Savimbi's UNITA in Angola, and domestic political candidates. While one associate of the firm advised the presidential campaign of George Bush, another advised that of Jack Kemp. David Keene, a former president of the Young Americans for Freedom, who became an aide to Vice President Spiro Agnew and Senator James Buckley, and worked in the 1976 Reagan and 1980 Bush campaigns, set up his own firm. Keene's main client in 1988 became Bob Dole. At the same time, Keene served as chairman of the American Conservative Union.

II

In his pathbreaking 1969 study *The Emerging Republican Majority*, Kevin Phillips argued that the combined votes in 1968 of Richard Nixon and George Wallace represented a new Republican majority of economic conservatives with northern ethnic and southern white voters, united in resentment against civil rights, the welfare state, and liberal cultural assaults upon flag and family. Reagan's victory in 1980 appeared to demonstrate Phillips's thesis. In the late seventies, a dramatic convergence occurred between public opinion and conservative programs. What mattered to conservatives over the prior two decades suddenly seemed to matter to many, if not a majority, of Americans. During the Reagan years, conflicts between conservative doctrine and popular opinion have reemerged, but considerable common ground remains. If there is no longer a conservative Republican majority, there is a significant conservative minority that might in certain circumstances expand into a majority.

The three issues that triggered the development of a conservative movement in the fifties and sixties were opposition to federally imposed racial integration; opposition to the welfare state; and support for the "rollback" (not merely the "containment") of Soviet Communism. In the movement's early years, conservative politicians had difficulty winning elections because they expressed their views in an extreme manner—for instance, Goldwater's attacks against Social Security during his 1964 presidential campaign—or because the public was still wedded to the programs conservatives opposed. As political scientists Lloyd A. Free and Hadley Cantril showed in their 1967 study *The Political Beliefs of Americans,* Americans had remained resolutely "conservative" in their overall ideology—"they continue to accept the traditional ideology which advocates the curbing of Governmental operations"—while becoming increasingly liberal in judging the worth of programs "at the practical level of Governmental operations."

But in the seventies, the public became increasingly willing to try conservative approaches, and conservative politicians became increasingly discriminating in the way they advanced their own program—emphasizing what was popular and understanding what was unpopular. Continuing inflation and unemployment eroded popular support for government intervention in the econ-

omy and contributed to support for conservative attacks against
government regulation, spending, and taxes. The racial backlash
also inflamed antiwelfare sentiment. In the University of Michigan's National Election Survey, for instance, the percentage of
Americans who believed that government was "getting too powerful" rose from 30 percent in 1964 to 41 percent in 1972 to 49
percent in 1980. By late 1980, according to a *Washington Post /
ABC* News poll, more Americans favored decreasing rather than
increasing unemployment insurance, food stamps, and loans and
grants to college students.

By the late seventies, popular disquiet about America's place
in the world had been fed by the defeat in Vietnam, the energy
crisis, the growing trade imbalance with Japan and West Germany, and the perception, carefully nurtured by Cold War lobbies, of Soviet military superiority. Many voters blamed the party
in power, the Democrats. By the end of the Carter administration,
two decades of civil rights struggle had also fragmented the Democratic coalition. Fueled by school-busing and affirmative-action
hiring, opposition to racial integration had spread north. Conservatives, who opposed the Supreme Court's integration decisions
and the civil rights acts—and now opposed affirmative action and
busing—were able to draw upon the racial backlash that George
Wallace had fanned in his 1964 and 1968 presidential campaigns.

Reagan crystallized this conservatism in his 1980 campaign.
He decried Democratic spending and taxes, attacked affirmative
action and busing, and promised, in his words, to restore America's "place in the sun." In 1984, faced with the perfect oppo-
nent, Carter's vice president, Walter Mondale, Reagan recast the
election in the same terms, only declaring this time that "America

is back" and holding out the implicit threat that if Americans elected Mondale, the country would revert to its former chaos.

Over Reagan's two terms, however, popular support for conservative approaches to the economy and foreign policy diminished. With inflation under control as a result of the 1982–83 recession, popular distrust of government and government programs noticeably decreased. According to a 1987 *Washington Post* / AP poll, more Americans favored an increase rather than a decrease in food stamps and unemployment insurance. But there was still considerable support for conservative economic approaches. For instance, the *Washington Post* / AP poll also found that 49 percent of Americans still believed that "federal government is trying to do too many things that should be left to individuals and private business."

Support for conservative foreign policy also diminished. According to a 1981 *Washington Post* / AP poll, 72 percent of Americans favored an increase in military spending; by 1987, only 31 percent favored an increase. With the accession to power in 1985 of Soviet Premier Mikhail Gorbachev, popular support for a posture of unremitting hostility toward the Soviet Union also declined. But Americans continued to be anxious about their place in the world. In pollster Stanley Greenberg's 1987 study of American attitudes toward military spending, he found above all "doubts that America was still 'number one' or that she was a 'first-rate power.' "

In his *Study of History*, Arnold Toynbee describes a political peculiarity of declining empires that he calls the "idolization of institutions." When a nation begins to fall from the pinnacle of world power, its people seek to restore the conditions that had made possible its rise. Thus, the British in the 1920s restored the gold standard even though it undermined British industry and contributed toward the outbreak of world depression. As the United States began to lose its preeminence, Americans turned to the economic policies of the twenties and the foreign and military policies of the forties—even though, it could be argued, these approaches accelerate American decline. The conservatism of the eighties was, above all, based upon this appeal to imperial nostalgia. And this accounts for the depth of its popular appeal.

In an important respect, the basis for conservative support may have widened during the Reagan years. The racial antagonisms that underlay the Reagan landslide in 1980 have, if anything, been exacerbated. The election of black mayors in major northern cities like Chicago and Philadelphia hastened the emigration of middle-class whites from the cities and toward the Republican Party. White political leaders like Chicago's Edward Vrdolyak and Philadelphia's Frank Rizzo defected to the GOP. In the 1984 election, Jesse Jackson's influence within the Democratic Party scared many Southern whites into voting for Reagan. "The effect of Jackson's campaign was to raise racial consciousness rather than class consciousness," said Jack Bass, coauthor of *The Transformation of Southern Politics.* "Reagan appealed to white prejudices and made them respectable. His promise to cut back social programs could be taken as a code word."

In a study prepared for the Michigan House Democratic Campaign Committee in 1985, pollster Stanley Greenberg concluded that Democratic defectors shared "a profound distaste for blacks, a sentiment that pervades almost everything they think about government and politics." Remarking upon the support for Reagan among thirty-to-forty-five-year-old union men, Greenberg wrote that "the depth of racial sentiment and regard for Reagan's leadership and strength" outweighed their opposition to a "whole range of specific Reagan programs." These voters, Greenberg notes, will support conservative candidates regardless of whether they agree with them on specific economic proposals.

In the next decade, the fundamental sources of conservative popular support—the nostalgic reaction to American decline and racial tension—will remain.

III

Not everything that occurred during the Reagan years was, however, beneficial to conservatives. In spite of their gains, conservatives found themselves, at the end of Reagan's second term in 1988, in the throes of a political identity crisis similar to that which afflicted them after major setbacks in 1964 and 1974. The cause for this identity crisis was partly the boom-bust cycle that affects all political movements.

Having emerged in the mid-fifties as a politics of antistatism and militant anticommunism, conservatives were forced to redefine their program and strategy after Goldwater's defeat in November 1964 and after Nixon's resignation in August 1974. After Goldwater, conservatives adopted a more pragmatic—even opportunistic—public stance. They eschewed open opposition to Social Security and focused on issues like crime and welfare fraud, which were attracting new voters to conservative candidates. Reagan's 1966 California campaign—managed by Nelson Rockefeller's former campaign consultant Stuart Spencer—was the paradigm.

After Nixon's resignation, a group of activists who eventually became known as the "New Right" made an explicit push for George Wallace's segregationist constituency and for small-town Protestants offended by the new sexual morality of the sixties and seventies. At the same time, former leftists, who came to be called "neoconservatives," sought successfully to reconcile right-wing politicians to a minimal definition of the welfare state. In 1978 and 1980 elections, these new approaches brought new voters into the conservative camp and helped revive conservative fortunes.

But what worked in 1980 won't necessarily work in 1988 and 1990. Both Reagan's economic policy and his foreign policy— dubbed by neoconservative *Washington Post* columnist Charles Krauthammer the "Reagan Doctrine"—have exhausted their political usefulness. In the wake of the 1988 election, conservatives will have to redefine their approach no matter who wins the presidency.

Reagan's economic policy, or Reaganomics, evolved out of the political failure of the old conservative economics. In the 1976 New Hampshire Republican primary battle between Ronald Reagan and incumbent President Gerald Ford, Reagan was defeated largely because he introduced a vague and threatening plan for transferring $90 billion in federal programs to the states. That plan was traditional conservative economics. It drew an enthusiastic response from conservative activists, but the Ford campaign used it to scare voters into believing that vital government services, including Social Security, would be cut under Reagan. Although Reagan tried to deny that Social Security would be affected, the damage was already done. He lost New Hampshire, and by the time he recovered his momentum, it was too late.

In 1980, Reagan adopted a new approach to economics. In the mid-seventies, *Wall Street Journal* editorialist Jude Wanniski, aided by Kristol and maverick economists Arthur Laffer and Robert Mundell, promoted a new theory that appeared to resolve the contradiction between conservative doctrine and popular support. According to the new theory, worldwide inflation and unemployment could be attacked by a simultaneous program of regressive tax cuts and reduction in money-supply growth. Wanniski and the supply-siders argued that tax rates could be cut across the board without reducing revenues. Thus, it was possible to cut taxes—a long-held conservative goal—without violating conservative strictures against budget deficits *and* without requiring unpopular cuts in social spending. Supply-side economics appeared to have squared the political circle.

In 1980, Reagan, prodded by Representative Jack Kemp, made supply-side economics a central plank of his campaign. One Reagan campaign commercial promised that "if we cut tax rates deeply and permanently, we'll be removing many of the barriers that hold everyone back. Those who have the least will gain the most." When Reagan assumed office, he made Wanniski's original program of tax cuts and reduced money-supply growth the centerpiece of his economic program. The trouble was that reducing the money supply through raising interest rates canceled out whatever stimulative effects the cut had on the economy. By 1982, the United States had plunged into the worst recession since the thirties. For the first time, the federal budget deficit rose above $100 billion. By 1983, it reached $200 billion.

After the economy began to recover, supply-side advocates claimed that the tax cuts had worked all along. It is indeed true that the cuts, combined with military spending, probably did

stimulate the economy in 1983 and 1984—in time for Reagan's
reelection campaign. But the tax cuts also helped create record
deficits and laid the groundwork for a series of tax increases (or
"revenue enhancements," as Reagan's White House staff eu-
phemistically labeled them) that eventually canceled out much of
the original tax cut. The administration felt compelled to use the
traditional conservative program of cutting spending to reduce
the deficit. But by 1983, there was little more that it could cut
without sparking a political revolt in Congress; its attempts to
reduce Social Security spending had already contributed to Republican defeats in the 1982 election.

At the beginning of Reagan's second term, he did not advance
a coherent conservative economic program. Rather, the administration backed a tax-simplification measure that was originally
devised by Democrats—Senator Bill Bradley and Representative
Richard Gephardt. And, alerted to opinion polls favoring certain
kinds of government spending, the administration proposed a
catastrophic-illness insurance plan that closely resembled a plan
introduced by the Carter administration. The administration even
repudiated in practice its own free-trade stance by backing sanc-
tions against Japanese firms accused of unfair trade practices.
Reaganomics became a dim memory.

The October 19, 1987, stock market crash exposed the fragility
of the Reagan recovery. Tax cuts and deregulation had fueled a
speculative boom in stocks and real estate without stemming the
erosion of the country's industrial base, which was evidenced in
a rising trade deficit in manufactured goods. As pressure mounted
for action, the administration found itself hedged in by the budget
deficits it had created. Foreign bankers and many economists
blamed the deficit for high interest rates and for undermining

confidence in the stock market. They urged the administration, unwilling to reduce military spending or cut entitlement programs, to cut the deficit with increased taxes. But many conservatives advocated cutting taxes and reducing stock market regulation to encourage stock investment and prevent a recession. Kemp advocated further reducing capital-gains taxes. In an editorial, *National Review* even advocated reducing the margin costs for stock purchases from 50 to 25 percent—a measure that seemed to invite further debt and speculation.

The prevailing confusion was epitomized by a debate that appeared in the *Wall Street Journal* between two founders of supply-side economics—economic consultant Arthur Laffer, inventor of the Laffer Curve, and Paul Craig Roberts, a former Treasury Department official. Once of a single mind, they now disagreed about why the crash had occurred and what to do about it. Laffer argued that the Federal Reserve's "recent acceleration" of the money supply was the cause while Roberts contended that it was the Federal Reserve's slowing of money supply. Laffer called for the Fed to "slow the growth" of the money supply, while Roberts called for the Fed to accelerate it.

The administration and conservatives were faced with a genuine dilemma but one that was of their own making. If they followed the supply-side prescriptions of 1981—reducing margin costs and capital-gains taxes, and accelerating the money supply—they risked an even more serious speculative crash down the road. But if they returned to the old conservative orthodoxy of tight money and balanced budgets, they risked an immediate recession. The administration muddled through an election year delegating the hard choices to the next president—but conservative economic doctrine remained badly in need of repair.

. . .

Since the mid-fifties, conservatives had faced similar difficulties reconciling their foreign-policy convictions with popular attitudes. While their militant anticommunism appealed to both patriotism and fear of Soviet attack, it also raised unwelcome anxieties about U.S. entanglement in foreign wars, or even nuclear war. In 1964, Lyndon Johnson's successful campaign against Barry Goldwater was epitomized by a television ad featuring a little girl whose picture faded into an H-bomb mushroom cloud. In 1980, even as Reagan was exploiting a decade of popular resentments against the United States being "pushed around" in the world and carefully nurtured fears that this country was falling behind the Soviet Union militarily, he had to calm the worry that he might plunge the country into war.

Once in office, Reagan pursued a mammoth military buildup. In undertaking an aggressive foreign policy, however, he found himself stymied at every turn, torn between conservative doctrine and the realities of both domestic politics and international power. The administration could not stop the Polish military, acting under pressure from the Soviet Union, from suppressing the Solidarity movement. Its thwarting of arms control sparked a nuclear-freeze movement. Its effort to create a guerrilla army to fight the Sandinistas in Nicaragua aroused popular fears of a Central American Vietnam and led to a congressional cutoff of contra funds.

Public opinion studies during Reagan's two terms revealed that the public feared Russia but was unwilling to commit tax dollars to foreign wars whose outcome was uncertain. Popular attitudes reflected the persistence of isolationism rather than sympathy for the Sandinistas or dislike of the contras. The public tolerated the use of military force only when the action was quick and decisive, as during the invasion of Grenada and the air strike against Libya.

Some conservatives were almost as critical of the administration's foreign policy as liberals. Reviewing Reagan's first term in *Foreign Affairs,* Norman Podhoretz, the editor of the neoconservative *Commentary Magazine,* accused the administration of practicing "rollover" rather than "rollback" with respect to the Soviet Union. The Heritage Foundation held a symposium in its journal *Policy Review* urging the administration to move "beyond containment." But in its second term, the administration, faced with conflicting priorities and new challenges, fell apart completely.

In the late seventies and early eighties, the behavior of the Soviet Union in Africa, Afghanistan, and Poland and the bellicose statements by the Soviet military lent a certain credibility to the conservatives' militant anticommunism. But when Mikhail Gorbachev assumed power in 1985, he reoriented Soviet policy toward economic and political reform at home and a kind of détente abroad. Moreover, the U.S. found itself suddenly outflanked in arms control negotiations.

The administration split internally between those favoring accommodation and those favoring a continuing push for military superiority through a "Star Wars" program. After Reagan appeared to commit the United States to a far-ranging reduction of nuclear weapons at the Reykjavik negotiations in October 1986, conservatives themselves became hopelessly divided. When the administration and the Soviet Union began to edge toward a treaty on intermediate nuclear forces in Europe, *National Review,* usually one of the administration's most loyal supporters, termed the pact "nuclear suicide" even though it had endorsed the treaty's terms five years before when they had been proposed by the United States. In the Senate, the treaty's chief supporters were liberal Democrats rather than conservative Republicans.

Administration attempts to "roll back" communism overseas also ran aground. Lacking public and congressional support for the Nicaraguan contras—in opinion polls, opposition to contra aid hovered between 60 and 70 percent—the administration attempted to accomplish covertly what it couldn't openly by using the CIA and the National Security Council (NSC) secretly to sustain and direct the contras. The Iran-contra scandal was more than the result of duplicitous individuals in the NSC; it was again the outcome of the conservatives' attempt to square their own political circle.

When the administration in August 1987 tentatively backed a peace accord for Central America that would have ruled out contra funding, conservative activists and the Republican presidential candidates denounced it. If Reaganomics had become a memory, the Reagan Doctrine increasingly became a reproach leveled by conservatives against the administration. But the conservatives failed to propose programs that would resolve the contradiction between their own foreign-policy aims and public opinion. Instead, they contented themselves with arousing their own faithful.

Aware that their movement lacked a coherent program, a number of conservatives urged a focus on cultural issues rather than on economics and foreign policy. "The most important political idea of the mid-eighties is cultural conservatism," wrote Paul Weyrich in May 1986. Lewis Lehrman, the millionaire founder of Citizens for America, expressed a similar view in a 1986 cover story for *National Review.* Comparing abortion to slavery and the present era to that before the Civil War, Lehrman predicted that "national politics during the late 1980s and the 1990s will be dominated by the great constitutional, moral, and social issues of our time."

But this perspective may offer little relief to conservatives in the years ahead. The success of the New Right in using abortion as a political issue has depended on unique circumstances. The threat of feminism and the sexual revolution had to be sufficiently vivid to scare socially conservative Democrats into voting for Republicans, and the dissatisfaction with Democratic economic and foreign policy had to be sufficient not to frighten away cosmopolitan Republicans and baby-boom Independents. If conservatives focus on cultural issues in 1988 and beyond, they might scare off Republicans and Independents without attracting many Democrats. The signs were already visible in 1986 in several elections, where Republicans who ran on "cultural issues" generally fared poorly. As primary challenges from the religious right demonstrated, an emphasis on cultural issues tended to destroy the Nixon-Wallace coalition between traditional Republicans and Wallace Democrats.

Even more important, Weyrich's and Lehrman's focus on cultural issues obscured the conservatives' lack of an actual political program to govern the country. Even if many voters agreed that supply-side tax cuts and 10 percent real increases in the military budget served a useful purpose in 1981, few believed that by the end of Reagan's second term. The conservatives' lack of an economic and foreign policy for the 1990s was central to their predicament.

During the Reagan years, conservative organizations multiplied rapidly, but there were significant symptoms of decay and stagnation. By the end of Reagan's second term, there were signs that conservatives were losing their grip on the Republican Party. While conservative ideas dominated the Republican presidential race, the two leading candidates, Vice President George Bush and Minority Leader Robert Dole, displayed little loyalty to the conservative movement itself. Bush, the son of Connecticut Senator Prescott Bush, put moderates like Richard Bond, a former aide to Manhattan Representative Bill Green, in charge of his campaign. Dole, who had initially employed movement conservatives like David Keene and Donald Devine, shifted control of his campaign to former Labor Secretary and RNC Chairman William Brock and former NATO Ambassador Robert Ellsworth. The New Right was virtually shut out of both campaigns.

Neither Bush nor Dole represented the return of the liberal Republicanism of the fifties. Dole's roots were in the anti–New Deal Old Guard midwestern party, while Bush was a hybrid of an austere Yankee Republicanism and Texas conservatism. But both men are Republicans first and conservatives second. And both were more likely to seek policy guidance from Wall Street and corporate Republicans than from the policy experts of the Heritage Foundation. If either man became president, conservatives would have to resume the battle they waged in the seventies for control of the party.

Not all conservative organizations fared well during the Reagan years. The national groups most responsible for the conservative Senate victories in 1978 and 1980 either folded or lost most of their clout. In 1980, the Life Action Political Action Committee (LAPAC) led the campaign against the twelve liberal senators it labeled the "dirty dozen." Six years later, deep in debt, it moved its offices from the Washington D.C. suburbs to Everett, Washington, where it played a minor role in state politics and none at all at the national level.

NCPAC, the National Conservative Political Action Committee, once the most feared New Right PAC, suffered a similar fate. In 1984, it went deeply into debt as a result of a mailing on behalf of President Reagan. In 1986, its founder and director, John (Terry) Dolan, died from AIDS. (Dolan's homosexuality had also divided the libertarian NCPAC from other sections of the New Right that were virulently antigay.) The next year, Dolan's chosen successor Brent Bozell III and Bozell's top aide quit in a dispute with the organization's board of directors and set up a rival group. NCPAC remains in Washington, but no longer targets senators for defeat. It has virtually no impact on politics.

After the 1984 election, direct-mail specialist Richard Viguerie, who helped create a network of New Right lobbies and PACs in the late seventies, laid off hundreds of employees and sold his magazine, *Conservative Digest.* Viguerie was also embroiled in a number of bitter disputes with organizations that had used his services. In 1986, for instance, he was sued by the National Tax Limitation Committee, which claimed that Viguerie was using its mailing list to collect money for "bogus entities."

The American Enterprise Institute also endured financial losses, forcing the resignation of the institute's president in 1986. AEI's losses reflected both the flagging enthusiasm of corporate America for the conservative cause and the growing disenchantment of wealthy conservatives with an organization that was trying to position itself closer to the political mainstream. In 1986, the highly conservative John M. Olin Foundation, which had given AEI $300,000 the year before, decided on political grounds to give it nothing.

Other organizations suffered from a combination of waning

political demand for their services and internal corruption. In 1984, the Young Americans for Freedom (YAF), the first major conservative youth organization, nearly ceased to exist. A group of YAF leaders charged that the YAF director was siphoning off the organization's money—more than $150,000—for purely personal expenses. The director finally quit, but the organization was wracked by the bitter fight. The religious right, in the meantime, was rocked by the sex and financial scandals of televangelists Jim and Tammy Bakker, who had been protégés of presidential candidate Pat Robertson. And the administration was rife with scandal, the most notable being that of the former White House aide closest to the Reagans, Michael Deaver, who was convicted of perjury for lying to Congress about his lobbying activities.

Writing in the Heritage Foundation's *Policy Review,* Irving Kristol suggested that the Republican Party, "when in office, always finds itself floundering in one squalid financial scandal after another—it does after all take money (as distinct from sex) seriously." But the Reagan administration was easily the most corrupt administration since that of Warren G. Harding. Neither its scandals nor those of conservatives could simply be explained by a natural interest in money. Instead, these scandals reflected a movement that has lost its idealistic purpose. In Washington, conservatism increasingly became a business rather than a cause.

As the organizations that helped engineer the conservative victory in 1980 floundered or folded, new organizations came forward to take their place. Some of these were highly problematic. For instance, the *Washington Times* became the main conservative newspaper in the country, with a daily circulation of a hundred thousand, but the *Times*—and two other conservative publications, the magazine *Insight* and the journal *World and I*

—are owned and controlled by an originally South Korean religious cult, the Unification Church, which is based on the belief that Sun Myung Moon is a son of God and the Messiah; its goal is a global theocratic dictatorship. Besides anticommunism, Andrew Ferguson wrote in the *American Spectator,* "there is little else in Unificationism that American conservatives would find compelling." In April 1987, editorial-page editor William Cheshire and four other editorial-page employees quit to protest the church's interference in the paper's editorials. Yet prominent conservatives like Paul Weyrich and William Rusher defended the church's increasingly pivotal role in American conservatism.

Viguerie's *Conservative Digest,* meanwhile, was purchased by a Colorado millionaire, William Kennedy. When editor Lee Edwards, an experienced journalist and widely respected conservative, quit, he was replaced by Scott Stanley, for twenty-five years the editor of the John Birch Society's *American Opinion.* The Birch Society had been ostracized from the conservative movement because of the charges of its founder, Robert Welch, that Dwight Eisenhower was a Communist and that the U.S. government was in Communist hands. Under Stanley, the *Conservative Digest* became a shrill voice of the New Right's social agenda.

A movement's health is reflected in its intellectual life. The birth of conservatism in the fifties coincided with a burst of theoretical work and the founding of two important journals, *Modern Age* and *National Review.* In the early fifties, important books and articles were published by Russell Kirk, Whittaker Chambers, James Burnham, Robert Nisbet, Leo Strauss, and William F. Buckley, Jr., that helped lay the foundation for the movement. At each stage in the movement's growth, new magazines and new thinkers came forth to help revitalize the movement. In the late sixties and the seventies, Kevin Phillips and Irving Kristol were important in defining the conservative strategy; Kristol's *Public Interest* and Norman Podhoretz's *Commentary* became influential conservative journals. In the early eighties, the conservative movement also had its intellectual innovators. Wanniski and George Gilder helped inspire the administration's support for supply-side economics. Richard John Neuhaus and Allan Bloom provided a respectable gloss on the fundamentalist reaction against modernism and the sexual revolution.

But the signs of intellectual stagnation and drift were clear, as the movement's thinkers were increasingly unable to reformulate their ideas in the light of changed experience. The supply-side thinkers are a case in point. Rather than revise their basic ideas, Kemp and Wanniski insisted that the recession of the early eighties would not have occurred if the administration had prevented Federal Reserve Chief Paul Volcker from braking the money supply. These supply-siders did not acknowledge that Reagan and Volcker had followed their original policy recommendations exactly. Now, as a remedy, they and other supply-siders urged a return to the gold standard. Other economists and public officials debated the proposal, but in the hands of the supply-siders it became a magic wand that could wave away all economic ills. Their version of the gold standard was not economics, but sorcery.

George Gilder, the author of *Wealth and Poverty*, one of the key supply-side texts, was particularly oblivious to the relationship between his ideas and reality. In 1984, he published *The Spirit of Enterprise*, a paean to American entrepreneurialism and an attack on government intervention in the marketplace. One of Gilder's model enterprises was Micron Technology of Boise, Idaho, a five-year-old firm that had captured the U.S. market in 64K RAM chips. By the time Gilder's book came out, Micron was reeling from Japanese competition. In February 1985, it laid off 625 employees—half of its total—and in June, it filed an anti-dumping suit with the government against Japanese companies. Indeed, Gilder's model of unfettered free enterprise was the very first U.S. chip manufacturer to ask for government protection against the Japanese.

Of course, theorists make mistakes. In Gilder's case, theory had become dogma. The blind commitment of the supply-siders to their doctrine became even more evident after the stock market crash. Alan Reynolds, the chief economist for Jude Wanniski's consulting firm Polyconomics, attributed the crash not to the artificial boom created by administration politics, but to the threat of a "return to heavy-handed and unpredictable government regulation." In a *National Review* article, Reynolds contrasted the "constructive" contribution of supply-side economics in the United States and the United Kingdom with the "forces of darkness [that] have appeared to be gaining the upper hand in the United States, Germany, and Japan." Reynolds's postcrash prescription for the American economy: more supply-side economics.

Conservative intellectuals found themselves equally unable to adapt their view of the world to the changes that Gorbachev was making in the Soviet Union. Since the early fifties, conservatives had viewed the Soviet Union as a totalitarian monolith incapable of change. In 1956, conservatives denounced Soviet Premier Nikita Khrushchev's attack against Stalin as a ruse. Now they interpreted Gorbachev's programs of *glasnost* and *perestroika* in

the same light. In a three-part series in the *Washington Times,*
Martin Sieff tried to demonstrate that *glasnost* was "being used
to mask repressive measures aimed at disciplining the labor force
and smothering human rights activists and those seeking religious freedom." Columnist George Will wrote that *"glasnost* can
never be more than a carefully controlled tactic to confuse the
West and motivate the Soviet masses with a tantalizing mirage of
freedom just over a forever receding horizon."

They took the same attitude toward any changes in Soviet
foreign policy or in the policy of countries that they believed to
be Soviet satellites. Writing in *Commentary,* neoconservative Eugene Rostow declared that the Soviet Union's apparent arms-
control concessions were really intended to gain an "offensive
first-strike capability." Podhoretz, for his part, compared Gorbachev to Hitler.

What was distinctive about these opinions was not their conclusion but their reasoning. Indeed, one could note, for instance, the
tenuousness or precariousness of Gorbachev's *glasnost.* But it is
one thing to remark upon the difficulty of change and another to
rule out its existence on *a priori* ideological grounds. Like the
supply-side economists, the foreign-policy conservatives betrayed
a rigid dogmatism that brooked no contradiction.

Conservative views of social policy also stiffened in the late
eighties. Beginning in the late sixties with Irving Kristol's highly
influential collection *On the Democratic Idea in America,* conservatives had staked out a position in opposition to the cultural
assumptions of the New Left and of modern feminism. In the
eighties, the movement's view of culture appears to have been
intellectually corrupted rather than inspired by its association
with the Reagan administration. Neoconservative intellectuals

increasingly allowed political imperatives to dictate their own thinking on highly philosophical issues. And traditional conservatives waged a bitter and often petty two-term battle with neoconservatives over appointments, a battle that by 1986 dominated the proceedings of the philosophically oriented Philadelphia Society.

William Bennett, the former philosophy professor and liberal turned neoconservative bureaucrat, was one of the administration's more thoughtful officials, but as he became more entangled in internal disputes and more beholden to conservative pressure groups, his own views became increasingly compromised. An initial foe of fundamentalists who wanted to replace the theory of evolution with creationism, he defended their judgment—"the judgment of the community"—against "experts" in a 1986 speech.

Bennett's equivocation was apparent also in Irving Kristol, who in a *New York Times* column advanced the novel thesis that the fundamentalist opposition to the doctrine of evolution was the result of the "dogmatic crusade" against creationism by proponents of evolution. Kristol argued that "the current teaching of evolution in our public schools does indeed have an ideological bias against religious belief—teaching as 'fact' what is only hypothesis."

In the conservative movement's first decades, the dominant religious trend among conservatives was toward a kind of aesthetic English Catholicism, epitomized by Buckley and by Catholic convert Russell Kirk. But in the late eighties, a highly anti-intellectual Pietist fervor swept conservatives. Its arch proponent was *Washington Times'* staff columnist John Lofton, a convert to a bizarre form of born-again Christianity devised by R. J.

Rushdoony. Rushdoony's followers, the Reconstructionists, seek to recreate their image of a Biblical social order in which sodomy, incorrigibility, blasphemy, and breaking the Sabbath are capital crimes. In his columns and public appearances, Lofton took upon himself the task of questioning the Christian credentials of other conservatives, including Buckley. Rather than being isolated as a crank, Lofton was accorded respect and even deference by other conservatives.

Lofton was an extreme case, but other prominent conservatives displayed variations on the same evangelical spirit in which one's religious—or political—beliefs accord a person membership in a godly elect. Reagan's top domestic adviser, Gary Bauer, argued that Georgia's laws making oral or anal sex a felony—even in private, between consenting adults—should be adopted by other states. His report on the family treated welfare as a form of self-inflicted injury.

This kind of evangelical fervor isolated the right in the fifties and early sixties; its replacement by a more political and ecumenical politics was key to the movement's success from 1966 through 1984. If it becomes a dominant strand in current conservatism, it may prevent conservatism from adapting to the politics of the 1990s.

IV

Modern conservatism's historical trajectory has been similar to that of modern American liberalism. Liberalism emerged in the thirties during Franklin Roosevelt's New Deal. It both incorporated and modified the program of prior historical movements—

populism, socialism, middle-class progressivism, corporate reform. It was a new synthesis that could not be identified with any
of its parts.

American conservatism also incorporated and redefined the
program of past movements. It shared the old right's fervent
anticommunism, its hatred of the New Deal and the welfare state,
its xenophobia, and its small-town morality. But it repudiated the
old right's anti-Semitism and anti-Catholicism, and substantially
modified its isolationism. The result was a new conservative
movement—one that had never existed before and that bore only
a distant resemblance to movements of the same name in Great
Britain and Europe.

Both movements endured cycles of success and failure, growth
and stagnation, roughly at ten-year intervals. Liberalism suffered
decline from the late thirties through World War II, but revived
and was redefined during the first Truman administration, when
the Americans for Democratic Action was formed. By the late
forties, it was again on the defensive. It revived in the late fifties,
and enjoyed an Indian Summer during the Kennedy and Johnson
administrations.

Both movements were able to sustain their influence even when
they were out of power nationally. From 1932 through 1952,
liberals were able to transform the judiciary and the major government institutions in their image. They were also able to establish a political infrastructure of lobbies and think tanks in
Washington that would continue to defend liberal ideas even
when liberals were not in office. Thus, the influence of liberalism
persisted during the Eisenhower years; and when Kennedy took
office in 1961, liberal policy-makers were ready to step in and run
the government. Conservatives have had only eight years in

power, but they have gained experience in the federal bureaucracy, and have established a network of pressure groups, think tanks, and consultancies that will survive even if a Democrat replaces Reagan.

Finally, both movements succeeded because their leading ideas reflected the imperatives of the nation. Liberalism enabled America to escape the threat of recurring depression and to assume a role as the leader of Western capitalism; it was an optimistic philosophy that stressed the power of Americans to remake their country and the world. Conservatism is a defensive philosophy that seeks to arrest America's decline in the world. Its optimism is rooted entirely in the fantasy of a recovered past. It is a deeply irrational faith, but appeals to a large public that is riven by social discontent and intoxicated by imperial nostalgia.

The conservatives of the late eighties, however, are weaker than liberals of the late forties in several respects. The liberals could constitute themselves as the governing arm of the Democratic Party and take advantage of its deep local roots. Indeed, Democrats have not lost the House since 1952, and lost the Senate for only eight of thirty-six years. To the conservatives' chagrin, the Republican Party has not been able to become a national majority party. It remains a marginal local party in much of the South, despite the popularity of some conservative ideas, and it is losing influence in local and state elections in the Northeast. "We have no power," writes Paul Weyrich. "Having power presupposes holding 'territory.' Nowhere in America today are conservative agendas moving through state legislatures."

Liberalism was also a far more varied and spontaneous movement than the conservatism of the eighties was. The spread of liberal institutions reflected the spread of liberal ideas. In the late seventies and during the Reagan years, conservatives were doing consciously what liberals did largely on an ad hoc spontaneous basis.

The conservatives, in addition, continued to lack mass institutions comparable to the labor movement. As the travails of Viguerie and the New Right demonstrated, organizations based on economic commonality could endure where those based on ideological mailing lists fell apart. In the late eighties, the only conservative institution capable of playing the same role is the religious right, but it tended to divide rather than unite the movement. And it had a strong separatist impulse, rooted in the fundamentalist suspicion of worldly affairs.

Perhaps most important of all the distinctions, liberalism had an underlying program of Keynesian intervention in the economy and free trade that for three decades satisfied Americans' desire for a rising standard of living. It remains to be seen whether the conservative program can achieve more than a selective and limited prosperity. If indeed conservative economics becomes identified with a depression, then conservative politics could suffer the same fate as Republican politics did during the Great Depression.

In the absence of such an economic crisis, however, the ultimate question for conservatism after Reagan is not whether it will muddle through, but whether it can enjoy the kind of revival that the liberalism of the forties enjoyed in the sixties. This will depend on the movement's ability on the one hand, to avoid the shoals of right-wing sectarianism and, on the other hand, the ability to establish political power in the cities and the states. This will not be easy.

REAGAN'S FOREIGN POLICY
AND THE REJECTION OF DIPLOMACY

DAVID IGNATIUS

I

The Rambo movies of the mid-1980s provided an easy caricature for Ronald Reagan's foreign policy. Here was the raw imagery of American power, a nation seemingly free at last from the pain and self-doubt of Vietnam, personified by a muscular hero with an oversize machine gun. The "America Is Back" theme of the Rambo movies was pure Reagan. And ironically, so was the reported off-screen behavior of the movie actor who played Rambo, Sylvester Stallone. According to one perhaps fanciful news report, Stallone—the embodiment of the new tough-guy American style—didn't attend the Cannes Film Festival in 1986 because he was worried about the threat of terrorism.

The Reagan years produced a similar disjunction in foreign

policy: the United States sought to project an image of strength in the world through hawkish rhetoric and a vast military buildup. But during the Reagan years, America often displayed a reality of weakness. The rhetorical assertion that "America Is Back" was accompanied, in practice, by an actual foreign policy that was often vacillating, ill-planned, and poorly executed. In most areas of the world, the administration was lucky if it succeeded in treading water and maintaining the existing pattern of alliances; in some areas, like the Middle East, it suffered chronic reversals; overall, the administration seemed unable to translate America's vast military power into concrete diplomatic gains.

Reagan himself epitomized the failure of judgment and competence in his humiliating sale of weapons to Iran, a nation he had repeatedly denounced as a sponsor of international terrorism. The arms-for-hostages deal was characteristic of a broader problem that afflicted his administration, and the entire country, in dealing with the world. America in the 1980s was in many ways a nation of armchair Rambos: a country of tough-talking second-guessers who wanted to confront terrorism in principle, but not in Lebanon; who wanted the rousing display of American military power without having anyone killed, who wanted to be respected as a superpower without paying the price.

Reagan's approach to foreign policy has been characterized as "lucky" by Michael Mandelbaum, and likened by Phillip Geyelin to Willy Loman's belief in "a smile and a shoeshine" in the play *Death of a Salesman.* But the enduring metaphors for Reagan really ought to come from the state where he made his name as an actor and a governor. So perhaps the high point of Reaganism was the 1984 Olympic Games in Los Angeles, where all the artistry of the entertainment industry combined to produce a pageant of national narcissism, with crowds waving American flags and chanting, "We're number one!" It mattered little to the crowds that we were achieving our magnificent Olympic victories largely because the other side—the Soviet Union and its allies—wasn't playing. And it mattered not at all that a few months before this celebration of national vigor, American troops had fled ignominiously from Lebanon, chased out by truck bombers and ragtag militiamen. To Americans in the 1980s, it was the show of power that mattered, not the substance. Ronald Reagan understood better than anyone that America wanted the exhilaration of a president who talked like Rambo—without the risks.

Reagan's foreign policy was driven in part by a desire to "win one"—to achieve symbolic victories against the Soviets and the Iranians that would satisfy the public hunger for low-risk, high-emotion successes. The invasion of Grenada was a perfect opportunity: it allowed Reagan to win one in near-perfect laboratory conditions and thereby erase some of the bad taste left by the bombing of Marine headquarters in Beirut the same week. Similarly, in Nicaragua, Afghanistan, and Angola, the administration could play at rolling back Soviet power without directly committing American troops or prestige. These covert operations were never much more than holding actions, however. CIA operatives in the field argued, sometimes bitterly, that the American goal wasn't to win in Afghanistan or Nicaragua but to hold the Soviet-backed forces to a draw.

The American show of power in the 1980s had its own drawbacks, quite apart from the failure to use that power successfully. The military buildup of Reagan's first term was immensely costly, poorly managed, and added only marginally to America's military readiness and security. Indeed, the costs of this pell-mell military spending—which, like the Vietnam buildup of the 1960s, was never adequately funded with tax revenues—produced economic dislocations that, by the stock market crash of October 1987, were themselves a leading national security problem.

Reagan's hawkish rhetoric, another aspect of the show of power, also caused problems. The arms-for-hostages deal, for example, would not have been so catastrophic had it not been preceded by so much overblown verbiage about terrorism. The antiterrorism speeches of 1985 created in the public mind an impression that the United States should never, ever negotiate with terrorists—an untenable proposition that has been rejected by most governments, including that of Israel. During the Iran-contra investigation of 1987, this rhetoric came back to haunt the president. Similarly, the president's first-term tirade against the Soviet Union as an "evil empire" made him appear both a war-monger and a hypocrite—since Reagan proved by the December 1987 summit with Mikhail Gorbachev to be as willing to deal with the Soviets as his predecessors had been.

What made the military posturing and rhetorical excesses of the Reagan era so troubling was that they were accompanied by a loss of flexibility and subtlety in foreign policy. That was obviously true in intelligence operations, where a combination of administration zealotry and congressional nit-picking joined to weaken further the Central Intelligence Agency. As Bob Wood-ward documented in his book *Veil*, the agency under William Casey became the vanguard of administration fantasies of rolling back Soviet power. The more Congress tried to curtail these covert operations, the deeper Casey pushed the struggle under-ground. The locus of action moved from the agency itself to the National Security Council staff and then to a network of private operatives. Some operations were subcontracted entirely to "friendly" intelligence services from other countries, such as Israel and Saudi Arabia, often with disastrous results. By 1986, incredibly, the American government was relying for its most sensitive operations on a motley group of ex–military officers and Iranian prevaricators who might have been drawn from an Eric Ambler novel. It was a pathetic sight, and it signaled a depressing fact of life: from Lebanon to Moscow, the United States intelligence agencies were losing their ability to operate effectively in the shadows. The professionals had become timid and demoralized; the amateurs now running the show were making a mess.

The State Department fared little better than the CIA. For the skills of successful diplomacy were in especially short supply during the Reagan years. Indeed, one remarkable fact about the administration is that for most of its first seven years, it failed to produce a single successful U.S.-led diplomatic accord. Compared to the Reagan record of nonachievement, former President Jimmy Carter looked like a master diplomat, with his success in negotiating the Camp David accords, the Panama Canal Treaty, and the SALT II agreement. Even in arms control, where the Reagan administration finally began to make progress during its final eighteen months, the breakthroughs were largely the result of aggressive Soviet diplomacy rather than American efforts.

The arms-control bargaining with the Soviet Union illustrated the most intriguing paradox of all about the Reagan legacy in foreign policy. Reagan's triumphs, in the end, were in the areas that mattered most to liberals: Reagan kept the country out of war; he grudgingly accepted the inevitability of the arms-control process and negotiated, in the INF (Intermediate Nuclear Force) agreement, the first true disarmament treaty of the nuclear era; he used military force sparingly and withdrew it at the first sign of serious trouble, as in Lebanon; and he helped remove undemocratic regimes in the Philippines and Korea.

In the areas that mattered most to conservatives, Reagan's

record was spotty: he failed to project American power successfully in Lebanon and Central America; he failed to modernize
America's strategic arsenal; he failed in his much-vaunted goal of
reversing the advance of Soviet power. Indeed, by the end of
Reagan's presidency, the United States appeared in some ways to
be weaker, relative to the Soviet Union, than when Reagan took
office. The Iran-contra affair symbolized the wreckage of a foreign
policy that was, at its core, confused and hypocritical.

The blame for the foreign-policy breakdown during the Reagan
years should be shared among all the players: the president and
his inept national security staff; the feuding and ineffectual Cabinet departments and intelligence agencies; an often-irresponsible
Congress; and a press that failed to live up to the responsibilities
it claimed for itself during the 1980s as a participant in the
foreign-policy process. This problem of shared responsibility was
highlighted in *Our Own Worst Enemy,* a 1985 study of the foreign-
policy deadlock by I. M. Destler, Leslie Gelb, and Anthony Lake.
They argued: "Our whole society has been undergoing a systemic
breakdown when attempting to fashion a coherent and consistent
approach to the world. . . . And the breakdown has produced
policies with a peculiar blend of self-righteousness and self-
doubt."

The Reagan legacy in foreign policy is hardly encouraging.
Because he concentrated so much on image rather than substance,
Reagan leaves behind an array of unresolved substantive problems. His successor will inherit a collection of outdated strategic
premises, alliances that don't quite adhere, roles and expectations
for America that no longer hold. By the end of Reagan's term,
for example, there was an emerging consensus among policy
experts that NATO's strategic doctrine was no longer credible,
that in the Middle East the era of unilateral American diplomacy

was ending, and that in superpower diplomacy the Soviet Union would be a far more subtle and creative adversary in the next decade. Yet because of the breakdown in the foreign-policy process, there was no consensus about how to address these problems, and precious little real debate about them within the government. When criticized for this state of affairs, weary Reagan administration officials remarked: If you only knew how much worse it might be if the conservative zealots within the administration had their way! Such comments illustrated the sad fact that American foreign policy during the Reagan years was largely a holding action. Perhaps it was inevitable that an administration that rejected diplomatic solutions for problems could show so few diplomatic achievements.

The goal of this essay will be to examine how the foreign-policy process broke down during the Reagan administration. The responsibility for fixing what went wrong is shared by the entire country, but the blame belongs first of all to Ronald Reagan—a charismatic but profoundly flawed president who wanted to close the book on the post-Vietnam era of American weakness and disorientation but instead added several new chapters.

II

The National Security Council was the seat of the Reagan administration's disorganization and failure in foreign policy. The Iran-contra scandal gave the country an inside look at the NSC's antics. We met Lieutenant Colonel Oliver North and his mysterious network of covert operatives. We read over Ollie's shoulder as he sent his "PROF" notes on the NSC computer system to his bosses, National Security Advisers Robert C. (Bud) McFarlane and John Poindexter. The message traffic showed a sleepless and often exhausted North racing to and fro with ill-considered schemes, putting his own memos—and, ultimately, American foreign policy—through the shredder.

The details that emerged during the Iran-contra investigation were so strange and sinister that they obscured the more mundane problem that had hobbled the NSC during the Reagan administration—its inability to produce an interagency consensus on foreign policy. It was this inability to make the normal channels work that drove McFarlane and Poindexter to the desperate and counterproductive measures revealed by the Iran-contra investigation.

The NSC during the Reagan years was a machine that had broken down. The purpose of the machine was to accomplish the routine but essential business of foreign policy: soliciting policy proposals from the various cabinet departments and agencies, refining them into clear options for presidential decision, and then imposing the decisions on the bureaucracy. That, in simple terms, was what the NSC was created to do. Though its functions had long since been embellished by a string of national security advisers with large egos and ambitions—particularly Henry Kissinger and Zbigniew Brzezinski—the NSC's central purpose was to make the bureaucracy work by mobilizing the various cabinet agencies and making them speak with one voice.

From the first, the Reagan NSC failed in this task. Through most of the first term, the State Department and the Pentagon disagreed strongly about major policy issues. On arms control, the interagency bickering was so chronic that it produced a stalemate that continued for most of Reagan's presidency. (The office politics of arms control was so rich in detail that it formed the basis of a best-selling book, Strobe Talbott's *Deadly Gambits*.)

The same divisions were evident on less visible issues: from trade policy to arms sales, from the Mideast to Central America. Alexander Haig, who fancied himself a bureaucratic operator, was eased out as secretary of state in mid-1982 in the hope that his departure would reduce the internal feuding between State and the Pentagon. It didn't. George Shultz, the new secretary of state, was soon locked in a bitter public quarrel with Secretary of Defense Caspar Weinberger over the use of American military power. The debilitating Shultz-Weinberger debate extended to the most vexing issue of Reagan's second term—how to frame a viable antiterrorism policy—with Shultz taking a tough line and Weinberger counseling restraint. The Iran-contra affair revealed yet another layer of the interagency feuding, with George Shultz and William Casey attempting to conduct independent—and radically different—policies for dealing with Iran.

Resolving such disputes quietly and efficiently is the job of the national security adviser and the NSC staff. But the Reagan administration gave this responsibility to a series of men who lacked the intellectual horsepower or the political skills to accomplish the job. It made sense to choose less flamboyant national security advisers after the turbulence and backbiting of the Kissinger-Brzezinski years. But the first four Reagan appointees—Richard Allen, William Clark, Bud McFarlane, and John Poindexter—proved to be so lacking in political clout that they were unable to make the NSC system work. As a result, the administration either spun its wheels, as on arms control and Mideast diplomacy; or it adopted an ad-hoc, muddle-through approach, as on the Philippines; or it pushed policy underground, as in the Iran-contra affair.

The NSC's problems stemmed in part from Ronald Reagan's

loose management style. Detached from and in many cases uninformed about the substantive issues of policy, Reagan ignored the
growing discord within his administration. Indeed, he seemed
almost unaware of the bickering that was taking place out of his
sight. In 1984, at a time when his administration was bitterly split
over arms control, Reagan denied that there were any serious
internal disputes on the issue, saying, "I don't know where all
this talk comes from." The "talk," needless to say, was coming
from some of his most senior aides. But they preferred to share
their complaints with reporters rather than with the president.

Reagan let the mess fester. He would not impose order on the
feuding bureaucrats himself, and he would not hire a tough national security adviser who could do the job for him. The disorder
eased in the final year of Reagan's presidency, mainly because
two of the most aggressive infighters—Weinberger and Casey—
were gone, leaving Shultz as the dominant figure. By the end of
Reagan's term, it was hard to decide whose behavior had been
worse: the genial president who had tolerated disorder for so long
or the self-interested cabinet officers who had created and
manipulated it.

III

The Reagan years were not a happy time for the State Department and its cadre of foreign-service officers. The striped-pants
set was abused from every direction. Terrorism put American
diplomats in mortal danger overseas, and the State Department
spent much of its meager budget trying to protect embassies and
consulates. That left little money for anything else. The budget

was so tight that by 1987, foreign-service officers were unable to attend international conferences unless the sponsoring foundation paid their way, unable to invite their spouses to attend Fourth of July receptions in some embassies, unable at one embassy even to afford enough newspapers for the staff to read.

Meanwhile, to get their ill-paid and often dangerous postings overseas, foreign-service officers had to run a Capitol Hill gauntlet organized by Republican Senator Jesse Helms. Some ambassadorial appointments languished a year or more while Helms and his staff examined nominees in minute detail and used them as hostages to bargain for the appointment of conservative cronies to State Department posts.

The diplomats' problems stemmed partly from the simple fact that the Reagan administration didn't much like diplomacy. Among the Reaganites, there seemed little understanding that military power was useful because it could help achieve specific diplomatic and political gains; instead, the Reaganites regarded military power as something to be valued in itself, independent of any actual uses. When Philip Habib became the administration's negotiator in Central America, for example, he hoped to use the military leverage that had been built up by the CIA-backed contras to achieve some lasting diplomatic gains in the region. But he soon found that conservatives in the administration regarded "negotiation" as a dirty word. Habib resigned in August 1987 when it became clear that the White House wouldn't allow its Central American negotiator to do any real negotiating with either of the parties. Habib complained bitterly, in private, that it would be our nominal allies, the contras, who would pay the price for the administration's disdain for diplomacy.

The most awkward problem, some foreign-service officers

began to suspect, was the inadequacy of the secretary of state himself, George Shultz. Supposedly the champion of moderation and diplomacy within the Reagan administration, Shultz proved to be more a caretaker than an active diplomat. Some of his senior aides grumbled about the difficulty of dealing with Shultz's Buddha-like presence. Aides would come to visit him to recommend innovative policies in the Mideast or Central America or Asia and Shultz would sit silently—his eyes narrowed, his face impassive—until they were done. "You never know what he's really thinking," a senior State Department official complained after one frustrating and unsuccessful effort to penetrate the Buddha presence.

Shimon Peres told American friends about one agonizing visit he had with Shultz in 1986. Peres was Israeli prime minister at the time, and he had come to Washington to try to persuade Shultz to support an international peace conference on the Middle East. Peres talked on and on, presenting argument after argument about the need for peace, without budging Shultz. What a spectacle, remarked one State Department official later. Here was an Israeli leader who seemed more interested in peace negotiations over the Palestinian issue than the American secretary of state! When Shultz finally decided to get serious about the peace process more than a year later, Peres was gone as prime minister and the situation was far more intractable.

The Middle East was probably the best example of the failure of American diplomacy during the Reagan years. The administration began with high hopes, eager to continue the role of peacemaker begun by Henry Kissinger in his shuttle diplomacy and sustained by President Carter in the Camp David accords. The key to success, the administration understood, was to maintain the appearance of evenhandedness and independence. To that end, the administration sold AWACS radar-surveillance planes to Saudi Arabia in 1981, over intense Congressional opposition, and sent Habib on a successful diplomatic shuttle that year between Damascus and Jerusalem that led to an understanding about Syrian missiles in Lebanon and a de facto cease-fire by the PLO. But the administration couldn't sustain the momentum of these bold opening moves.

The 1982 Israeli invasion of Lebanon began a chain of events that had disastrous consequences—most of all for Israel. Israeli General Ariel Sharon raced to Beirut, armed with a half-baked invasion plan that relied too much on wishful thinking about the ability of his Lebanese Christian allies to impose a pro-Israeli Christian government in Lebanon. The Israelis reached Beirut quickly enough, and then settled into a long and—in public-relations terms—disastrous siege of West Beirut.

In midsummer 1982, the Americans stepped in to help clean up the mess and to provide the Lebanese government with an alternative to the machinations of Israel and Syria. The Marines arrived in Beirut in August to escort Yasser Arafat out of the city, ending Israel's frustrating siege of Beirut. The American troops returned a few weeks later when hundreds of Palestinians were slaughtered by Israeli-backed militiamen at Sabra and Shatila, despite American assurances that they would be safe.

For the Arabists at the State Department and the CIA, September 1982 was high tide. Early that month, before the Marines returned to Lebanon, President Reagan announced a well-crafted plan for resolving the Palestinian problem based on U.N. Security Council Resolution 242 and the Camp David accords. Israeli Prime Minister Menachem Begin was furious. He would have

been even angrier had he known that an American operative had
secretly delivered a copy of the Reagan peace plan to Yasser
Arafat in Beirut—some days before it was announced publicly.
The events of September 1982 put the United States sharply at
odds with Israel. Not only was the Reagan administration pushing
a peace plan denounced by Begin; it was also stealing Mossad's
man in East Beirut—Bashir Gemayel—and putting American
troops on the ground to save Lebanon from Israel!

The American defiance of Israel didn't last long. A year after
the Marines arrived in Lebanon, independent American policy
there was already giving way to a new U.S.-Israeli security-coop-
eration agreement. The Lebanon mission was complicated from
the start by the fact that it never had solid political support. And
as America began to get a taste of terrorism in Lebanon, our
Israeli allies looked better and better. The Reagan administration—from George Shultz to Bud McFarlane to Bill Casey—
seemed increasingly envious of Israel's hard-nosed and expedient
approach to foreign policy and eager to emulate it.

The Lebanon policy itself was a study in confusion. The Marines were sent on what was called a "presence mission," whose
purpose was never adequately described. Their first real confrontations in Lebanon weren't with Lebanese terrorists but with
Israeli tanks. The situation soon changed. Rather than push for
political reforms in Lebanon that would benefit the Moslem majority, the Americans embraced Israel's Lebanese Christian clients. To Lebanese Moslems, it looked as if America was taking
sides against them in the long-running Lebanese Civil War. So the
Moslems, backed by ruthless strategists in Damascus and Tehran,
began attacking the Marines and seeking to drive the Americans
from Lebanon.

Shultz at this point committed the biggest diplomatic mistake of his career: the ill-fated May 17, 1983, accord for withdrawal of Israeli troops from Lebanon. The agreement was premised on an unrealistic assumption that the Syrians would tolerate an openly pro-Israeli Lebanon. Shultz badly misread Syria's intentions, and he had no fallback plan when Syrian President Hafez Assad announced his opposition to the agreement. The United States flailed around in Lebanon for nearly another year in an unsuccessful search for a policy. There was a brief period in which the Reagan administration, seemingly ready to go to war with Syria, shelled and bombed its positions in the Lebanese mountains. There was even a hawkish faction within the administration that talked of sending an airborne division to secure the entire Shouf Mountain area. But America hadn't the staying power for this Lebanese campaign—not Congress, not the public, not the Pentagon. We were, as Syria's foreign minister aptly remarked, "short of breath." And soon enough, the Americans were gone, turning Lebanon back to the wiles of the regional superpowers, Syria and Israel.

Shultz recognized that going against Israeli policy in the Middle East amounted to swimming upstream. By late 1983, the Reagan administration had tired of the struggle and decided to go with the flow. For the remainder of Reagan's presidency, the Israelis maintained unusually close relations with the United States. Their long-standing war against terrorism was now our war, too.

Unfortunately, the most striking outgrowth of this period of American-Israeli cooperation was the Iran affair. The NSC staff, desperate to "win one" by getting the American hostages in Lebanon released, turned to the Israelis for help. In walked a cast of characters that included Israeli arms dealers Jacob Nimrodi and Al Schwimmer, Saudi billionaire Adnan Khashoggi, and Iranian middleman Manucher Ghorbanifar. The Israelis urged the Americans to join them in selling arms to Iran, a consistent Israeli goal for decades. The Reagan administration agreed, at the cost of its own foreign-policy credibility.

In the panic about terrorism and hostages, the United States nearly lost sight of its traditional role as peacemaker in the region. The Reagan peace plan of September 1982 collapsed in the uproar over Lebanon. When a chief architect of the plan, CIA case officer Robert Ames, died in the Beirut embassy bombing in April 1983, Shultz seemed to lose heart. He waited until late 1987 before showing even modest interest in Mideast diplomacy again.

The regional actors kept trying. Jordan's King Hussein met secretly with Shimon Peres (and there were even rumors that he met secretly in the Israeli desert with Likud leader Yitzhak Shamir), to no avail. At one point, King Hussein was reduced to asking an American friend whether the United States still supported its own nominal Mideast policy—the exchange of land for peace, as outlined in Resolution 242. Could it be true, the King asked, that America now regarded 242 as "folklore"? The administration eventually decided that, yes, it did still support its own policies, and Shultz embarked on a new round of shuttle diplomacy with a retinkered version of the 1982 peace plan. But Shultz's efforts seemed, to many analysts, to be too little, too late.

In sum, the Reagan years saw the demise of the Great American Mediation Machine in the Middle East. The Lebanon debacle marked the end of a decade of intense American effort to negotiate a comprehensive peace in the Middle East. When the Americans became involved again in the region in 1987—sending an armada to the Persian Gulf to protect Saudi and Kuwaiti shipping and renewing discussions on Arab-Israeli peace—it was partly to head off similar efforts by the Soviet Union, which was playing a much more clever and aggressive diplomatic role in the region. The Soviets seemed to have learned what America had once understood about the Middle East and then forgotten: that diplomatic success in dealing with the Arab-Israeli conflict is based on maintaining the illusion that the mediator—once the United States but now increasingly the Soviets—can ride two horses at once.

The Middle East was the clearest example of the Reagan administration's incapacity in foreign policy, but it wasn't the only one. The competence problem affected even the area that seemed to matter most to Ronald Reagan—Central America.

From the beginning, the Reagan administration was never able to match its ambitious goals in Central America with the modest means available. The president, from the start, seemed determined to topple the Sandinista regime in Managua. A paramilitary covert operation was duly set in motion in 1981, piggybacking on an Argentine-backed operation involving former members of Somoza's National Guard. It was the worst sort of vehicle for American aid: a group of right-wing Nicaraguans, who had been detested by most of their countrymen, trained by right-wing Argentines from an antidemocratic junta that would soon be driven from power itself. These were our freedom fighters!

In Miami and Tegucigalpa, CIA officers encouraged the contras in their fantasies of seizing power in Managua. Yet from the beginning, neither Congress, which appropriated the money for the operation, nor the CIA brass who supervised it believed the contras had any real chance of winning. Indeed, the CIA's inspector general concluded at one point in 1983 that the operation didn't violate a congressional ban against overthrowing the government of Nicaragua because the contras were too feeble to achieve their goals.

From year to year, from congressional amendment to amendment, that basic picture never changed. The contras never had a strategy that could plausibly have led to military victory and seizure of power in Managua. For that reason, the only rationale for the contra operation was to gain leverage that could be used in negotiations with the Sandinistas. In these talks, the United States might be able to achieve its primary goals of containing the Nicaraguan revolution within its borders and democratizing the Sandinista regime. Negotiations eventually came, pushed by Costa Rican President Oscar Arias. But since the Reagan administration scorned diplomacy, it missed its opportunity to shape the diplomatic agenda to its own ends. As a result, the administration gained little for its trouble—and wasted thousands of lives.

The State Department recognized the weakness of the U.S. effort to support the contras and tried from time to time to encourage a more sensible course. There was an occasional show of diplomacy, with the appointment of a new negotiator or new lip service from Shultz to the Contadora process. But Shultz and his aides recognized that they had little influence over Central American policy. The contras were Ronald Reagan's toy. Lieutenant Colonel North told one acquaintance that the president listened to briefings on the secret war with fascination, studying maps that showed the latest combat operations and hearing colorful war stories from some of the contra fighters. The survival of the contras—the "freedom fighters," as the president and his men called them—became a sentimental goal that overshadowed America's actual strategic goals in Central America. American policy toward Mexico—the real strategic prize in the region—was subordinated to the make-believe war against the Sandinistas.

Reagan's determination to stick by the contras was admirable in its way, but it didn't alter the fact that his Central American policy was fundamentally misconceived. So when Arias prodded the leaders of the Central American states to craft a peace plan of their own, Reagan's policy seemed to run out of gas. The administration publicly backed the peace plan and privately worked to sabotage it. When Congress finally pulled the plug on military aid in early 1988, the contras were left to negotiate the terms of their surrender on their own.

A similar ideological confusion afflicted the administration in southern Africa. Assistant Secretary of State Chester Crocker crafted a policy of "constructive engagement" in the region that drew the administration closer to white South Africa—but also to the Marxist regimes of Mozambique and Angola. Crocker's aim was to accumulate the diplomatic capital that might allow the United States to broker a settlement in the region. But these subtleties were too much for the administration's ideologues. Crocker's policy smacked of "negotiation." So the administration succumbed once again to its fantasies of military victory against the Soviets and began a covert-action program to support South Africa's man in Angola, Jonas Savimbi. The diplomatic opening to Mozambique languished. It was another sorry example of the administration's rejection of diplomacy.

The State Department seemed to do better in other areas— such as Asia—that were less visible than the Mideast, Central America, or southern Africa. In its Asian diplomacy, the administration triumphed over its own ideology and succeeded in some important initiatives that are likely to boost American security for years to come.

The first and most important Asian success was in China. In the first several years of his administration, Reagan seemed on the verge of blowing it. His pro-Taiwan sympathies threatened to unravel the American opening to China begun by Nixon and Kissinger—thereby destroying what is arguably America's most important strategic relationship. But by visiting the Peoples' Republic in 1984, Reagan triumphed over his own anti-Communist rhetoric and put his own conservative stamp of approval on the Sino-American relationship.

The administration also showed skill and steady nerves in pushing Ferdinand Marcos out of power in the Philippines and helping Corazon Aquino take his place in early 1986. Here the professionals ran the show with élan and success. The American ambassador in Manila, Stephen Bosworth, and the CIA station chief worked closely together—holding Marcos's hand when necessary, giving him a firm shove at the right moment, and calming the fears of the Philippine military about the new government. By 1987, the American embassy in Manila appeared to have contact with nearly all elements in the Philippines and seemed well positioned to deal with Aquino or any of the possible successor regimes. This was precisely the sort of contact and flexibility the United States had lacked a decade earlier in Iran. The Philippine example showed how crucial diplomacy can be in maintaining America's strategic interests and in fostering its democratic ideals.

The key to American success in the Philippines was that in place of the rigid anti-Sovietism that characterized some aspects of administration policy, there was a loose, nonideological approach that might be termed "ad-hoc-ism." The administration adopted a similar muddle-through style in dealing with South Korea. There, as in the Philippines, the United States sought to ease out a dictatorship and encourage a democratic transfer of power—without alienating pro-American elements in the military and the security service. The electoral process worked and installed a new regime that was at once pro-American and backed in democratic elections by the Korean people. In Asia, unlike the Middle East, the administration still seemed able to manage the trick of riding two horses at once.

IV

Arms control with the Soviet Union proved to be the crowning achievement of the Reagan administration in foreign policy. This was a bizarre turn of events, since two guiding lights for the Reaganites had been anti-Sovietism and mistrust of arms control. In precisely this spirit, they had put on the table in 1981 a proposal for removing medium-range missiles in Europe—the so-called zero option—that administration officials privately described as nonnegotiable. Arms control appeared to be in the deep freeze, precisely where many of the Reaganites wanted it. Then along came Mikhail Gorbachev.

When Gorbachev became general secretary in 1985, he apparently concluded that the long-run benefits of reaching arms-control agreements with Reagan—the most conservative American president in modern history—justified any short-term sacrifices. Such agreements would lock in arms control as a permanent feature of the superpower relationship and allow the Soviets to plan defense spending in a way that would help Gorbachev reform the Soviet economy. The new Soviet leader thus began a relentless quest for agreement: he literally would not take no for an answer.

Consider the chain of Soviet concessions that preceded the agreement on medium-range nuclear forces: when the United States deployed its Pershing II missiles in West Germany in late 1983, the Soviets broke off INF and START negotiations and said they wouldn't resume talks until the missiles were withdrawn; when that approach failed, the Soviets said they would return to the bargaining table, but only to talk about banning space weapons; when that failed, they agreed to resume START and INF talks, but only if they were linked to a ban on SDI; when that failed, they agreed to "delink" the negotiations and reach a separate INF accord, but only covering Europe; when that failed, they agreed to ban medium-range missiles worldwide.

The INF talks weren't the only area where the Soviets offered major concessions. In the START talks, they agreed in principle to cut the number of strategic weapons in half and accepted subceilings that would impose these cuts on "heavy" land-based missiles, where the Soviets had been dominant. In talks on limiting strategic defense, they dropped their demands for a flat ban on research and testing of SDI systems. In chemical-weapons talks, they moved toward the American positions on on-site inspection and monitoring. In conventional-arms talks, they appeared to accept American arguments that Warsaw Pact forces should be cut more than NATO forces.

These startling Soviet concessions indicated that Reagan and his hard-line advisers had been right in their contention that if the American side stuck to its guns—and stopped negotiating with itself—we could achieve far more favorable agreements than we had in the détente era of the 1970s. The Soviet concessions also made clear, even to Reagan's opponents, the enormous leverage that Reagan's defense buildup had given the United States at the bargaining table. SDI, above all, seemed to have frightened the Soviets and convinced them to bargain in earnest.

Reagan had truly pulled a rabbit out of his hat with SDI. He had, in effect, gotten something for nothing. Few scientists believed that SDI as envisioned by Reagan would actually work, and Congress clearly wasn't eager to fund it. Yet Reagan had somehow managed to use the threat of this nothing of an SDI program to obtain Soviet concessions that were something very tangible indeed.

The arms-control process was the clearest sign that a role reversal had taken place in Soviet-American relations. During the 1960s and 1970s, the United States had been the initiator and *demandeur* in the bargaining process. We had supplied the categories, specified the units of account, proposed the innovative ideas—and thereby drawn the Soviets into a web of our own design. In this role, we were sometimes overeager, offering concessions larger and sooner than was necessary, in part to elicit responses from the poker-faced Soviet negotiators who sat across the table. But we dominated the process and shaped it to our own interests.

By 1987, the tables had turned. Now it was the Soviets who initiated the arms-control dialogue and offered concession after concession to the sullen and unyielding Americans. In one sense, this change benefited the United States. But it was also true that we had lost the initiative, that we were being drawn into a web of Soviet design. Public-opinion polls in mid-1987 showed that in Europe it was the Soviets and not the Americans who were seen as the architects of the new arms-control regime.

Gorbachev posed a new and different challenge for an America that had grown used to aged, ailing Soviet leaders whose chronic ill health seemed to symbolize the failings of their system. Facing the geriatric team of Brezhnev, Andropov, and Chernenko, the Reagan administration had a free ride during its first term. Gorbachev changed that. His visit to Washington in December 1987 showed Americans that they were dealing with a master politician—charming, humorous, thoroughly opportunistic—who was able, by the force of his own personality, to rewrite the traditional rules of the game in Soviet-American relations. The wily and adventurous new Soviet leader seemed likely to pose an entirely new set of problems for the West in the 1990s. Indeed, there were signs that this new, American-style leadership in the Kremlin could prove more volatile and willing to take risks in a crisis. If so, we may look back more fondly than we expect on the Reagan years—and Reagan's taunting of a weak and decaying Soviet leadership.

V

America's difficulty in foreign affairs during the 1980s was partly the responsibility of two groups that had demanded a greater role in the foreign-policy process: Congress and the press. Neither acquitted itself especially well during the Reagan years, though, to be fair, Reagan offered little opportunity for a meaningful partnership.

Congressional involvement in foreign policy has been increasing since Vietnam. Congress made its claim in the 1970s in the War Powers Act, in the establishment of the House and Senate Intelligence committees, and in the tougher oversight role claimed by the Foreign Affairs committees. The expanded Congressional role was in many ways beneficial: it reflected the growing worldliness and independence of members of Congress. The old congressional stereotype—the rube who was interested only in the pork-barrel aspects of foreign policy—had mostly vanished. The congressman of the 1980s spent his free time drafting op-ed pieces for the *New York Times* and the "Outlook" section of the *Washington Post.* Now members of Congress were among the leading foreign-policy experts in the land: Senator Albert Gore of Tennessee on arms control; Senator Sam Nunn of Georgia on defense issues; Senator Bill Bradley of New Jersey on international economics; Representative Stephen Solarz of New York on Asia.

The problem was that when it came to a crisis, members of Congress tended to act like politicians. They ran for cover. When a policy seemed to have popular support, like the initial commitment of American Marines in Lebanon in 1982, Congress was all for it; but when Americans began to get killed and the public mood changed, congressmen often bailed out. There was initially broad support, for example, for reflagging and escorting Kuwaiti tankers in the Persian Gulf when the idea was first floated in early 1987. But after the attack on the USS *Stark* made clear the obvious fact that the Persian Gulf was a dangerous place, members of Congress began to panic and there was talk of immediately invoking the War Powers Act. When our armada in the Gulf began bashing the Iranians and public support for the policy increased, congressional criticism became muted once again. The same pattern of on-again, off-again support was evident in the case of the contras. Congress, in effect, declared its support for popular, winnable wars.

The problem, of course, is that a superpower can't conduct foreign policy by public-opinion poll. Many of the things that a nation does to protect its interests are bound to look frightening to the public—especially in the initial phase—and may cost lives. Similarly, most bold and innovative strategies run some risk of failure. One obvious example was Britain's decision to contest Argentina's seizure of the Falkland Islands in 1982. During the long, slow passage of the British fleet to the Falklands, many skittish members of parliament and the press questioned the policy. The Thatcher government refused to heed their warnings and won a stunning victory.

The lesson is obvious: the fact that a policy may cost lives or may fail shouldn't be a sufficient reason to scuttle it. Yet during the Reagan years, Congress seemed obsessed with such dangers and wary of all but the most muddled and mealymouthed foreign involvements.

On the Middle East, Congress turned the policy-making process into a rite of lobbying and influence-peddling worthy of the Lebanese parliament. With large campaign contributions from pro-Israeli PACs at stake, members of Congress battled to outdo each other in denouncing arms sales to Arabs and delivering new benefits for Israel. The America-Israel Public Affairs Committee became, by many accounts, the most powerful and feared lobby on Capitol Hill. The moment the Reagan administration began drafting plans for a new arms sale to, say, Jordan or Saudi Arabia, AIPAC lobbyists began gathering signatures from members of Congress opposing the sale. The scramble to be seen as pro-Israeli had become so intense by 1987 that it seemed to have passed beyond AIPAC's control, and several former AIPAC officials questioned privately whether the congressional zealotry truly served Israel's long-run interests.

Congressional skittishness was a problem in part because it reinforced a long-standing problem in American foreign policy: our impatience and unreliability. The United States, as a democracy, has trouble being a consistent and reliable ally even in the best of circumstances. But the problem seemed to get worse in the 1980s: a contra who risked his life in a secret war financed by Congress, and who then found himself without food or ammunition because Congress had changed its mind, might reasonably question the reliability of the United States. So might a Jordanian or Saudi military officer who had planned his nation's future defense strategy on the promise of American weapons and then found that Congress refused to deliver them.

The Intelligence committees constituted a special case of the congressional desire to share responsibility for foreign policy, unless it became unpopular. The panels had been established in the mid-1970s, following the investigation of CIA misdeeds by the Pike and Church committees. The dubious premise of this new oversight effort was that congressional supervision could make the dirty business of spying clean—by wrapping it in legalism and democratic procedures.

This new American approach to intelligence stood the usual model on its head. In most countries, intelligence matters are kept far away from the institutions that embody the legitimacy of the state, such as the legislature and the courts. The reason is simple: intelligence work is dirty; it involves, at a minimum, the systematic violation of the laws of foreign countries. In most countries, politicians accept this dirty work as an inevitable fact of life, and ask only that they be shielded from it. But not in America. Here our politicians want to know the details of the dirty work and claim that they will exercise the same discretion and discipline—and accept the same corrupted standards—as intelligence officers.

But in dealing with intelligence matters, members of Congress have, understandably enough, behaved like members of Congress. That is, they have supported operations as long as they remained secret and posed no political danger, but they have tended to jump ship whenever the operations have surfaced and produced a flap. This shouldn't be surprising: after all, how can you ask a politician who has to stand for reelection to condone publicly the mining of Nicarguan harbors once it becomes public, even if he was briefed on the operation before it was undertaken. That's what happened in April 1984, when members of the Senate Intelligence Committee ran for cover and claimed no knowledge of the mining, even though committee transcripts showed that CIA Director Casey had told them a month before, "Magnetic mines have been placed in the Pacific harbor of Corinto and the Atlantic harbor of El Bluff, as well as the oil terminal at Puerto Sandino."

Members of Congress complained, with considerable justification, that the high-handed policies of the Reagan administration didn't allow them to play a positive role in the oversight of intelligence or foreign policy. When the administration talked about bipartisan foreign policy, they argued, what it really meant was that it wanted congressional endorsement of what it had already decided to do. It was a fair point. A truly bipartisan foreign policy—responsive to the clearly expressed views of Congress—would have spared the nation the embarrassment of the secret war in Central America and the Iran affair.

Perhaps the best measure of the folly of the Reagan administration's foreign policy was that it made Congress look good. Watching Richard Secord and Albert Hakim talk about their secret dealings with Iran, who could doubt that the correct antidote was more oversight? Yet that is only part of the answer. A challenge for the next administration will be to solve the riddle of intelligence oversight in a way that satisfies the political demands of Congress while remaining faithful to the realities of the intelligence business.

The news media comprise the most jagged piece in the jigsaw puzzle of foreign policy. That's as it should be. An easy fit between the government and the journalists who cover it is the clearest mark of an undemocratic regime. And as journalists so often remind their critics, the free and sometimes bilious flow of information is what makes the miracle of American democracy possible.

But something was going badly wrong in the role of the media during the mid-1980s. Newspapers and television had become immensely more powerful. Thanks to modern technology, they were able to gather information around the globe and transmit it instantly to every American home. In the White House situation room during crises, for example, the television sets were often tuned to the network newscasters. At the State Department, diplomats often turned first to the Associated Press and Reuters telex machines for hot news—rather than to the top-secret cables arriving from American embassies around the world.

Yet the press hadn't developed the skill or sophistication commensurate with its new role. On major news stories, journalists often managed to be at once too arrogant and too meek: too quick to make snide and uninformed judgments about American policy, and too lazy to dig for the hard information that could help policy-makers and the public alike reach a clearer understanding of issues.

The best example of how the press was spinning its wheels covering foreign policy during the Reagan administration could be found every day in the White House press room. What a scene it was! Reporters screaming at the press secretary and at each other, making a show of asking tough questions but often letting the real stories slip through their fingers. As the network correspondents shouted their questions at the president over the roar of a helicopter on the White House lawn each weekend, it became increasingly obvious that the news media and the White House were locked in a cycle that ill served the public.

I saw a classic example of this in 1984, when Ronald Reagan went to China. I had gone to China a few weeks before as a reporter for the *Wall Street Journal* to get a sense of the place, so I was there when the 747 arrived in Beijing and the White House press corps tumbled out. Here they were, in one of the most exotic spots on earth, covering a trip that was truly a historic breakthrough—a conservative, pro-Taiwanese president visiting the People's Republic. Yet the White House regulars seemed oblivious. They went directly to the press room at the Great Wall Hotel, and within two hours of arriving in China, they were embroiled in a bitter argument with Larry Speakes about whether a senior White House official had or hadn't promised that there would be a live feed of an interview Reagan had scheduled with Chinese television. Incredible, and pathetic. Watching this scene, in the midst of China, you had to think: Something has gone wrong here.

The rejoinder of the press during the Reagan years was that it was all the fault of the news managers at the White House. The reporters wouldn't have to be so rude and obstreperous, they would explain, if only the president would hold more news conferences and open up his administration. Only by being so rude—by shouting questions at poor, deaf Ronald Reagan each day—could the news media obtain anything useful for the public. That argument had considerable merit, and the first task of any new president should be to establish—and maintain—a regular schedule of press conferences. Not because press conferences are good for the press, but because they're good for the public.

But the news media's whining about Reagan concealed an important problem. During the Reagan years, White House reporters began to confuse the appearance of adversarial journalism—rudeness, aggressive questions, an abrasive personal manner—with the reality, which is quite different. That mock toughness was especially evident on foreign-policy issues that lent themselves to television—like the endless fascination with summits or the daily attempts to catch the president in a gaffe on arms control or the Mideast (as if these misstatements mattered more than the substance of his policy). More complicated foreign-policy issues that were tougher to cover got little attention.

TV reporters imagined that shouting questions at the president was the same thing as digging for the truth, but they were mistaken. It's useful to recall, in this regard, that many of the best investigative reporters—from I. F. Stone to Bob Woodward—have been polite and modest people. They didn't bark; they bit.

One small example illustrates the point. It involves the archetypal modern TV reporter, Sam Donaldson. In his book *Hold On, Mr. President*, Donaldson boasted of his tough reporting. He explained the function of the press this way: "Our job is to challenge the president, challenge him to explain policy, justify decisions, defend mistakes, reveal intentions for the future, and comment on a host of matters about which his views are of general concern. . . . I have one goal: To find out what's really going on at the White House."

Donaldson was entirely right about the need to be skeptical of public officials and to dig for the truth. Without these qualities, journalists are lost. But he and other television reporters, with their question-shouting technique, didn't uncover the Iran-contra scandal, or any of the other chronic problems of the Reagan administration. And the subjects that did preoccupy television often seem, in retrospect, to have been trivial. Television was relentless in breaking the big story of August 1985. That story, if you forgot, was whether Larry Speakes had lied to the press about the cause of a blemish on the president's nose. Was it skin cancer or not? Television was tireless in tracking that one down. That month, we now realize, also saw the beginning of the Iran-contra affair, as President Reagan approved the first Israeli arms shipments to Iran. Television contributed little to the unraveling of that story. In fact, most of the supposedly tough-minded press corps missed the boat.

The point is obvious: the news media, in their show of toughness, were often overlooking the big story during the Reagan years. What was striking about the Iran-contra affair wasn't how powerful and aggressive the press was, but how weak and pliant. In covering Ronald Reagan, journalists tended to follow public opinion rather than lead it. They joined in the celebration of Reagan's leadership skills, as in a memorable *Time* magazine story that appeared in July 1986, two months before the disclosure of the Iran affair. *Time* described Reagan as "a Prospero of American memories, a magician who carries a bright, ideal America like a holograph in his mind and projects its image in the air."

Soon enough, this reverential tone changed to a snarl. But the sudden turnaround in coverage only reinforced the impression that the press corps was following public opinion. Journalists feared to challenge the foreign-policy decisions of a popular politician like Ronald Reagan when he was up in the polls, and piled on him when he was down. In this sense, the press corps during the Reagan years was part of the problem rather than part of the solution.

VI

The overriding challenge for American foreign policy at the end of the Reagan era is to find a stable relationship with the new Soviet leadership. This task is likely to be more difficult than most American analysts expect, in part because it won't be easy to repair the damage to American interests caused by the Reagan administration, and in part because Gorbachev is likely to be a skillful and potentially dangerous adversary.

This view isn't widely shared. Instead, there is a loose assumption that Gorbachev is good for the West—that a more modern Soviet Union that looks and acts more like the United States will pose less of a danger to our security. This sense of reassurance is based partly on an unstated premise that as countries grow more like each other, politically and economically, they are likely to be less of a threat to each other militarily.

The next American president would be wise to put aside this optimistic premise. He should remind himself that in the years before 1914, optimistic European statesmen tried to reassure themselves with the notion that Britain and Germany were becoming more alike, politically and economically.

Let's consider an alternative scenario: the possibility that as the United States and the Soviet Union grow more alike in the future, their rivalry may become more dangerous rather than less so. In this analysis, let's leave aside the complex issues of how Soviet economic modernization and political liberalization may affect Western security interests. And let's agree that Gorbachev and his advisers truly want a "breathing spell" in foreign affairs so that they can concentrate on modernizing the Soviet economy.

Let's focus instead on the nasty problem of what happens when things go wrong—when the superpowers face a sudden foreign-policy crisis that neither desired, like a new Middle East war. How will the new Soviet leadership behave in such a crisis? Will Gorbachev be less dangerous than his recent predecessors, or more? Here, the next president may have reason for concern.

Let me begin by offering a model for how Soviet-American crises have been resolved in the nuclear age. We might call it the "pushmi-pullyu" model, after Doctor Dolittle's mythical two-headed beast—which tugged in various directions but managed to avoid a dangerous break. The Soviet-American relationship has been a similar process of action and accommodating reaction, and this action-reaction process has been crucial to coexistence and stability in the nuclear era. When one side has pushed, the other has tended to give way.

What's interesting is that in most major superpower crises since the 1960s, it has been the Soviet Union that eventually gave way. Indeed, during the Brezhnev era, Soviet actions seemed to follow a pattern: belligerent rhetoric, occasional adventurous forays when America didn't seem to be looking, followed by generally cautious behavior during crises. The troubling question is whether this pattern will hold during the Gorbachev era.

We can describe the crisis-management problem with a simple

axiom: crises put a premium on rapid and bold decisions. The side that can act quickly and boldly has an enormous comparative advantage in crisis management. Until recently, the United States had just such an advantage, and that is one reason why we have managed to dominate the few nuclear crises that have arisen.

As evidence, let's examine Henry's Kissinger's account of superpower crises as outlined in his memoirs. Here are three examples:

- Jordan, 1970. The locus was the Washington Special Actions Group, or WSAG. Under Kissinger's direction, it sent carefully calibrated signals to the Soviets as Syrian tanks moved into Jordan, including improving the alert status of an airborne brigade in Germany; putting the 82nd Airborne on full alert, with the expectation that this would leak; and sending a reconnaissance plane to Israel to pick up targeting information, again with the expectation that this move would be detected by the Soviets and the Syrians. The United States moved promptly and boldly in a show of force and, in Kissinger's words, "the Soviets backed off."
- Cienfuegos, 1970. The crisis over Soviet construction of submarine-tending facilities in Cuba was a minireplay of the 1962 Cuban missile crisis. When the United States received intelligence evidence that such facilities were under construction in the fall of 1970, Nixon and Kissinger moved promptly—and in private—to force the Soviets to stop. This quiet diplomacy worked: the Soviets backed down. Kiss-

inger writes: "By great firmness in the early stages of construction, we avoided a major crisis, yet we achieved our objective. Military construction was halted. . . ."

- The 1973 Mideast War. This was probably the most dangerous superpower confrontation since the 1962 Cuban missile crisis. Here again, as in the 1970 Jordan crisis, the United States moved quickly and deliberately by using military alerts to convey determination. At the height of the crisis, on the evening of October 24, Soviet Ambassador Anatoly Dobrynin delivered a message from Brezhnev threatening to send troops unilaterally to Egypt to rescue the Egyptian Army. Shortly thereafter, Nixon fired a warning shot by ordering all military commanders to move to a higher state of readiness, known as "DefCon III." When this seemed an inadequate signal, Nixon ordered the 82nd Airborne on alert. Brezhnev got the message. About twelve hours later, Kissinger writes, "the Soviets had backed off."

Notice a pattern? In each case, it was the Soviets who, once the crisis was underway, gave ground. Not only that, but according to Kissinger and other participants at the time, the Soviet decision-making process was often sluggish. One official recalls that during the 1973 Mideast war, for example, the Soviets "seemed to be twenty-four hours behind events."

The Soviet sluggishness during the Brezhnev era stemmed in part from the collective-leadership ethos of the Soviet system. This was a generation that had seen the madness of Stalin's one-man rule and was determined that it shouldn't be repeated. For the Brezhnev generation, the Politburo was supreme—even if collective decision-making by such a large body slowed the Kremlin's ability to respond to crises.

Gorbachev is different. One NSC official who has observed the old Soviet style and the new remarked: "You have the sense that a bunch of younger guys may be capable of quicker decisions —and gutsier decisions. . . . Gorbachev probably has a self-confidence that his predecessors lacked. The older generation remembered how weak the Soviet Union had been. There was a sense that Brezhnev, for all his bluff, would back down. . . . It used to be almost a foregone conclusion that we would win in a crisis," this official concluded. "Now it's indeterminate, and that's a little scary."

Soviet crisis management may prove more robust under Gorbachev for several reasons. First, the new Soviet leader may be less deferential toward the Politburo as the seat of executive authority and more inclined to act "presidentially" in a crisis. Gone is the mentality that led Brezhnev to take the entire Politburo with him to negotiate with the Czech leadership in 1968. Gorbachev's advisers, especially former Ambassador Dobrynin, have seen the American presidential system in action and studied the crisis-management techniques of Kissinger and others.

Second, Gorbachev seems to be encouraging changes in the intelligence area that may give the Soviets quicker and better information in crises. For example, intelligence experts say that in the past, Soviet leaders have been hamstrung during crises partly because of a tradition of concentrating the analytical function at the very top. Where American intelligence agencies encourage analytical judgments at every stage of the process—so that it's not unusual for a mid-level bureaucrat to speculate about what the Soviets will and won't do in a crisis—the Russians have tended to give their decision-makers facts only. Deciding what these facts mean has been left to the Politburo and its most senior advisers. "Stalin was his own intelligence analyst," remarked one American official. "That's why he was surprised in 1941 by the Germans." In contrast, this official noted, "It's clear that Gorbachev wants his people in national security to behave differently."

Similar changes may be taking place in what Americans call the "interagency process"—the task of coordinating the activities of the various agencies involved in national security. Traditionally, experts say, the Soviet general staff and the KGB have worked separately, with consolidation of their views and activities taking place only at the highest levels of government. There have been few interagency groups and senior interagency groups ("IGs" and "SIGs" in bureaucratese) in Moscow, in other words. That may sound like an enormous advantage for the Kremlin. But experts argue that the Soviet approach has often meant an overload at the top. U.S. officials believe that Gorbachev may be changing this, too. Finally, there are signs that Gorbachev is continuing the expansion of Soviet air mobility and airlift capability—areas that are crucial in sending signals and projecting power in crises.

Soviet diplomacy is already losing the sluggishness of the Brezhnev years. During 1987, Moscow was on the move diplomatically around the world: negotiating quietly with the Chinese to ease border tensions; adjusting its policy toward South Africa to reassure whites there; expanding ties with South America; reestablishing diplomatic contacts with Israel after a twenty-year break; patching together a peace accord between the feuding factions of the PLO; improving relations with the Gulf Arabs; talking to both sides in the Iran-Iraq War. Lebanese politicians reported that the Soviet ambassador in Beirut was the most active diplomat in town, making the rounds among the warlords and dispensing proconsular advice in the way that the American ambassador had in earlier years. It was a small indication that the Soviets, in the new Gorbachev era, were playing America's game and winning at it.

This analysis isn't meant to imply that Gorbachev is a war-monger or that the danger of war with the Soviets has increased markedly. The point is simply that the free ride of the early Reagan years is over. The next American president won't have the luxury of negotiating with a weak and slow-moving Soviet Union. During a crisis that might escalate into nuclear warfare, a more efficient Kremlin leadership—with an American-style approach to crisis management—may be less willing to give ground than Moscow did in the days of Brezhnev and Gromyko. In the "pushmi-pullyu" model, that means that when the Americans push, the Soviets may push back—and quickly—straining the fabric of the relationship. Someone has to give, and it's less automatic under Gorbachev that it will be the Soviets.

What, then, should the next American president do? First, he should understand that however admirable *glasnost* may be, Gorbachev's accession hasn't necessarily made the world a safer place. In a crisis, Gorbachev may prove far more willing to take risks, and far cleverer in his actions, than his recent predecessors. His arms-control bargaining, for example, shows that he gives ground on small issues to gain a broader initiative.

The tensions inherent in Gorbachev's accession were defused during the Reagan years partly by the unlikely role reversal that took place in Soviet-American relations. As the Soviets grew more rambunctious, America assumed some of the characteristics of the Brezhnev-era Soviet Union: it was cautious, methodical, secretive, inclined to let the other side take the lead in negotiations. Reagan and Shultz seemed increasingly to be the stodgy oldsters and the Gorbachev team the impulsive youngsters. This role reversal may have eased tensions in the mid-1980s, but it isn't likely to last in a new administration.

Second, as the next president contemplates the prospect of a future superpower crisis, he should make sure that our own national-security process has the flexibility and the discipline needed to protect America's interests. At the same time, he should probably seek to expand, where possible, the number of rungs on the ladder of escalation, adding additional steps short of resort to nuclear weapons. Otherwise, facing a Soviet leadership better able to match the United States in climbing quickly and boldly, he may find himself too soon at the top of the ladder.

Finally, if the next president concludes that Gorbachev is likely to be a more formidable adversary in a nuclear crisis, he should take special steps to prevent such crises from happening. That means using diplomacy creatively to solve problems before they reach the level of Soviet-American confrontation. This is especially important in areas like the Middle East, where the next regional war could contain, literally, the seeds of World War III.

The tragedy of the Reagan presidency was that in rejecting diplomacy, the administration rejected the creative application of American power. The next president should understand what Reagan did not: that military force is a costly waste of money unless it serves American diplomatic goals.

THE REAGAN CHALLENGE
TO THE RULE OF LAW

LINCOLN CAPLAN

Since the start of the Republic, the rule of law has been enacted in three fundamental ways. First, there is the structure of the government. Its three branches were designed to check and balance each other, for the framers of the Constitution recognized that unbridled power in any one branch would jeopardize the government's overall equilibrium. The Congress was given the power to make law, the Executive Branch the duty to enforce it, and, as the third and "least dangerous branch," in Alexander Hamilton's phrase, the Supreme Court was made especially responsible for solving hard legal problems, as the final arbiter in legal disputes between the branches and between the citizens and the government.

Then, there are the contents of the Constitution. Besides establishing the structure of the government, it is the ultimate author-

ity for resolving American legal differences. In 1949, in a classic
called *An Introduction to Legal Reasoning,* Edward Levi (who
became attorney general in the Ford administration) explained
the traditional view that the meaning of the Constitution is neither
fixed nor self-explanatory.

"The Constitution in its general provisions embodies the conflicting ideals of the community," Levi wrote. "Who is to say what
these ideals mean in any definite way?" Not the framers, because
words they chose were often "ambiguous." Not any one Supreme
Court, because "an appeal can always be made back to the Constitution." Levi concluded that the Constitution's "words change to
receive the content which the community gives them."

This change in the contents of the "words" has occurred
through the mechanism of legal reasoning—most prominently
through the Supreme Court's interpretation of the text, structure,
and history of the Constitution, of prior Court rulings, and of the
experience of the nation. Because the meaning of the Constitution
is neither fixed nor self-explanatory, it is vital that legal reasoning
be marked by its own integrity, for otherwise the whole system
of government would collapse.

Legal reasoning is the black box of the law. As scholars often
note, it is sometimes possible to have two able judges apply the
same law to the same set of facts and reach quite opposite conclusions about the proper outcome in the case at hand. But each field
of the law, including constitutional law, is made up of rules of
reasoning that give it some coherence and enable it to contribute
to the law's general purpose of lending predictability and stability
to society. It is no exaggeration to say that consistent legal reasoning has been essential to American governance. Careful legal
reasoning has supplied the third essential ingredient to the rule
of law.

These elements have always been subject to another rule—evolution. "No Constitution is the same on Paper and in Life," wrote Gouverneur Morris, an author of the text, who, along with other framers, began to debate the meaning of the document almost as soon as it was adopted. In 1787, the Constitution was seen as a law with contradictory powers: it established the federal government, but severely constrained the government's actions. If the government sought to do something that would impinge on the lives of citizens, it had to justify its action by citing the constitutional passage that gave it the authority to do so.

In the past generation, Americans have come to take for granted the Constitution's energizing force as opposed to its constraints, and the power of Congress and of the president have spread enormously, confirming one of James Madison's deep fears. In a profound shift in the burden of responsibility, they have usually been checked only when a citizen convinces a court that one of the political branches has violated a constitutional right.

The Supreme Court is charged with the duty of protecting citizens from unlawful coercion by the government—especially protecting unpopular minorities from the tyranny of the majority—by applying the guarantees in the Bill of Rights. When the political branches expanded, it stood to reason that the Court would be asked to resolve an increasing number of cases dealing with civil rights and liberties—as it has. When the political branches failed to solve major social problems—racial discrimination being the most prominent example—it also followed that the Court would be asked to tackle them—and it did.

To solve these problems, the Court relied on what retired Justice Lewis Powell called "an evolving concept" of the Constitution. In the heyday of this activism, from the 1950s to the 1970s, conservatives like Felix Frankfurter cautioned the Court about expanding its authority too far and tried to restrain the Court by promoting conservative practices of legal reasoning. The Supreme Court and other federal courts should defer when possible, they said, to the judgments of democratically elected bodies. Since the states are the foundation of the Union, and the Constitution draws its power from them, the courts should defer to state over federal authority. Exercising passive virtues, the courts should decide no case unnecessarily. Except in unusual instances, they should avoid rash decisions by closely following precedent.

These canons were so compelling as tools of interpretation that in the past generation they have transcended legal politics and have stood for the essence of good lawyering. They have also expressed the idea of progress in the law, for, however cautious, Frankfurter and other conservatives joined their liberal colleagues in believing that the Constitution was a living charter whose meaning had to grow with the country.

The techniques of legal reasoning that conservatives favored did not compel agreement with either conservative or liberal views about social policy. Even after social reforms of the 1960s were enacted into law, for example, these techniques were often used to challenge liberal views and were used by the Burger Court to moderate some Warren Court decisions. (An example of this is subsequent rulings about the 1966 Miranda decision, guaranteeing certain rights to criminal suspects. The decision has been limited by the Court and, while it was worrisome at the outset to the police, they now welcome it.) But the techniques reflected the judgment that, once a decision is resolved in the law, and becomes part of the legal fabric, and is supported by a consensus, it should be widely honored. They also reflected the view that the law must resolve the tension between tradition and change while avoiding wholesale contradiction.

The Reagan administration sought to change each of these elements of the law and in effect to redefine the rule of law. It sought to alter the roles of the governmental branches in shaping the law, the meaning of the Constitution, and the nature of legal reasoning itself. Since America is a rule-of-law country, this effort was an attempt to alter the character of the nation.

Early in the Reagan years, it appeared that the administration sought to do no more than put into practice ideas associated with some legal conservatives since the days of the Warren Court. In remarks before the Federal Legal Council in October of 1981, Attorney General William French Smith declared, "We believe that the groundswell of conservatism evidenced by the 1980 election makes this an especially appropriate time to urge upon the courts more principled bases that would diminish judicial activism. History teaches us that the courts are not unaffected by major public change in political attitudes."

By the second term, the nature of the Reagan approach had become explicit and extreme. The main articulator of the president's outlook was the dominant legal figure in the administration, Attorney General Edwin Meese. After Meese left his post as counselor to the president and became attorney general in 1985, he began a highly publicized series of speeches about the proper role of the Judiciary, which culminated in an express challenge to a tenet of government resting on almost two centuries of American law—a tenet known as "judicial review."

In 1803, in *Marbury* v. *Madison,* Chief Justice John Marshall wrote, "It is emphatically the province and duty of the judicial department to say what the law is." The Constitution makes no

mention of the Supreme Court's authority to rule on the lawful-
ness of acts of Congress and of the president, but legal scholars
have long agreed that for an effective separation of powers between the branches of government the Court must have that
authority, and that the authority is ultimately derived from the
Constitution.

But Meese advanced a contrary idea—a theory he claimed was
already proved—for limiting the role of federal judges in the
performance of review. In his early speeches, he said that some
of the more vexing problems in American life—school-busing,
affirmative action—were the result of decisions made by judges
overstepping their bounds, making policy instead of interpreting
law. The attorney general proposed that courts correct these errors by using what he termed a "Jurisprudence of Original Intention."

The way to prevent Supreme Court justices and other federal
judges from making policy was to "resurrect the original meaning
of constitutional provisions and statutes as the only reliable guide
for judgment," he said. "To make certain the ideal of the rule of
law is given practical effect, the law must be fixed and known."
By Meese's lights, the widely shared view of the Constitution as
a living testament that takes "meaning from the circumstances of
each age" was mere "chronological snobbery."

Although these remarks were general enough to be construed
in different ways, and although they appealed to some students
of the Constitution who believe that the Supreme Court has not
been sufficiently mindful of its inherent limits, what Meese said
went far outside the bounds of mainstream thinking. Meese himself understood that this was a radical departure, for he said that
the long-dominant view of the Constitution as a living charter

"suffers the defect of pouring new meaning into old words, thus creating new powers and new rights totally at odds with the logic of our Constitution and its commitment to the rule of law."

Meese's "Jurisprudence of Original Intention" was dismissed by many in the legal community, including Supreme Court justices representing the philosophical left, center, and right of the bench. Justice Byron White, who endorsed some of the administration's most controversial positions, called the notion "simplistic."

By the time commentary on the "Jurisprudence" appeared, Meese had changed the focus of his statements. Now he concentrated on how the Constitution had structured the American government and how the government had strayed from that model. "Some of the chief problems of government today stem from the fact that how the federal government works in practice doesn't always resemble how it is supposed to work according to the Constitution," he said. The Judiciary had departed from its role as the interpreter, not the maker or the enforcer, of laws, and the two other branches had allowed it to expand its power. Meese lectured about the dangers of equating judges and lawgivers, and of submitting to government by Judiciary.

Pressing his argument further, he announced that "each of the three coordinated branches of government created and empowered by the Constitution—the executive and legislative no less than the judicial—has a duty to interpret the Constitution in the performance of its official functions." He seemed to use the word "interpret" in a very active sense. To the amazement of many, Meese declared that the Supreme Court's interpretations of the Constitution do "not establish a 'supreme Law of the Land.'"

While the framers were deeply concerned about the government's structure, they did not directly address the question of which branch would have ultimate responsibility for interpreting the Constitution, and they certainly did not resolve it as Meese claimed. They praised the wisdom of judges, and seemed to take for granted that judges would play this role. By voting down a proposal for a body called the Council of Revision, which would have given the president a role in judging the constitutionality of federal statutes, the framers rejected the idea Meese was proposing. But the attorney general was not deterred by history. He invented a new axiom of constitutional law: if the Supreme Court handed down a decision with which the Executive disagreed, then officials in the Executive should simply treat their own views as authority for the true meaning of the law. The same executive authority applied to acts of Congress with which the Executive disagreed, Meese maintained. Unlike the Nixon administration, which held that it was above the law during Watergate, the Reagan administration in essence asserted that it *was* the law.

The administration's approach to the law was vividly illustrated by its handling of voting rights for minorities. The Voting Rights Act of 1965 let voters sue state governments for unfair districting, unfair registration, and other discriminatory election practices, and it succeeded in increasing the number of black voters. By some accounts, the law was among the most important of the century because it assured that many formerly disenfranchised citizens would exercise their most basic democratic right. In the fifteen years after the law was enacted, the percentage of blacks registered to vote in the South almost doubled (29 percent to 57 percent by 1980), and the number of blacks holding office increased from fewer than three hundred to over twenty-four hundred.

In 1980, the Supreme Court held that in order to win suits under the original law, voters had to prove that legislators who set district lines intended to discriminate against them when they diluted the voting power of minorities. The voters could not rely simply on a showing that the effect of any gerrymandering was to dilute minority votes. In the wake of this ruling, Congress decided to amend the law. But the Reagan administration fought to have Congress retain the "intent" standard, on grounds that any form of an "effects" test would require "proportional representation" and lead to "a quota system for electoral politics." In 1982, both the House and the Senate rejected the president's view and voted overwhelmingly (389–24 in the House, and 85–8 in the Senate) to amend the law so that it allowed voters to use an effects test when seeking fairer elections. Under the 1982 amendment, voters had to prove that the "results" of redistricting denied them an equal opportunity to take part in elections and to choose the representatives they wanted. The amendment explicitly rejected the requirement of proportional representation.

The first case to test the 1982 voting-rights amendment was a challenge to a state redistricting plan for the North Carolina General Assembly. It was called *Thornburg* v. *Gingles.* A federal trial court found that the plan violated the new "results" standard. The case promptly rose to the Supreme Court, and it raised elementary legal questions. How should the Court interpret the new standard? What kind of evidence should it tell lower courts to rely on in making a judgment? The state of North Carolina argued that the "results" a voter had to show to get relief were the outcomes of elections in suspect districts. On that theory, if any blacks had been elected, the black voters could not have been victims of discrimination. The NAACP Legal Defense and Educational (LDE) Fund, Inc., on the other hand, attempted to give substance to the new law's "totality of the circumstances" test: even if some blacks had been elected, lawyers for the group contended, there were other factors to consider in assessing the "results" of an election.

In North Carolina, black communities had long been submerged in white districts, and blacks were only occasionally elected. The share of white voters who chose blacks on their ballots was extremely low. Blacks who won the highest number of votes from blacks regularly carried the smallest number from whites. After a century of official hostility to their voting in North Carolina, blacks still registered to vote less often than whites, and, according to the NAACP Inc. Fund, black candidates sometimes lacked the money and know-how to compete against whites. As the lower court acknowledged, blacks occasionally won in elections under scrutiny only because they picked up votes from whites who hoped to prove to the court that the new districts treated blacks fairly. The NAACP Inc. Fund pointed out that North Carolina had long had the smallest percentage of blacks in its state legislature of any state with a sizable black population (blacks made up 22.4 percent of the state's residents, but had never comprised more than 4 percent of either house of the state legislature), and the first black had not been elected to the state House of Representatives until 1968.

In the Supreme Court, the Reagan administration repeated arguments that it had made during the legislative debate about the voting-rights amendment in 1982. It said that blacks should get elected "the old-fashioned way—through politics." The administration agreed with the State of North Carolina that "results" meant "election outcomes." Because blacks had been elected to office, the new district scheme could not have impeded the rights of blacks to play a role in politics.

To strengthen its position, the administration departed from established practices of legal reasoning. As the NAACP, Inc. Fund put it, the Reagan lawyers offered "an account of legislative history" that was "substantially inaccurate." In 1982, the Senate Judiciary Committee had favored amending the Voting Rights Act as it was ultimately amended, and two-thirds of the full Senate stood ready to support the bill in case any of the remaining senators should consider holding the bill in committee until it was changed to suit them. But the administration's brief focused on the views of a few New Right senators who were overwhelmingly outvoted: it called the result of their stubborn maneuvering a "deadlock" instead of acknowledging the general harmony of the decision. After the amendment was passed, the Senate followed its usual procedure and wrote up the history of the new voting-rights legislation in an official Senate Committee Report. But in its brief to the Supreme Court, the administration urged the justices to pay slight attention to this report and chided the Republican Party of North Carolina; the then Senate majority leader, Robert Dole, Republican from Kansas; Senator Charles Grassley, Republican from Iowa; and eight other cosponsors of the 1982 voting-rights amendment, who together had filed a friend-of-the-court brief siding with the NAACP LDE Fund against the government. In their brief, the members of Congress stated that the lower court had interpreted the new law as Congress intended, and that the administration had not.

When the Supreme Court decided the case in 1986, it rejected the administration's interpretation of the law and endorsed that of the NAACP Inc. Fund and the cosponsors in Congress. At forty-seven pages, the Court's majority opinion was notably long, and at least half of it was devoted to rebutting the administration's arguments, point by point. That portion of the opinion had the unanimous support of the justices.

In the voting-rights example, then, the Reagan administration sought to have the Congress adopt an "intent" standard in the 1982 amendment, and was soundly defeated. In 1985, when the new law was tested in the Supreme Court, rather than abiding by the will of the Congress, the administration sought to impose its contrary interpretation of the law. Putting aside established practices of legal reasoning, it did so by misrepresenting the amendment's legislative history and the official Senate report about the amendment.

But the administration's pursuit of its chosen ends at the expense of accepted means did not stop there. In 1986, soon after the Supreme Court handed down its voting-rights decision, the administration announced a major change of policy in implementing the 1982 law. Under the law, nine southern states and parts of eight other southern states with histories of discrimination against minority voters (measured by low voter participation in elections and the use of literacy tests to keep minorities from voting) were required to ask the federal government in advance for approval of any changes in local election practices. This "pre-clearance" requirement was designed to avoid the need for complicated litigation that almost certainly would have arisen if the federal government had not been charged with policing the states, and it contributed notably to the law's success. Although the 1982 Voting Rights Act Amendments had established discriminatory "results" as the standard for violations of the act, and the Supreme Court had explicitly endorsed "effects" as the meaning of that standard, the Reagan administration announced that it was going to abandon the "results" standard altogether in its enforcement of the "preclearance" requirement. In essence, the administration unilaterally gave up its legal duty of policing election-law changes and rewrote the law by executive fiat, on the grounds that the "results" standard was set forth in one section of the law (two) and the "preclearance" requirement in another (five), so that the Court's recent ruling was not binding. Even if the government formally required states to "preclear" changes, as it continued to do, by requiring the states to meet an "intent" test as opposed to a "results" test, the administration assured that all but the most egregious election-law changes would be approved.

The administration elaborated on Attorney General Meese's axiom about constitutional law: if the Congress passed a law with which the Executive Branch disagreed, and the Supreme Court handed down a decision interpreting that law as Congress intended with which the Executive disagreed as well, then officials in the Executive should treat their own views as authority for the true meaning of the law. The administration demonstrated how comprehensively its legal outlook affected the rule of law. One definition of respect for the rule of law is that it constrains a citizen, a lawyer, and, most importantly, an official who has sworn to uphold the Constitution, from taking an action he would otherwise take. When faced with adhering to an established practice of legal reasoning that would lead to the opposite result from one favored by the president, or abandoning that practice to pursue a Reagan goal, the administration's lawyers chose the latter. They undermined the integrity of legal reasoning and the legal process, and thus the rule of law.

The official who argued on behalf of the government in the

voting-rights case was an important but little-known figure called the solicitor general. Of all the nation's public officials, including the attorney general and the justices of the Supreme Court, the solicitor general is the only one required by statute to be "learned in the law." Although he serves in the Justice Department, and his title, like the attorney general's, is displayed in large bronze letters on the facade of the department's building, he also has permanent chambers in the Supreme Court.

The fact that the solicitor general keeps offices at these two distinct institutions underscores his special role. Since the post was established in 1870, the solicitor general's principal task has been to represent the Executive Branch in the Supreme Court, but he is sometimes called the tenth justice because the nine actual justices count on him to look beyond the government's narrow interests. They rely on him not only to help guide them in the case at hand, but to counsel them about the long-term impact of the case on the law itself.

To fulfill this "dual responsibility," as Justice Lewis Powell called it, it has been important for the solicitor general to be independent. The word "independent" does not mean that he should be free to argue points of view that regularly diverge from the administration's. The Executive Branch is in a real sense the solicitor's client, and within the bounds of the law he must strive to represent its interests as they change from one administration to the next. In any event, he is not likely to disagree often or by much, because a president will not appoint or, if he does, will not retain a solicitor who does not share his vision of the law. Yet by tradition, and because of his responsibilities to the Court, a solici- tor must be free to reach his own carefully reasoned conclusions about the proper answer to a question of law, without second-guessing or insisting that his legal advice regularly conform to the politics of the administration he represents. A solicitor must have the independence to exercise his craft as a lawyer on behalf of the institution of government without becoming a partisan spokesman for the president.

In 1977, during the Carter administration, the Justice Department issued the only official statement about the role of the solicitor general that has been made in the history of the post. It explained why the solicitor's independence had long served both the administration and the law, and what duties he had to fulfill in order to do so. He had to coordinate conflicting views within the Executive Branch, to "protect" the Supreme Court by presenting arguments professionally and screening out ones that lacked merit, and to " 'do justice,' " by ensuring that "improper concerns do not influence the presentation of the Government's case in the Supreme Court." The attorney general couldn't do the same, because his political responsibilities might "cloud a clear vision of what the law requires." The major safeguard against errors of an independent solicitor general was the Supreme Court, but if the justices upheld him, "then all the better, for his legal judgment and not that of his superiors was correct."

The Reagan administration's view of the law explained why it didn't accept this traditional definition of the solicitor general's role, and why it used the solicitor's post as it had never been used: the administration did not accept the Supreme Court as the final arbiter in American law, so the solicitor's special responsibility to the Court lost its point. Philip Heymann, a professor at Harvard Law School, who was head of the Criminal Division of the Justice Department during the Carter administration and served as an assistant to the solicitor general during the Kennedy administration, noted this connection: "When you get to the Reagan Administration, you find that the Solicitor General is in a different position. It is basically the view of this Administration that courts, including the Supreme Court, have misbehaved, making law where they should not and doing social justice instead of law. The Administration regards it as an important responsibility of the Department of Justice to straighten out the courts, both through judicial appointments and through declarations in briefs that they should stop what they've been doing." There was no need for the solicitor to defer to the Court, if the Court's rulings did not establish what the law was any more than did the judgments of the Executive Branch, and the solicitor general might just as well carry to the justices the policies of the administration even where they conflicted with the law as previously expounded by the Court. This is what the Reagan administration did. Rex Lee was the first Reagan-appointed solicitor. Although he was an able, conservative lawyer, who enjoyed extraordinary success in terms of wins and losses as solicitor general and agreed fully with the president's views about social policy, he was hounded from office after his sense of the solicitor's obligations conflicted with that of the administration. Lee observed that the administration turned the post into that of a "pamphleteer general." The second Reagan solicitor was Charles Fried, and he made the same point in the negative. He said, "I'm not the Tenth Justice."

Fried drew wide notice in the summer of 1985, by filing a brief in an abortion case that asked the Supreme Court, only two years after it had strongly reaffirmed the right to abortion, to overturn *Roe* v. *Wade*, the landmark that established the right. In the estimate of some longtime observers of the solicitor's office, Fried's brief was more strident than any previously submitted by a solicitor general. It was an extreme sample of the Reagan submissions that had already eroded the credibility of the solicitor's office, and a warning of things to come. During the 1985 term of the Supreme Court, Fried presided over the continuing decline in the standing of the office. He helped drive away career attorneys who were committed to supporting the solicitor's traditional role, and the office had twice the normal staff turnover. It lost three of its four career deputies, who had a combined total of over forty years' experience as government lawyers and were almost uniformly respected, by members of the Supreme Court and lawyers in the Justice Department, as being among the government's finest advocates. The roster of cases on the Supreme Court's docket in which the government aggressively pursued the president's agenda (known as agenda cases) expanded from abortion, voting rights, and other familiar topics, to include medical treatment of handicapped infants, school discipline, and almost anything of interest to a member of the Reagan team. In case after case, Fried asked the Court to overturn established precedent. He put aside established legal reasoning and spurned the traditional notion of the solicitor's restraint in order to try for results. The cases strengthened a concern in parts of the American legal community that serious harm was being done to the solicitor general's office.

When the Supreme Court issued opinions that term, it confirmed the grounds for this concern. Its comments about the solicitor's arguments were prickly and virtually unprecedented in their criticism, and they were not restricted either to cases that the solicitor general lost or to agenda cases. The opinions were written by justices ranging from liberals (William Brennan and Thurgood Marshall) to centrists (Harry Blackmun and John Paul

Stevens) and moderate conservatives (Lewis Powell and Sandra Day O'Connor), to the Court's strongest conservative (William Rehnquist). Members of the Court also offered direct evidence about the tie between the changes in the role of the solicitor general under the Reagan administration and the Court's negative response.

According to some justices, the expressions of concern and disapproval in the Court's opinions gave only a hint of the sadness and distress that at least a majority of the justices (Brennan, Marshall, Blackmun, Powell, and Stevens, four of whom were appointed by Republicans) felt about the changes in the solicitor's role. Interviews with law clerks and other close observers of the Court also indicated that each of the four other justices was sometimes put off by the solicitor's advocacy. One justice said angrily in 1986: "There's no question we've taken this SG to task in our opinions more than any of his predecessors. What we're saying to him and the other people in the Justice Department is simple: 'Listen, you guys, you're just dead wrong. This is an abdication of your responsibility.' "

The justices confirmed that the Reagan administration had diminished the institution that, to lawyers at the highest reaches of the profession, once stood for the nation's commitment to the rule of law. It had done so, once again, by challenging the traditional relationship between the branches of government, the traditional approach to interpreting the Constitution, and by challenging established legal reasoning, all to advance the Reagan agenda.

One measure of the administration's true interest in results instead of what the president called "judicial restraint," and of the cynicism about the process by which laws are made and interpreted that this interest revealed, is how selectively the administration adhered to its stated views about the proper role of the Judiciary. As the solicitor general's story indicated, once the president's lawyers failed to persuade Congress to turn various parts of the Reagan agenda into law, they turned to the courts as the main forum in which to pursue his domestic policies. And more important, the administration tried to pack the courts with judges who appeared willing to put aside truly conservative canons of judging to reach results favored by the president.

According to Sheldon Goldman, a professor of political science at the University of Massachusetts, the administration pursued its goal in substance and process. Apart from applying distinct criteria for judges, it adopted a new procedure for judicial selection to assure that nominees for the courts shared the president's legal philosophy. In the past, the responsibility for picking judges had been the Justice Department's. In the first Reagan term, instead of leaving judicial selection to Attorney General William French Smith, the Reagan administration identified the task as a high political priority, moved it to the White House, and gave the lead to presidential counselor Edwin Meese. To the consternation of some Republican senators, as well as Democrats, the administration also abandoned the long-standing practice of following recommendations from the senior senator of the president's party in each state, and set up its own conservative network for identifying potential judges.

As to substance, the Reagan team demonstrated more interest in ideology as the primary test of a candidate's fitness for the bench than any administration since Franklin Roosevelt's in the 1930s and 1940s. The distinction made a difference because resignations from the lower federal courts and the creation by

Congress of eighty-five new seats on the bench gave Ronald Reagan the chance to join Roosevelt and Dwight Eisenhower as the only presidents this century to appoint a majority of the judges on the federal courts. (Roosevelt appointed 81.4 percent of the judiciary in four terms, and Eisenhower 56.1 in two.) By 1987, Reagan's selections were largely rich, male, white, and Republican, and made up over 42 percent of the bench.

On the courts of appeals, which are the courts of last resort for approximately 34,000 cases a year, compared to the 175 or so that are decided each term by the Supreme Court, the Reagan administration was especially careful to appoint judges who promised "to restore a philosophical balance," in the words of Fred Fielding, the president's longtime White House counsel who also headed a panel called the Federal Judicial Selection Committee.

The early Reagan appellate judges included Robert Bork, Richard Posner, and Antonin Scalia, and surveys about their performance by conservative organizations sympathetic to the president found that the administration's ideological standard paid off almost immediately. The Center for Judicial Studies, which publishes a bimonthly journal called *Benchmark,* found that the "overwhelming majority" of the Reagan judges supported the president's views in judicial opinions. More neutral observers, like the *Columbia Law Review,* corroborated this view. In 1987, the journal found that, while some Reagan appointees were only somewhat more conservative than the sitting judges picked by previous Republican presidents, the Reagan judges were considerably more conservative than those selected by President Carter. A small corps of Reagan judges—like Bork, Posner, and Scalia, of whom the administration was especially proud—

were extremely conservative, the journal concluded, and considerably more conservative than the judges picked by other Republicans.

During the second Reagan term, a new statistic emerged as a clue to the seriousness of the administration's commitment to appoint judges who fit the Reagan profile. In 1952, the Standing Committee on the Federal Judiciary of the American Bar Association began to rate candidates for judgeships. The committee evaluates the competence, integrity, and judicial temperament of candidates, and takes no account of political philosophy or ideology, except as they affect integrity or judicial temperament. The Senate has usually applied the same standards. In recent years, the fifteen-member, bipartisan committee has offered one of four ratings for a candidate for a lower federal court: "exceptionally well qualified," "well qualified," "qualified," and "unqualified." The "qualified" rating may be the uniform recommendation of the committee, or it may be "mixed." A candidate is placed in the last category when the ABA committee can't reach unanimous agreement whether he should be rated qualified or not. The rating signifies that the committee has disagreed over its judgment. Since the ABA offers its ratings for probable nominees who have not yet been officially named, its "unqualified" ratings often help the government avoid nominations that will prove embarrassing. The "mixed" category leaves a candidate in limbo between approval and disapproval, and is the most controversial in which the American Bar Association can place a would-be judge.

During the Carter administration, of fifty-six judges named to the courts of appeals, the ABA rated none "unqualified" and two "mixed." During the first term of the Reagan administration, of thirty-one judges named to the courts of appeals, the committee rated none "unqualified" and two "mixed." In the first year of the second term, however, the "mixed" rating took on new prominence. Of twenty-eight judges named to the appeals courts by June of 1986, eleven, or about two out of every five, were rated "mixed." Put differently, of the judges appointed to courts of appeals, half were rated in the mediocre category of "qualified," including the "mixed" group. By contrast, only about one-third of the administration's appeals-court judges were rated "qualified" in the first term; and just a quarter of the Carter administration's appellate judges were similarly ranked. Instead of clustering at the high end of the spectrum of quality, the Reagan judges ended up at the low end. The president's team seemed to have reached the bottom of the barrel among ideologues who were candidates for appellate judgeships. Senator Daniel Patrick Moynihan, Democrat from New York, expressed his views about judicial selection in the Reagan administration in plain terms: "There is a word for the ideological tests for the judiciary which are seemingly now in place in the White House and the Justice Department. The word is 'corruption.' "

In 1986, Daniel Manion was nominated for the U.S. Court of Appeals in the Seventh Circuit. To supporters of the administration and its critics, the debate about Manion was emblematic of the disagreement about judicial selection during the Reagan years. Manion was a forty-four-year-old lawyer from South Bend, Indiana, who stood out as a candidate for a judgeship almost entirely because of his ideological credentials. His father was a founder of the John Birch Society and a former dean of the Notre Dame University Law School, and he ran a small broadcasting network known as the Manion Forum. Daniel Manion was a supporter of the John Birch Society. ("Your members are cer-

tainly the people who are on the front line of the fight for constitutional freedom," he wrote in a letter to the society's Elkhart,
Indiana, bookstore.) He was also a trustee of the Manion Forum,
and, as a guest on his father's television show, he favored ideas
that Attorney General Meese eventually promoted: limiting the
jurisdiction of the federal courts to deal with certain social issues;
overturning the Supreme Court's ban on spoken prayer in the
schools; and making the Bill of Rights inapplicable to the states
by outlawing a legal principle called the incorporation doctrine,
which applies to the states most of the bill's protections by incor-
porating them in the Due Process Clause of the Fourteenth
Amendment.

After his father died in 1979, Daniel Manion endorsed his
father's ideas when he wrote to the pastor of a Baptist church in
his city (the misspellings are his): "There is no question that he
was certainly a champion of the cause of Christian education and
separation of church and state. But one thing that Dad often
critized was the misnomer of that separation. While it is true that
therewas to be a separation of church and state, he constantly
fought against the false premis that there should be a separation
of God and Country. He fought for prayer in school and for the
recognition of God in all public places. That was the basis of our
constitution and Declaration of Independence, and for those with
the misguided idea that our whole society must be secularized, he
had much contempt."

As an Indiana state senator, Manion turned his father's contempt for the idea of a secular society into disrespect for established law. In 1980, the Supreme Court ruled that the State of
Kentucky could not allow the Ten Commandments to be posted
in public schools, because it violated the prohibition against a

state's endorsement of a religion in the Establishment Clause of the First Amendment. Two months later, Manion defied both the Court and his oath to uphold the Constitution and the laws of the United States by sponsoring a bill to let the Ten Commandments be displayed in the Indiana schools. The bill was virtually identical to the one outlawed in Kentucky and obviously unconstitutional and, Manion said later, he didn't expect it to be passed into state law. He sponsored it as a "protest" against the Supreme Court. According to the logic of a generation-old landmark decision called *Cooper* v. *Aaron,* the Manion "protest" amounted to "a solemn mockery," for as Felix Frankfurter wrote then, "no state legislator or executive or judicial officer can war against the Constitution without violating his undertaking to support it."

On the Manion Forum, Daniel Manion praised a book called *We Hold These Truths.* The contents of the book suggested a different explanation from the one Manion gave for the reason behind his support for the Ten Commandments bill. The volume was by then Representative Larry McDonald, Democrat from Georgia, a member of the John Birch Society, who wrote, "Please understand that a Supreme Court decision is not the law of the land. Indeed it is not a law at all. Only a legislature can make laws. The Supreme Court decision is a rule that is binding only on the parties involved in the case, and it is enforceable only on that limited group if the executive and legislative branches choose to enforce it."

Manion called the book "one of the finest summaries of the history of our country that I have ever read," and during his confirmation hearing before the Judiciary Committee he was asked about the meaning of this praise. Did he agree with McDonald about the limited reach of Supreme Court law? Manion's answer was imprecise, but he seemed to say that his oath as a state senator bound him to respect the opinions of the justices as law for the federal courts but not as the law of the land. "You are bound by oath to support the Constitution," Senator Joseph Biden, Democrat from Delaware, repeated back to him. "And you said that means as interpreted by the Supreme Court. And yet you vote the other way. You vote against the Constitution. Is that correct or incorrect?" Manion replied, "The vote is as it appears."

At the request of the Judiciary Committee, a bipartisan group of trial attorneys known as the Chicago Council of Lawyers took five briefs submitted to the senators by Manion as his best writing samples and asked members of the bar to study them. Since Manion had not been lead counsel in a federal case, not handled a case involving a constitutional issue, not argued in the Seventh Circuit to which he had been nominated, and had not published either an article or a speech about the law, the briefs were the best available evidence of his intellectual abilities as a potential judge. The Chicago Council found Manion wanting on the most elementary grounds. "The numerous typographical errors, grammatical mistakes, and syntactical errors in the brief raise concerns about Mr. Manion's ability to write," wrote the chairman of the council's evaluation committee about one brief. "Moreover, in addition to the errors noted above, the brief lacks precision in its expression and argument. Putting aside the grammatical and syntactical errors, many of those who reviewed this brief for the Council commented that the quality of its content fell far below what one should expect from a candidate for the Seventh Circuit." In his own defense, Manion pointed out that he had won four of the five cases in which he had submitted the briefs and that the errors were the price he paid for the pressure that comes with a successful law practice. The Council praised the nominee's "high reputation for integrity, conscientiousness, and fairness," but, judging him "not qualified," the lawyers concluded they were "not confident that Mr. Manion will be able to deal adequately with the difficult legal issues which are routinely presented to the Seventh Circuit."

President Reagan addressed the Senate vote on the Manion nomination as a battle he could not afford to lose. In June of 1986, the president focused on the nomination in his weekly radio address. He said that his administration had nominated for judgeships "only those with high qualifications," including Manion. "Some are doing just about everything they can think of to prevent Daniel Manion's confirmation. Believe it or not, they're even tried to make a major issue of a few typographical errors in several of his briefs and the fact that he practices law in a small town," said the president. "Let's be honest. The real objection to Dan Manion is that he doesn't conform to the liberal ideology of some Senators." Reagan told the Senate that it should confirm Manion. "It's the right thing to do," he said. "He's the kind of judge the American people want—and I think they know it." The Republican-controlled Senate approved Manion by one vote.

Besides indicating the ideological standard for judges that dominated the selection process in the Reagan years, the Manion debate also showed how unprepared, in an era of new criteria for judges, the Senate was to advise and consent, as the Constitution requires. From 1981 to 1986, when the Republicans controlled the Senate as well as the presidency, and Strom Thurmond, the former Dixiecrat presidential candidate and Republican from South Carolina, chaired the Judiciary Committee, the Senate served as a virtual rubber stamp for Reagan nominations to the federal bench except in extreme instances. Part of the explanation for this was politics, but another was the inability of Democrats to articulate how traditional standards for judges had been modified by purely ideological standards, which accounted for the Reagan selections made.

The Manion appointment of 1986 was a rehearsal for the nomination of Robert Bork to the Supreme Court in 1987 in the intensity of its controversy and partisanship. Both events revealed that the Reagan judicial selections were based on an interest in results rather than restraint. In those ideological results, the administration exposed its view of the law.

At its peak, the controversy about Bork turned into a bitter debate about whether Bork was right or wrong for the Court. But the pro- and anti-Bork advocates reached a surprising degree of consensus about what the prospective justice's convictions were. They agreed, first, that he was critical of the role that the Supreme Court had played in relation to the other branches of government for the previous fifty years: second, that he contended that the Supreme Court, in interpreting the meaning of the Constitution, should restrict the reach of its protections; and, third, that he believed it was sometimes necessary to put aside established practices of legal reasoning in order to correct the mistakes represented by what he once called a "large proportion" of the "most significant Constitutional decisions of the past three decades."

Whatever the characterization of Bork's views, there was wide agreement that if he became a justice he would almost certainly have a deep impact on the meaning of the rule of law in the United States, for his views about constitutional law were at odds with current assumptions about each of the key ingredients of the rule

of law. As a critic of the "imperial judiciary," he had long contended that, except where he believed the Constitution clearly
states differently, the Supreme Court must defer to the will of the
majority, as it is expressed in presidential decisions, congressional statutes, and state law, or else the Court robs the majority of
the most basic liberty in a democracy—the liberty to enact the
will of the people.

As a believer in "original intent," Bork had argued that when
justices look outside the text and structure of the Constitution
their judgments are constrained by nothing but personal values,
which means they are not constrained at all.

As to legal reasoning, while Bork told the Senate that a "judge
must give great respect for precedent," he made clear how limited
his expressions of this respect were likely to be if he became a
justice. He might not aggressively overturn precedent, he indicated, but he was unlikely to extend the reasoning and reach
of prior decisions as traditional conservatives had done, on
grounds often stated by the Reagan administration: if the Court
was strictly bound by established law, it would end up strengthening decisions of the past generation that Ronald Reagan and
Robert Bork considered wrong.

For Bork, an evolutionary approach to the law—what Frankfurter called the need to put meaning *into* the Constitution—had
led American law to a dangerous impasse—"a tipping point for
democracy," Bork called it. He sought to save the American
government from what he described as the "tyranny of the minority," and return the government to the proper balance that he
contended the framers designed. Bork didn't consistently reject
this evolutionary approach, since he relied on it as the basis for
his expansive view of presidential power, sometimes at the ex-

pense of the "majority" will expressed through Congress. (Senator Arlen Specter, Republican from Pennsylvania, asked Bork during his confirmation hearings, "Why not organic development for liberty? Why only organic development for executive power?") But Bork was adamant about rejecting an evolving concept of the role of the Judiciary. He advocated cutting back the role of the Supreme Court and the lower federal courts, as he had tried to do as an appeals-court judge between 1982 and 1987.

As an appellate judge, Bork challenged basic doctrines (about the separation of powers, for example) and more technical-seeming ones (about access of individuals to the courts). He put aside forty years of sustained precedent that led to an outcome he didn't like (in a case about rate-setting by utilities). He chose to reach far beyond the issue before him as a judge, "to conduct a general spring-cleaning of constitutional law," according to the disapproving judges who otherwise concurred with his decision about a narrow question before them (whether the navy could exclude homosexuals). While for seventy-five years the debate about the constitutional right of privacy had focused on the scope of that right, Bork set himself apart as a jurist by questioning its very existence. In word and deed, he apotheosized the Reagan outlook on the law. In the hour of Bork's defeat in the Senate by 58 votes to 42, there was considerable irony to a charge by the president that Bork's critics had turned the confirmation process into a partisan struggle. The terms of the Bork fight were the result of the administration's seven-year partisan effort to cut back the role of the courts, which compelled consideration of a basic question in law and politics: the place of the Supreme Court in American life.

Some observers concluded that the Bork defeat was an endorsement for the role of the Supreme Court defined by the Warren Court, and that it signified a new legal consensus. The intense, bitter, and divisive nature of the debate about Bork told otherwise and fit a pattern that had been developing in American law for many years.

The most significant indicator of this pattern may have been rulings of the Supreme Court. As the Court's work shifted from resolving common-law questions of torts, property, and contracts (in the nineteenth century) to interpreting statutes and ruling on the meaning of the Constitution (during the twentieth), the justices became increasingly divided on the substance of the law. In each term from 1801 to 1900, the average number of Court cases decided by a bare majority was one. In the 1986 term, forty-three cases—fully 30 percent—were decided by a bare majority of five to four. Not surprisingly, the law was most often marked by controversy when the issues were political. During the past generation, cases dealing with important social policies, like school-busing and affirmative action, became the centerpieces of each Court term. In these cases, the law sometimes appeared indistinguishable from politics and, when the justices struggled unsuccessfully to articulate legal principles that transcended political terms, the results were as divisive.

The breakdown in consensus at the Supreme Court was matched by extraordinary polarization among legal scholars. Disputes between scholars representing the conflicting movements of Law and Economics, on the right, and Critical Legal Studies, on the left, summed up this split. Law and Economics is often associated with the University of Chicago Law School, where a corps of scholars began to apply some of its tenets in the 1940s and 1950s. When Robert Bork was a student there, he took a course that used free-market economics to refute the law's traditional antitrust doctrine. "A lot of us who took the antitrust course or the economics course underwent what can only be called a religious conversion," he said at a symposium about Law and Economics in 1981. "It changed our view of the entire world."

The seminal work in the field was a piece of writing called "The Problem of Social Cost" that was published in 1960 by an economist named Ronald Coase, before he joined the Chicago faculty. Say the spark from a train sets fire to some woods, Coase proposed. According to traditional legal thinking, the question of who should pay for the damage had to be resolved by deciding who was at fault. But as Coase saw the problem, both the train and the woods "caused" the fire. To prevent another, the railroad would have to buy a spark guard or the owner of the woods would have to cut back his trees. In many instances, forcing the railroad to pay for the damage as well as a spark guard would be too costly to society, because the railroad would have to increase its rail rates to cover those costs. "In devising and choosing social arrangements," Coase concluded, "we should have regard for the total effect."

Coase's argument that legal rules should minimize the economic costs to society was interpreted as a call for the law to foster the free market. His article became the most widely cited ever in journals of law and journals of economics, and beyond fields like antitrust and securities regulation, where economics had long aided understanding of the law, this form of economic analysis was also applied to fields like constitutional law, where it had long been considered irrelevant.

Instead of concentrating on the reasoning that defines a legal doctrine, many lawyers and legal scholars now analyze a law's purpose and impact in terms of economics: law-review articles are increasingly filled with mathematical equations and economic formulations. Where almost any law doesn't follow the logic of economics, devout Law and Economics scholars insist that it should. The wide popularity of this view helped ease the impact of the Reagan administration's approach to the law: it gave new currency to a focus on social results instead of traditional legal reasoning. The influence of the movement on the Reagan administration was widely apparent: in the appointment to the appeals court of Richard Posner, the movement's chief promoter and perhaps the most controversial legal scholar of the 1970s; of Frank Easterbrook, a protégé of Posner's; and other Law and Economics judges; and in the appointments to the appeals court and nominations to the Supreme Court of Robert Bork and Douglas Ginsburg, though each man, for different reasons, did not make it to the Court.

For all its influence, the ascendancy of Law and Economics in the face of equally vital opposition seemed to prove the claims of scholars who made up the left-wing movement called Critical Legal Studies. A premise of CLS, as it is known, is that the law is ultimately defined less by abstract principles than by the political and moral views of the judges and lawyers who apply the principles, and that, in the endless process of interpretation that it requires, the law becomes a forum for resolving larger social conflicts, rooted in passion, in reason, and, most of all, in power. The conflicting factions of Law and Economics, CLS, and other movements left an increasingly narrow mainstream of adherents to the ideas summed up by Edward Levi in 1949, and left American law without wide consensus.

Given the vigor of these factions and the differences of opinion they stirred, it is possible to see the Reagan administration as little more than a vehicle for one side, for an intellectual force that had been gathering momentum for two generations. However, many events indicate why the Reagan administration was particularly responsible for exacerbating this breakup in consensus and, in effect, challenging the rule of law. These events came to a head in 1985. In January, the administration went forward with the nomination of Edwin Meese to be attorney general. The president had first proposed him for the office the year before, and the Senate had put off hearings about Meese for ten months while an independent counsel investigated allegations of wrongdoing in his personal business affairs. After the counsel issued a 385-page report about Meese in September of 1984, the administration proceeded on the conviction that it had cleared and vindicated Meese. In fact, while the independent counsel found no basis for prosecuting Meese on most of the eleven charges leveled against him, in some instances the counsel found a basis for prosecution but chose not to bring charges. As chairman of Common Cause, former Watergate Special Prosecutor Archibald Cox wrote: "The Attorney General must symbolize the highest standards of honor, integrity, and freedom from self-interest in the performance of public office." In the dealings chronicled by the report of the independent counsel, Cox concluded, Meese showed himself either contemptuous of these standards or oblivious to them.

Meese was confirmed as attorney general after intense hearings, and began a campaign to pursue the Reagan legal outlook with fresh enthusiasm and a group of like-minded lieutenants. The most important colleague for Meese at the Justice Department was Assistant Attorney General William Bradford Reynolds, the head of the Civil Rights Division. Meese chose

Reynolds to be associate attorney general, the third highest officer in the department, and in June the Senate Judiciary Committee began hearings about Reynolds.

The nomination was controversial, and the administration claimed that opposition to Reynolds rested on two counts: first, they said, his critics misrepresented his record, since, in the administration's eyes, he had vigorously enforced civil rights; second, they said, Reynolds was the victim of a misperception, because the only major differences between the views of past administrations and the current one came in the areas of school desegregation and affirmative action. Extensive hearings about Reynolds—the report on them filled 1,037 pages—showed that the administration was wrong about these claims. The Lawyers' Committee for Civil Rights Under Law submitted an 85-page report documenting how Reynolds, in every area of government responsibility, reaching far beyond school desegregation and affirmative action, had reversed a record of progress in civil rights that began during the Truman administration and continued through every Republican and Democratic administration until Jimmy Carter's. For the first time in its two-decade history, the Lawyers' Committee felt compelled to oppose a nominee of the president to an Executive Branch position.

The hearings also demonstrated that the case against Reynolds went deeper. Events recounted to the senators showed Reynolds to be a lawyer whose dedication to the Reagan agenda made him headstrong and often insensitive about his choice of means. The Judiciary Committee documented the performance of a radical conservative whose impatience for results made him deaf to the appeals for craftsmanship forwarded by Justice Department lawyers. The senators also heard substantial testimony that went to the issue of character. It appeared to some senators that Reynolds pressed to have his way as expeditiously as possible and that at times he overlooked or hid the truth to get it.

After the Judiciary Committee rejected the Reynolds nomination, some senators were astonished when Attorney General Meese went out of his way to praise Reynolds, give him the expanded duties that he would have assumed had he been confirmed, and eventually to make this special role official by naming Reynolds counselor to the attorney general as well as assistant attorney general. This challenge to the Judiciary Committee was accompanied by one to the Supreme Court. In the summer of 1985, soon after the Reynolds hearings, three significant events occurred: the attorney general began his series of speeches about the Reagan view of constitutional law; Solicitor General Charles Fried began submitting his series of briefs that prompted the Supreme Court to go out of its way to reject administration positions; and the president stepped up his efforts to fill the courts with judges who shared his legal outlook. In retrospect, this multifront campaign seemed driven by the knowledge that time was running out for the administration: even with a Republican-controlled Senate, the president encountered strong resistance to his legal program from the outset, and the Reagan team knew that if the Senate turned Democratic, as it did in 1986, the election would represent a firm denunciation of the legal ideas that the president and his aides repeatedly presented as a fundamental part of the administration's agenda.

What the Reagan team did not acknowledge were the grave implications of this approach. At its most extreme, the Reagan legal outlook could be described in terms of corruption: of ideas at the heart of legal discourse and of the ideal of the rule of law;

of the legal process by which it has long been observed; and of the literal kind. The reports of the independent counsel about the Meese affairs and of the Senate Judiciary Committee about the Reynolds hearings documented what also occurred in scores of other instances, for members of the administration compiled a record of misdeeds, improprieties, and unlawful behavior that defied comparison with that of any of its predecessors, including the Grant, Harding, and Nixon administrations that were marked by egregious scandals. (Elliot Richardson, the former Nixon attorney general, exclaimed in 1987, "For God's sake, are we not entitled to hope that the next administration will be a little less sleazy?") To take one measure: by the count of the *Washington Post*, between January 1981 and April 1986, 110 senior Reagan officials were accused or found guilty of unethical or illegal conduct. This was months before the Iran-contra affair was exposed, and before the Wedtech scandal implicated yet another group of top officials, including Edwin Meese.

The 1987 report of the House and Senate Select Committees on the Iran-contra affair indicated how far-reaching the administration's corruption of the processes of government could be. The report narrated how, to carry out a clandestine foreign policy, a small group of senior aides in the White House and, it appeared, the director of the CIA arrogated power to themselves; displayed contempt for the workings of democracy by breaking the law and circumventing restrictions established by Congress; hooked up with self-described patriots who considered it their due to make large profits as middlemen; and, once the enterprise unraveled, misrepresented its purpose and operations in a deliberate cover-up. It also faulted Edwin Meese, William Bradford Reynolds, and others for the incompetence of their inquiry into the affair, and indicated that these Justice Department officials had aided the cover-up. The report by the select committees was a reminder of how the administration's challenge to the rule of law was set apart from past challenges by its breadth and audacity. It left to the investigation of an independent counsel the task of specifying the alleged crimes and perpetrators engaged in the enterprise.

The United States takes pride in its commitment to the rule of law, but Americans rarely discuss the meaning of that phrase. The Reagan administration made such talk a national practice. It challenged common views about each of the key ways in which the rule of law is enacted and in doing so raised serious doubts among many citizens about the government's adherence to that rule. It exacerbated the breakdown in consensus about American legal ideas and undermined the country's legal process. In dramatic examples, such as its reinterpretation of the Antiballistic Missile Treaty in order to pursue the Strategic Defense Initiative, or its defiance of the World Court's authority to judge America's role in the Nicaraguan war, the government also raised doubts in the world community about this country's adherence to legal principle. A significant part of the administration's legacy is that any American interested in broad legal questions has to reckon with its views.

REAGANISM AND THE NEOKITSCH AESTHETIC

SIDNEY BLUMENTHAL

The truest event of the Reagan presidency was the first inauguration. It was a celebration of wealth, by the wealthy, for those who wanted to be wealthy (the rest of us). The line between fantasy and reality was constantly blurred, and the glitz of new money was presented as the heart of tradition. Style was substance, fashion was power: with sequins on parade, the strength that waned during the plebeian Carter years would be restored.

In January 1981, this was the authentic vision of the Reaganites, advanced without shame or irony. The inauguration planners designed the event on a clean slate; no confusion or ambiguity from the past clouded it. They meant for it to happen just as it did, and on its own terms it was a resounding success. It was such an arresting tableau, in fact, that White House public-relations specialists spent years afterward trying to erase the initial impression. But no matter the agility of the White House at shifting superficial images, the superficial values of the inauguration remained the bedrock of the Reagan public aesthetic. The Reaganites never really escaped the tone set at the beginning; the White House effort to submerge it was part of the failure to transcend it.

It began on the steps of the Lincoln Memorial, on the evening of January 18, 1981, with a laser light show and the Mormon Tabernacle Choir, the flash of the new and organ notes of the old. The master of ceremonies was Efrem Zimbalist, Jr., former star of "The F.B.I.," a long-canceled television series. He set the mood by piously reading excerpts from Ronald Reagan's acceptance speech at the Republican convention.

Zimbalist was an inspired choice for the role of preliminary master of ceremonies. He was, in effect, playing the role of Ronald Reagan before political stardom. Zimbalist was a second-level handsome leading man, whose presence evoked memories of forgettable past performances. His most recent unmemorable role was that of the FBI agent. This persona was implicitly recruited for the public performance in the Reagan gala. As the FBI agent manqué, Zimbalist embodied the law and order that the new administration promised to impose; as the tanned Hollywood denizen in the capital for the winter festivities, he represented the phalanx of second-rank celebrities that Reagan mustered to surround the new administration as it assumed office.

At the Lincoln Memorial, master of ceremonies Zimbalist prepared the crowd for the national master of ceremonies. Reagan, the old host of "Death Valley Days" and "General Electric Theater" (and in real life, from those days, an FBI informer), would soon take over the role Zimbalist was rehearsing. Zimbalist's cameo appearance also suggested that what was happening was about more than a transition of power in the Executive Branch. His reading from Reagan's partisan oration implied that the partisan was becoming national. This Reagan speech was not merely rhetoric to arouse the Republican faithful, but the new tropes of patriotism. It was the dawning of the Age of, well, perhaps not Aquarius, but at least Mergers and Acquisitions.

The cochairmen of the first Reagan inaugural were ideal figures of this new age: Charles Z. Wick, Reagan family friend, formerly named Zwick, former talent agent for fifties kids'-show star Pinky Lee, bandleader, producer of a movie entitled *Snow White and the Three Stooges,* nursing-home chain operator, director-designate of the United States Information Agency; and Robert K. Gray, big-business lobbyist, operating out of a building with a brass plaque advertising itself as THE POWERHOUSE. For both of these self-made men, perception was reality.

Tickets to the various inaugural events were priced up to $500. In 1977, at the Carter inaugural, all tickets were democratically priced at $25. The slogan of that event: "Y'all come!" The new mood was perhaps best captured by Hugh Sidey, the White House columnist for *Time* magazine, eager to praise the incoming presidency: "Let's have some class this time around."

Indeed, "class" was very much in evidence. Many Fortune 500 companies laid out lavish spreads. "For $10,000 you get nothing in advertising," a partygoer told the *Washington Post.* "For $10,000 you can get a heck of a nice party and you get just the people you are targeting."

The publicity machinery around the Reagans proudly spewed out the information that Nancy Reagan's wardrobe for the inauguration cost $25,000. Money was power, and to be shy about it might be a sign of weakness. That would invite comparison to the despised Carter. We're number one!

But as the limousines clogged the capital's roads and the fur coats clogged its restaurants' checkrooms, even a few conservatives paused. "When you've got to pay $2000 for a limousine for four days," said Senator Barry Goldwater, "$7 to park and $2.50 to check your coat, at a time when most people in this country just can't hack it, that's ostentatious." Obviously, Goldwater was not in the new mood. His instinctive recoil revealed the fading Protestant ethic in which wealth was a sign of self-denial, hard work, and personal virtue. In spite of the repeated invocation by the celebrants of that ethic, which they pledged to restore, it was the antithesis of the Reagan aesthetic.

"This is the first administration to have a premiere," cracked Johnny Carson at the two-and-a-half-hour televised bash at the Capital Center on January 19. As the moment in which Reagan would be invested with his power approached, the stature of the master of ceremonies was heightened: from Zimbalist to Carson. Carson, however, had never played anyone but Carson; his only persona was himself, at least what he chose to expose. If he were reverent and sycophantic, he would have been out of character. And he did not betray himself. "Ron's economic emergency," he said, "is when they run out of goose liver pâté at Bloomingdale's gourmet department." The jest seemed good-natured and thus harmless; but by recasting Sidey's hope as a joke, Carson proved himself the more cogent analyst.

The stage was laid out before a raised platform on which were perched the Reagans, seated in velvet-covered wing chairs, like a royal couple viewing command performances. One after another they came: the comedian Rich Little; singer Debbie Boone; fiddler Mel Tillis; dancer Ben Vereen; the Naval Academy Glee Club;

Ethel Merman, belting "Everything's Coming Up Roses"; Charl-
ton Heston, in his inimitable mock-biblical mode, reading inspirational passages from great American literature; Donny Osmond,
redoing Chuck Berry's primal "Go, Johnny, Go," as a cheerlead-
ing "Go, Ronnie, Go."

And—Frank Sinatra. He sang "Nancy with the Laughing
Face," awkwardly altering the words to "Nancy with the Reagan
Face." He was her fancy—"Francis Albert," she called him
fondly. She wanted him to sit near her, escort her, dance with her.
But he was more than her favorite walker. He was something like
the administration's poet laureate, the court favorite, adorning it
with his specially crafted feuilletons: "Nancy with the Reagan
Face." Certainly, Sinatra was the greatest artist present, "the
chairman of the board" in the industry in which Reagan was most
influential as a union official arguing hours and wages; Sinatra
was a figure in popular mythology who drew upon sources far
more dramatic than the man about to be president. The Sinatra
story was about the rise of immigrants; the Mafia; the big bands;
the sexual conquest of the most glamorous women in Hollywood;
the left-wing politics of the 1940s; the fraternity of the Rat Pack;
Las Vegas; and the Kennedys.

Now, at this moment, it was especially about the Kennedys. For
Sinatra, the Reagan inaugural was a remake of the Kennedy
inaugural. Two groups of men, two bands of brothers, had surrounded Kennedy as he prepared to run for the presidency. One
was mostly composed of thoroughly assimilated Irishmen, including his brothers, who were masters of politics. The other was
composed of the preeminent lounge lizards of the day—Sinatra's
Rat Pack. Just as Kennedy's campaign was the assertion of the
young men of World War II coming to power in politics, Sinatra's
entourage was a reflection of the same generational process in the

field of entertainment. The ultimate Rat Pack movie, *Ocean's Eleven,* about the last patrol of war comrades reconvened to raid a Vegas casino, was the green felt underside of the New Frontier.

Kennedy's brother-in-law, Peter Lawford, a Rat Pack member, had gained him entrée to this exclusive world. (Lawford, according to Kitty Kelley in *His Way: The Unauthorized Biography of Frank Sinatra,* said that Sinatra had served as Kennedy's "pimp." And Sinatra indeed introduced Kennedy to one of his dalliances, Judith Exner, a mistress of Mafia boss Sam (Momo) Giancana.) In honor of Kennedy, Sinatra renamed the Rat Pack the Jack Pack. At the 1961 inauguration, Sinatra was the producer of the inaugural party, and escorted Jacqueline Kennedy to her seat. Two Broadway show casts appeared; the lights dimmed on the Great White Way, but brightened in Washington. At the show's conclusion, the new president took the stage: "The happy relationship between the arts and politics which has characterized our long history I think reached a culmination tonight. I know we're all indebted to a great friend—Frank Sinatra."

Sinatra convinced himself that his Palm Springs home would become the western White House. He spent hundreds of thousands of dollars constructing a helicopter pad in his backyard to receive the president. A guesthouse on the grounds was built. One room in Sinatra's home was turned into a Kennedy shrine. On the door was a brass plaque noting that Kennedy had slept there. The room was filled with memorabilia, mainly pictures of Sinatra and Kennedy. Then the FBI told Kennedy of Sinatra's associations with Mafia figures, which must not have been much of a surprise, and this "happy relationship between the arts and politics" was abruptly terminated.

Sinatra was embittered. And over the years, he attempted to ingratiate himself back into political favor. In the Nixon era, he became the close friend and ideological defender of Vice President Spiro T. Agnew, in almost every way the antithesis of Kennedy. To the degree that Kennedy was sophisticated and supple, Sinatra's new pal was crude and obvious. After Agnew attacked the press for being "nattering nabobs of negativism," Sinatra underlined the point by saying that "some newspapers dispose of their garbage by printing it."

Kitty Kelley wrote: "Frank agreed with Agnew about 'the disease of our time' being an artificial and masochistic sophistication, and said that was what concerned him most about American life. 'It's the amorality,' said Frank." On this subject, there could be no more unconvincing a spokesman. But he seemed to savor the role of Agnew's echo chamber.

For Sinatra, Agnew must not have been the embodiment of a dream, like Kennedy, but of an antidream, the personification of his curdled resentment. Sinatra was now rising through self-destructiveness; he was obliterating his own past, his previous affections and longings. The guest house built for Kennedy became the "Agnew House." A parade of show-business personalities lurched through whenever Agnew was in residence. Among those who appeared at the Sinatra soirees for Agnew were the Ronald Reagans. But when Agnew pleaded nolo contendere, Sinatra's massaging of power came to naught.

The Reagans offered Sinatra the opportunity to recapture what had been lost twice. What had gone haywire in the past would have a happy ending. Reagan's themes were of restoration: America would be number one in the world again; the free market of the pre–New Deal era would be revived. Sinatra's elevation to the Reagan court was the illustration of the restorationist theme in the cultural domain.

Just as Sinatra the Rat Pack leader had been in harmony with a certain level of the New Frontier, he was now in tune with Reagan's New Beginning. Sinatra had become an older man, with hair implants, his skinny frame bulky with age, his voice a shadow of itself. Ideologically, he had traveled from left to right. That journey was marked by more than the loss of convictions, but of conviction itself. As a left-winger, he was ardent in his beliefs, belonged to many liberal organizations, crusaded for unpopular causes, and had confronted the Hollywood blacklist. Unlike Reagan, who had also made the odyssey to the right, Sinatra seemed to lack all commitment. He sought to reassert the glory of a past he had already rebuked. He appeared merely to want acceptance, willing to say almost anything to flatter those who might grant it to him. At the cultural center of the Reagan universe stood this void. (The most penetrating and apt commentary on this Sinatra incarnation and the aesthetic he now celebrated was offered by Sid Vicious in his insane punk cover of "My Way.")

"The greatest collection of talent America could offer to any audience!" exclaimed Sinatra to the Reagans as they sat in their regal thrones on inauguration eve. Once again, he was the host to a president-elect. Once again, the spotlight signaled his status.

Reagan himself arose to speak, to thank his great friend, as Kennedy had, and to say something more. He hailed the theatrical profession for the "pure pearl of tears, the gold of laughter, and diamonds of stardust they spread on an otherwise dreary world." In praising the actors before him, he implicitly praised himself. For wasn't he once one of their company? But this was more than self-congratulation. It was a statement of his intentions for the future, too. He was promising that he had the magic to make us cry and laugh and turn us into stars. As for the "dreary world," that might be a reference to the "malaise" that Carter had claimed infected our psychology. That was then, this was now: time for "stardust."

Ronald Reagan sought to use his presidency to do more than cut taxes and increase the military budget. From the beginning, his handlers spoke of their ultimate goal of fostering a political re-alignment that would lock in Republican power on the presiden-tial level into the twenty-first century. To make this an enduring feat, they sought to control more than the dynamic of elections; they wanted to transform society as well. Reagan seemed ideal to serve as the instrument for this ambitious venture. He was, after all, more than a pure-bred politician; he had descended to politics from the ether of popular culture. In his first race, he finessed the "actor issue" by casting himself as a "citizen-politician," assert-ing his lack of qualification precisely as his salient qualification. He aspired to be the enchanting ruler of society, over which he would spread "stardust." But the White House political director-ate thought little about culture, which in any case was not as malleable as the White House press corps. The Reagan managers never went beyond public relations, never beyond acts such as negotiating for a cover photo on *Parade* magazine of the oldest president in a white T-shirt lifting weights.

At its height, before the Iran-contra scandal, Reaganism put the country in a warm bath, which may have had a short-term therapeutic effect. This was not a continuation of what Harold Rosenberg called "the tradition of the new," a tradition that is more than twentieth-century modernism: it is the cultural essence of American progress. Nostalgia was at the center of the Reaganite aesthetic, which fed upon the cultural debris of the past. Because it was inherently backward-looking, Reaganism had no redemptive power and was ultimately disabling. There was no cultural realignment on which to rest a presumptive political realignment.

The aesthetic of Reaganism was promulgated chiefly by Ronald Reagan and his family through public spectacles. Through them, the charismatic leader mediated his relationship with the people, rising above the Congress and the press. The spectacles were a peculiar blend of forms, one prescribed by the obligations of office, such as the inauguration, and the other rooted in the vaudeville variety show. Virtually all the dimensions of that aesthetic were established at the first inauguration and the subsequent gala.

In this aesthetic, the beautiful was the familiar. The best artists, or more aptly, the best entertainers, were those who were familiar, whose period of greatest creativity and authenticity was in the past. As remnants of another era, they were reassuring, not only about the past, but about the future. Their presence was an indication that what lay ahead was already experienced. But the virtue of familiarity extended beyond the familiar personalities. The best songs were familiar. The best jokes and stories sounded familiar. And the best images were familiar.

The familiarity of art was far more important than the artist's inspiration because the source of creativity might be uncontrollable—critical rather than uplifting. The familiar, by contrast, is predictable. It can attempt to inspire by evoking familiar sentiments, especially a celebratory patriotism. But the familiar may be threatened by the plural. Conservatives of the Reagan era often blamed the sensation of vertigo they felt in a pluralistic

America on "moral relativism." This phrase was less an empirical description of what they deplored than a symptom of their anxiety. If expression can come from unexpected places, then what happens to the common center? The notion of what is native, what is American, may be thrown into question. If we haven't already experienced it, how do we know if a spontaneous expression from a previously unheard-from quarter is legitimate? When the familiar is abandoned as the yardstick, all standards of judgments are gone.

In the aesthetic of Reaganism, the beautiful was also the expensive. What looks good is what is costly. It is something to wear, to display, to purchase, to bask in for its price tag. The Kennedy inauguration, of course, was not cheap. But the act of spending was not paramount. After all, the Kennedys had so much money, and it had all been earned by Joseph P. Kennedy a generation earlier. Money was a means, not an end. In the aesthetic of Reaganism, however, the expense was the ideal itself. The exorbitant ticket prices for inaugural events, for example, were very much the point.

Winning was also beautiful. But it was a particular kind of winning. It was simply the victory. The Reagan aesthetic cut optimism off from the struggle, innocence from effort. Winning was immaculate; it was a form of wish fulfillment. Believing became doing, as long as one had the right beliefs, like Reagan. A focus on the struggle could produce the unhealthy psychological condition known, according to Reagan, as "gloom and doom," which was how he described the outlook of his 1984 Democratic rival Walter Mondale, who was all work and no play. And Mondale lost every state but one.

The need for acclaim was another aspect of the aesthetic. At many of his State of the Union addresses, Reagan played the master of ceremonies, introducing heroes in the galleries, common folk who had performed admirable individual acts. They had been recruited by a diligent White House staff to draw applause in the middle of Reagan's speeches so that the acclaim would also be his. These heroes were neither inspired by his ideals nor part of a general spontaneous movement. Some of them were not really heroes: a spelling-bee champion, for example. But they made us feel good about ourselves without demanding that we do anything. The uplift, if not artificial, was vicarious. Simply being ourselves was wonderful enough, providing an existential smugness. Reagan challenged us to stay the same—offering the virtue of familiarity.

The aesthetic of Reaganism arose at a moment of cultural transition. Modernism was largely a spent force. For the first half of the twentieth century, it had been the movement of the experimental avant-garde, self-consciously staking out the role of leading the culture against the philistinism of the bourgeoisie and the masses. Now, it had been completely absorbed by the bourgeoisie and was taught in the universities as orthodoxy. Whenever any new trend emerged, it was almost instantly assessed and assimilated. On its own terms, the modernist success removed its point. To be viewed as classic rendered it no longer the vanguard. High culture was also no longer insulated from popular culture, if it ever was. The postmodernist synthesis was an attempt to combine elements of both.

But Reaganism, which had a symbiotic relationship with the popular culture, was not really postmodernist. It lacked the irony and self-consciousness that was intrinsic to the style. Moreover, the aesthetic of Reaganism was not a postmodernist transcendence of the high and the low. It was still very much rearguard, but in a context without a vanguard.

The idea of the rearguard was formulated by Clement Greenberg in his seminal 1939 essay, "Avant-Garde and Kitsch." His categories, which were the basic categories of the modernist construct, would seem to have become obsolescent in the postmodern environment. But the aesthetic of Reaganism gave at least the lower realm renewed relevance.

Greenberg's tone was drenched with the condescension of the avant-garde critic, but his insights remain acute. Kitsch, he wrote, is "ersatz culture . . . destined for those who, insensible to the values of genuine culture, are hungry nevertheless for the diversion that only culture of some sort can provide.

"Kitsch, using for raw material the debased and academicized simulacra of genuine culture, welcomes and cultivates this insensibility. It is the source of its profits. Kitsch is mechanical and operates by formulas. Kitsch is vicarious experience and faked sensations. Kitsch changes according to style, but remains always the same. Kitsch is the epitome of all that is spurious in the life of our times. Kitsch pretends to demand nothing of its customers except their money—not even their time.

"The precondition for kitsch, a condition without which kitsch would be impossible, is the availability close at hand of a fully matured cultural tradition, whose discoveries, acquisitions, and perfected self-consciousness kitsch can take advantage of for its own ends. It borrows from it devices, tricks, stratagems, rules of thumb, themes, converts them into a system, and discards the rest. It draws its life blood, so to speak, from this reservoir of accumulated experience."

The Reaganites were the standard-setters of a new kitsch.

Unlike the old kitsch, which was simply the popular culture, neokitsch involved an effort to become an artifact of kitsch itself—the glittering, ephemeral object that might impress both the newly affluent and those who aspire to that station. It was, as Greenberg suggested about the earlier kitsch, less a sensibility than an insensibility; a video-age substitute for folk culture, yet familiar. It was little cause, a lot of effect. The Reaganite aesthetic was a vast scavenger operation, drawing upon the images of kitsch past and present. It was at the same time surreal and instantly accessible to the average viewer; the relentless drizzle of kitsch imagery was a kind of geriatric MTV.

Reagan himself was the aesthetic's chief practitioner. His rhetoric was filled with shards of kitsch, ripped from the context of popular culture. On budget policy, Reagan threatened Congress by quoting Clint Eastwood: "Make my day." Here the president played Dirty Harry, the vigilante cop. On terrorism, he said he would act like Rambo. On taxes, when the movie *The Untouchables* was in commercial release, he cited Eliot Ness: "If any tax hike ever comes across my desk, my handling of the veto pen will make the way Eliot Ness went after Al Capone look like child's play." Then he referred to Vanna White, the comely *Playboy* featurette and letter-turner on the television game show "Wheel of Fortune": "I'll veto it in less time than it takes for Vanna White to turn the letters V-E-T-O." Did he have worries of meeting with Mikhail Gorbachev at the Washington summit of 1987? No, Reagan said, he had once acted with Errol Flynn, a really big star.

The stream of kitsch allusions emanating from Reagan was endless. But it was kitsch once removed. Reagan used such tidbits as in-jokes that everybody would get. He was also augmented by those people and things he endorsed. He became a composite figure without doing anything more than posturing—familiarity through association with the familiar.

This was not, however, the apotheosis of Norman Rockwellism. Rockwell, perhaps the most original artist of kitsch, crystallized clichés in a storytelling pictorial style, a sentimental realism, without a hint of the modernist trends raging through the art world of his time. The small-town life Rockwell depicted in all its foibles was the one Reagan promised to restore. Between the dream and the desire lay the ultimate predicament of the aesthetic of Reaganism. In Rockwell's ideal small town everybody was more or less of the same social class; neighborliness was not frustrated by economic cleavage. There was no evidence in Rockwell's *Saturday Evening Post* cover art of limousines, furs, or diamonds. He never painted the portrait of an arbitrageur.

But in the Reaganite aesthetic, as it was lived, rather than imagined, the realities of the *nouveau riche* clashed with the projections of the traditional village. The costly had greater value than the homespun; the amenities of class were more urgent than the needs of community. Reagan's references to popular culture, making him seem familiar and, by extension, his policies more acceptable, were mostly lifted from the entertainment world that had supplanted much of genuine small-town culture. Reagan himself was part of that irreversible process. It was all familiar, but Frank Sinatra and Sylvester Stallone and Vanna White, whatever their humble origins, were not exactly plain folk. The overriding of community by class and of the homespun by show business made the Reaganite cultural realignment mainly a matter of fantasy.

Though there was no upsurge of Rockwellism, there was a

swelling of celebrity-mongering Warholism. Andy Warhol was the polar opposite of Norman Rockwell. His heritage was East European and he grew up in the depressed industrial regions of eastern Pennsylvania, but when he landed in Manhattan, he presented himself as a blank. His hair was dyed white, his existence was nocturnal, and his sexuality was androgynous. He seemed to be from nowhere and his mission nothing. His art consisted of flat representations of objects of consumption, the most well known of which were his serial paintings of Campbell soup cans. His films, in which the camera, for instance, focused on a sleeping man, unreeled for hours. His best-known line was that "in the future everyone will be famous for fifteen minutes." During the 1960s, his "Factory," a demimonde clubhouse of talented, half-talented, and untalented hangers-on, staged "happenings"— events of no particular purpose that captured media attention, epiphanies of his nonphilosophy.

In Washington, attending Reagan's first inauguration, Warhol announced at a party that he had "become a Republican." In fact, he had not changed at all; he remained a chameleon. His feel for the 1980s was as sure as it had been for the 1960s. Now he founded a new magazine, *Interview,* featuring the wealthy and the celebrated, a forerunner of the slick magazines for the wealthy and their voyeurs that flooded the racks in the Reagan years. On the cover of an early issue appeared Nancy Reagan's face. (Among those working on *Interview:* the wife of Ron Reagan, Jr.)

On January 8, 1986, the *Washington Times,* the Moonie-owned right-wing newspaper that had become an arbiter of conservative politics and taste in the capital, ran a long piece on Paul Morrissey, a former worker in Warhol's Factory, director of his 1968 film *Trash.* Morrissey was glowingly described as "a conservative whose art explores the aesthetic possibilities of blood on concrete." Morrissey's new cultural hero was Sylvester Stallone in his Rambo mode: "I like seeing him kill commies because that's the best thing you can do in a movie now, is mow down the Kremlin, because the liberal minds are protecting them right and left."

Was it parody, or was it Memorex? It was sheer Warholism —an eagerness to shock in the effort to gain attention: the spotlight, if anything, being the point. Morrissey, like Warhol, had not changed at all. But the conservatives were delighted to promote him as long as he mouthed what seemed to be the appropriate opinions of the moment. This was hardly evidence of cultural realignment, but a vacuum into which were rushing people who were themselves vacuums. Their opportunism was not greeted with skepticism, but as proof of the righteousness of the cause. Because of the worthiness of the goals, all conversions were treated as heartfelt, following the religious pattern of sin and redemption. So the nihilist Morrissey was stamped "a conservative," a true believer. The ideological impulse behind the embrace of Morrissey was, as Greenberg suggested about kitsch, less a sensibility than an insensibility.

Neokitsch was located somewhere in the gray zone between kitsch and camp, between Rockwell and Warhol. Both Reaganism and Warholism, the highest stage of camp, drew life from decayed kitsch. But neokitsch Reaganism was camp without the wink.

Camp, as Susan Sontag pointed out in "Notes on 'Camp,' " is an aesthetic sensibility that views certain forms of banality as fantastical. It is serious, but purged of tragedy; out-of-date, but liberated from time; dandyism for the age of mass culture. "Indeed," writes Sontag, "the essence of Camp is its love of the unnatural: of artifice and exaggeration." It is self-conscious about the naive, which is considered comic: "it's good because it's awful." Reaganism was the epoch-making union of kitsch and camp.

Rockwellism and Warholism were myth-mongering incitements to envy of opposite sorts, if not to feelings of personal inadequacy. Reaganism drew from both. It was hooked on celebrities, especially those who had come to devote more of their energies to investment portfolios than to performance, who carried themselves with the gravity of the chief executive officer—or the swagger of the "chairman of the board." At the same time, worshipful obeisance was made to small-town imagery, the Eden to which Reagan promised to return us. But Reaganism had a tincture of cynicism that was nowhere present in Rockwellism. And yet Reaganism was not as cunning about either the superficial or the profound as Warholism.

The representative figures of the Reaganite aesthetic happened to be the Reagans themselves—Ronald and Nancy, Ron and Patti. They did not resemble the traditional family gathered around the Thanksgiving turkey in the famous Rockwell painting. As the parents sought to captivate the public, the children offered a disenchanted commentary on the cost of status-seeking and the conservative pieties about the family.

For a short time, Ron, the younger son, was a member of the corps de ballet of the Joffrey company. After he retired, still in his twenties, he pirouetted through the popular culture. He knew he was a creature of kitsch, and he made no apologies. He also made no attempt to present himself as a misunderstood artist, miscast by an accident of birth. "I've got one of those cheap kinds of celebrity," he told *Vanity Fair* magazine. "No question about it."

Ron was represented by the William Morris Agency. "Do you think he's the most successful First Child ever?" his agent asked the *Vanity Fair* interviewer. This hopeful statement accompanied a spread of full-color photographs of the First Child. In one shot, Ron appeared in a red, white, and blue suit. In another, he leapt in the air, demonstrating his balletic prowess, attired in red underwear, white socks, unbuttoned white shirt, his bare chest exposed, his eyes shaded by sunglasses, his hair spiked in the punk mode. Here was the camp comment on the previous picture, which was straight patriotic kitsch. From Ron's smirk, one knew he was in on the joke. This Ronald Reagan winked.

The joke involved his identity. In an American Express card ad, Ron played himself using his "cheap celebrity": "Every time I appear on a talk show, people ask me about my father. Every time I give out an interview, people ask me about my father. Every time I pull out the American Express card, people treat me like my father. Come to think of it, that's not so bad! Hello, Dad?" Ron shuts a phone booth door. What the hell. The Wizard of Oz's son was matter-of-fact.

(The other Reagan son, Michael, an adopted son, from the president's first marriage to Jane Wyman, popped up during the 1980s with occasional bitter remarks. Of Ron's American Express ad, he said: "Frankly, if I were going to use somebody's name, I would use my mother's. She makes more in one month [as the star of the television series "Falcon Crest"] than my father makes in a year." This unhappy family was really like no other.)

On February 9, 1986, Ron was the guest host of "Saturday

Night Live" and presented two visions of his parents as refracted through two crucial films of the Reagan era. The show opens with Ron on the phone at the White House. On the other end of the line are his parents, off at Camp David, assuring him that he has their trust in caring for the house. He hangs up, grabs a broom, pretends it's a guitar, as he lip-syncs the screeching lyrics of a rock song. He jumps in the air and does a full split to tumultuous audience applause. He is wearing a pink shirt and underpants.

In this scene, Ron acted out the 1983 movie *Risky Business*, in which a young man, left at home by his affluent parents, becomes the operator of a prostitution ring. By the end, he manages to disentangle himself, but has proved himself a successful entrepreneur—a tale of the 1980s.

Later in the show, Ron acted out the 1985 movie *Back to the Future*, in 'which a young man, disillusioned with his nerdy, unsuccessful parents, passes through a time warp and winds up in 1955, where he discovers them as youths. A Ronald Reagan movie is playing at the local theater, and nobody believes the young man when he says Reagan is the president in the 1980s. Through his involvement in his parents' past, he transforms their future. When he returns to the present, his hapless wimp of a father has become a confident businessman and his alcoholic, nagging mother has become a svelte tennis lady. In the "Saturday Night Live" version, Ron's parents are depicted as dim and out of touch—and then magically transformed. The audience is left laughing with the thought that the dopey Reagans are the real ones.

Just a week before, in his State of the Union address, Reagan had announced that the country was going "back to the future." He even quoted a line of dialogue from the movie: "Where we're going, we don't need roads." Thus, a movie that poked fun at the notion of Reagan as president became the fodder for presidential rhetoric and, in turn, a vehicle for a parody of both film and reality, acted by the son of the actor-president. Ron's "Saturday Night Live" sketch was among the highest expressions of the neokitsch aesthetic.

A few months later, Ron's older sister, Patti Davis, published a novel, *Home Front*—perhaps the only novel of the era to deal directly with Reaganism and the family issue. "If he sounds like my father—he's the only father I have," Patti told the *Washington Post*. About reports that her mother was upset by the book, Patti said: "And if she is so hurt—okay, let's say she's hurt—but how else could I have written the mother, the character so she wouldn't be hurt?"

The book's plot was familiar: a governor of California becomes president. He is Robert Canfield, a man of "hardy good looks," whose "persuasive voice sold an awful lot of cars for National Motors." As governor, he calls out the National Guard against student demonstrators. And like the Reagan portrayed in the David Stockman and Alexander Haig memoirs, Robert Canfield is a distant and passive figure.

His wife Harriet is obsessed with status and appearances. The author writes about Harriet's first impression upon entering the White House: "My mother was carrying on conversations as she ducked in and out of rooms, inspecting furniture, drapes, walls. 'There's so much history here! Imagine all the people who have been within these walls. But, good grief, I just can't wait to redecorate.' "

Beth is their alienated daughter, who joins anti–Vietnam War protests, to her mother's consternation. "Families should stick together," says Harriet, "but you just insist on ruining it. We were so happy when you were born. You were such a lovely little girl . . . What went wrong?"

Beth reflects: "I wanted so much to smooth things out with my parents, but I didn't know how. It seemed that our relationship had deteriorated to little more than a clash of political views, ideologies milling around bumping into each other. The gap that separated us had become a chasm . . . now the pain of being strangers was so great I couldn't even spend twenty-four hours under their roof."

"Interesting fiction," said Reagan about his daughter's book. He added that he hoped she "makes a lot of money." But Patti's publicity tour was disrupted when her appearances on the Joan Rivers and "Merv Griffin" shows were suddenly canceled. There were reports that Nancy Reagan had applied pressure.

Like Ron's "Saturday Night Live" satire, Patti's novel blurred the line between fiction and reality. Her book was more than a First Child's complaint about her place in the family. It was also a harsh criticism of her parents' superficial aesthetics and acquisitive values. Patti was playing Jane Fonda playing Patti's life. But who had more authority to cast the part?

During the early Reagan presidency, Nancy Reagan was consumed with the effort to transcend precisely the image of Harriet Canfield. She was dubbed "Queen Nancy," said to be concerned above all with her new $200,000 White House china, interior decorators, and clothing designers—which, of course, she was. Transforming her image literally required a song and dance.

On March 28, 1982, at the Gridiron Club dinner, before the national press corps, the First Lady put on a bravura performance. Wearing a plumed hat, baggy pants, and yellow boots, she slinked onto the stage and belted a song to the tune of "Second Hand Rose": "Second hand clothes / I give my second hand clothes / To museum collections and traveling shows . . . I never wear a frock more than just once / Calvin Klein, Adolfo, Ralph Lauren, and Bill Blass / Ronald Reagan's Mama's going strictly first class / Rodeo Drive, I'll be back, Rodeo Drive / In 1985."

According to Donnie Radcliffe of the *Washington Post,* she "brought down the house. . . . The sophisticated audience of journalists, politicians, and their friends responded to her performance as though she had undergone a major change." In fact, she had not changed, but had simply given a camp performance. Her self-parody was also a mocking of the homespun and a self-conscious embrace of the luxurious; her use of public relations simply demonstrated her desire for popularity and her skill at manipulating the press. This was neokitsch of a high order.

In the June 1985 issue of *Vanity Fair,* William F. Buckley, Jr., paid tribute to the Reagans as paragons of married bliss, the ideal Mr. and Mrs. America. A full-page close-up picture showed them kissing. Buckley explained that he had prompted them by playing a tape of Frank Sinatra crooning.

"Keep Audrey Hepburn, and keep Liz Taylor, Nancy's the feature, they're just the trailer," said the president, placing his wife in the pantheon of popular-culture icons. Now he and his First Lady were the ultimate film royalty, something they could achieve only through politics.

Oddly, Buckley felt moved to explain this apostle of optimism and his "Nancy with the Reagan Face" in tragic terms:

"The last time I heard the legend of Philemon and Baucis adduced seriously was in the final paragraphs of Whittaker Chambers's book *Witness.* Chambers was given to melodrama, but those who knew him and his wife Esther never doubted . . . that it was so between them. It is always hard to think it might indeed be so when one thinks of public figures, where posturing is one of the professional obligations. But it is so also of them, as it proved to be so of Arthur and Cynthia Koestler. Chambers wrote of how the god Hermes in disguise had been treated hospitably by the poor, elderly couple, who shared with him their board and hut. In the morning, Hermes asked them what was their most secret wish, and it transpired that it was for both the same, that they would leave life together, inasmuch as life apart would be unendurable.

" 'The god, now gleaming through his rags, raised his staff— the caduceus with the twined snakes, interlacing good and evil. Where Philemon and Baucis had stood, two trees rustled up whose branches met and touched when the wind blew.' People curious to know how it is between the man and wife dancing together on the cover of *Vanity Fair* this month are going to have to put to one side their political feelings and recognize that that is the way they are."

The subtext to the Reagans' apparently carefree behavior, he suggested, was really the tragedy of conservatism, always thwarted in the end—an apocalyptic and fatalist attitude personified by Chambers, a founder of modern conservatism and Buckley's early mentor. Yet Buckley's treacly recounting of this tale of aging and death, highlighted by reference to the Koestlers' double suicide, was not quite apt. The Reagans did not fit Buckley's construction. Their performances never reached the portals of tragedy. They demanded to be understood through other references—"Calvin Klein, Adolfo, Ralph Lauren, and Bill Blass," and Audrey Hepburn and Liz Taylor, too. They were not "the trailer" to a Greek myth, but "the feature."

. . .

The themes promoted by the president were given their greatest elaborations in certain television series and films. On TV, the family, riven by conflict in the 1960s and 1970s, was restored: *Home Front* with a Hollywood ending. The message, however, varied from show to show and was not necessarily simple.

"Dynasty" and "Family Ties," about two very different families, were two of the 1980s' most popular and durable television series. "Dynasty," which began airing in January 1981, carried the spirit of the Reagan inaugural forward through the 1980s. The show centered on a *nouveau riche* family in Denver—plutocrats from Pluto. Their wealth was equated with an outrageously camp and deadbeat glamour. No distinction was made between the family and the family business; there was no haven in this heartless world. The family struggle and the money struggle were the same. Greed was depicted at its most snarling and grasping, a view of Reagan-period parvenus as if scripted by Thomas Hobbes. The show was make-believe and yet utterly deadpan; it was glittery and banal at the same time. "The appeal to 'dreams come true'—meaning luxuriant wealth and true love—is one basis for the remarkable success of Ronald Reagan, who taps 'Dynasty' themes in ordinary Americans' imaginations," wrote Debora Silverman in *Selling Culture.* "Dynasty" was a documentary of Reagan-era fantasy.

"Family Ties," by contrast, featured a humorous and sympathetic portrait of an ambitious young Reaganite, Alex Keaton, played by Michael J. Fox, the star of *Back to the Future.* The treatment of his values was gently satiric. (Adding to the irony was Reagan's declaration that it was his favorite show.) Yet, for all the appeal of the diminutive yuppie character, Keaton/Fox, the anchor of the family in "Family Ties" was the parents, just like real life. These video parents were 1960s campus protesters attempting to adjust to the realities of the 1980s. They had not rejected their past selves, but were constantly seeking to balance work and home, ideals and realities. The father, who had once edited a radical newspaper, worked for the Columbus, Ohio, public television station. The mother was a career woman, whose work did not diminish her centrality in the home. Their son's Reaganism was often laughable, a phase of immaturity. Like most teenagers, Alex frequently made claims of omniscience, but father—and mother—still knew best. The triumph of these parents, week after week, might have been a victory for common sense, but it was not necessarily the triumph of Reaganism.

The ultimate Reaganite cultural hero emerged, not on television, but in the movies. At the heart of his struggle was doubt and anxiety about his potency. The hero was almost always obsessed with the American defeat in Vietnam, and tried to erase the past and alter the present by subduing savages on the frontier—a process the historian Richard Slotkin, writing about colonial America, called "regeneration through violence." The latest Leatherstocking lived by a personal code of honor that compelled him to seek vengeance. His mission usually involved rescuing captives from the Indians—or rather the Vietnamese, Iranians, or Latins. The hero always succeeded, after a series of escapades, in reconciling families. Variations on this scenario were familiar in World War II movies and Westerns, most notably in John Ford's classic *The Searchers.* But now the old warhorse was responding to new cries for help.

The hero first snapped to attention in *An Officer and a Gentle-*

man, a military-school story told as romance: the troubled kid is redeemed by the discipline of the army and literally sweeps the girl off her feet. The 1960s were over; the 1980s had begun.

In *Uncommon Valor,* a father assembles a paramilitary team to rescue his son, still held as a prisoner of war in Indochina. The team, a kind of good-guys Dirty Dozen, is stabbed in the back by the CIA, which takes away their exotic weaponry. It's back to basics in the jungle.

In *Iron Eagle,* a boy is rebuffed by the State Department and must enlist a retired fighter pilot to rescue his father held hostage in Iran. This family reunion is accompanied by the blasting of many mullahs.

And these were only two of a rash of rescue-mission movies: *POW, Missing in Action, Missing in Action II, Delta Force, Commando, Predator.*

Clint Eastwood, the law-and-order icon from the late 1960s and 1970s, also returned for two films of typical 1980s heroism. In *Firefox,* the hero is a troubled ex-military officer, enlisted by the U.S. government to steal a jet from the Russians that operates by mental telepathy. Why are the Americans the ones stealing technology? We are falling behind. Single-handedly, Eastwood closes the window of vulnerability.

In *Heartbreak Ridge,* Eastwood is a Vietnam veteran who fears he's becoming obsolete. He whips a bunch of snot-nose kids into a tip-top unit—they are a kind of family redeemed by discipline—and in the end they invade Grenada and slaughter Cubans. "It's time to go to war," says the hero.

War isn't hell; it's fun. In *Top Gun,* the young hero swoops around in a jet as the rock score throbs, tests his manhood against his peers who are equally jacked-up on racing hormones, wins the blonde, and beats the Russians in the big game over the Indian Ocean. Make love, make war.

Nobody was more ready to go than Sylvester Stallone. In *First Blood*, the hero, Rambo, is an inarticulate, disturbed Vietnam veteran who cannot adjust to civilian life. He single-handedly holds off the police and National Guard, expressing his inchoate discontent through gunfire, until he's captured and taken away to prison.

In the second Rambo movie, the pathetic but lunatic victim has become a lunatic *Übermensch*. He is enlisted by the U.S. government to rescue hostages in Vietnam. "This time, do we get to win?" he asks. The answer is yes. His performance is a veritable triumph of the will. He defeats the Vietnamese army and its Russian adviser, but discovers that the U.S. government intended all along to betray him. We lost in Vietnam, after all, because we were stabbed in the back on the homefront. The evil of the Russian adviser is exceeded by the evil of the American bureaucrat.

In *Rocky IV*, the familiar working-class boxer, who always comes from behind to win, battles a mean Russian. As in *Firefox*, the Soviets are technologically superior. Their champ trains with the latest computerized equipment; Rocky drags sleds and lifts logs. But he wins because he is made of better fiber. He drapes himself in the American flag to the cheers of the Russian fight crowd.

In *Cobra*, the hero is a former Special Forces soldier, now a special police unit of one, who battles an evil terrorist to the death. Along the way, the press and the police bureaucracy, who insist on adherence to stupid rules (the Bill of Rights), try to frustrate his mission. Only the hero knows that every law must be broken to save civilization; only he can do so.

And if we are not saved by the hero? Two films suggested the alternative: *Red Dawn,* in which high-school students turned guerrillas fight a Soviet invasion (interestingly, the warfare is all conventional—no nukes); and *Invasion U.S.A.,* in which Chuck Norris, a veritable one-man army, defeats an invasion by an unnamed drug-running terrorist organization led by a Russian adviser.

Finally, in February 1987, ABC, at the instigation of right-wing critics, aired a seven-part, fifteen-hour variation on the invasion theme—*Amerika.* The time is 1997. The United States has lost World War III to the Russians, although exactly how is never explained. There is no evidence of nuclear warfare. "You lost your country before we ever got there," says the principal Russian villain. "You had political freedom, but you lost your passion." If we had only felt better about ourselves, none of this would have happened.

No matter what was on the small screen or the silver screen, the main "feature" of the Reagan era was always the Reagans, who promised to make us feel good. The public spectacle that had the greatest effect on the tone of the Reagan presidency in its halcyon middle period was one in which he played only an off-stage part—the 1984 Olympics. They were held in Los Angeles, the Soviets and the eastern-bloc countries did not participate, and the United States won many medals. Reagan blessed the U.S. team as they went in, telling them to "win one for the Gipper," referring to one of his most popular movie roles. The post-Olympic party, staged for television at the Los Angeles Coliseum by Hollywood producer David Wolper, was a celebration of good vibrations.

The scavenger aspect of the Reaganite aesthetic surfaced early in the 1984 campaign. In June, Bruce Springsteen released his album *Born in the USA,* with its driving lead cut. The Reaganites interpreted Springsteen's cry about the woes of a Vietnam veteran in a declining industrial town as an upbeat anthem, and they sought to appropriate it for their own use. But Springsteen refused. (In 1986, in his live three-album set, his cover of "War" was preceded by a long spoken introduction about how he evaded the draft during the Vietnam War and how the administration had not learned the lessons of Vietnam.) Next to Mondale, Reagan was Springsteen. But next to Springsteen, he was Mondale. Rebuffed by Springsteen, his campaign hired a less well known substitute, a country-western singer with a slightly seedy appearance named Lee Greenwood, whose tune "I'm Proud to Be an American" became the Reagan campaign hymn.

Reagan was neither the first to use the mood generated by the Olympics, nor the last. Several sponsors of the event, such as Pepsi, had especially produced ads for airing during the competition. (One of the chief creative influences on the Pepsi spots, Phil Dusenberry, helped frame Reagan's ads, too.) After the Olympics, the uplifting patriotic theme was widely used to sell beer (Miller: "Made the American Way") and automobiles (Chrysler: "Made in the USA"). This advertising both played off and reinforced the mood that Reagan was seeking to attach to himself. Reagan did not have a unique selling proposition, and that was a political plus. The theme's broadness made it seem that he was at one with American society. During his issueless reelection campaign, he floated in and out of popular culture and commercial culture with ease. His performance, though, was always structured. He never did well without a choreographed event and a script. Optimism

and self-confidence, it must be stressed, were not themes artificially pasted on Reagan. He had these qualities in immense
quantities, qualities the public generally believed connoted
knowledge and mastery. It was unthinkable that the smiles meant
ignorance and passivity.

The 1985 inauguration was planned as a contrast to the 1981
affair. This one was called a "People's Inaugural." Then it leaked
out that Nancy Reagan's wardrobe cost forty-six thousand dollars.
And Frank Sinatra was back in town. "You're dead, every one
of you!" he shouted at the press, after an article appeared in the
Washington Post recalling the Rat Pack. "You're all dead!"

On January 18, at a show in honor of Vice President George
Bush, Frank Sinatra, Jr., performed a minioratorio about Francis
Scott Key's composition of the national anthem. In a bit of frac-
tured poetry, he called the beginning of the American Revolution
"that fateful shot the world heard round."

The next night was the big show for the Reagans. Frank Sr.
shared the hosting with Mr. T, Tom "Magnum" Selleck, and
Pearl Bailey. Jimmy Stewart declaimed that the Hollywood he
and Ronnie knew long ago was "a place where concepts like
patriotism and family were extolled." The world of entertainment,
which usurped traditional culture, was represented as its crucible:
the fantasy was real, at least as nostalgia.

At last, Sinatra took the stage, accompanied by his Rat Pack
sidekick Dean Martin, playing himself as a drunk.

"Did I win?" asked Martin.

"You weren't even running," said Sinatra.

"Then why am I tired? Who did win?"

"Mr. Reagan and Mr. Bush. That means four more years of
partying."

"Frank, I can't take four more years of partying, but I'll try."

Thus, with patter about being out of touch and in the way, the second Reagan term was launched.

The culmination of the Reaganite aesthetic as public spectacle was the Statue of Liberty centennial in 1986. The theme of restoration at last had been matched by a physical act of restoration; the merely symbolic assumed the shape of stone and metal. (In a 1984 Reagan reelection spot, the Statue of Liberty made an appearance surrounded by scaffolding.) David Wolper, the Hollywood producer from the Olympics, was back as the producer of the television spectacular. In its own way, the event was glorious, a tribute to the immigrants. But it was unlike the Olympics. This was a celebration without competition; the television screen was not filled with striving young athletes, but familiar stars. There was Elizabeth Taylor and Willie Nelson, over there Frankie Avalon—and two hundred Elvis look-alikes. Liza Minnelli, at the gala at Giant Stadium, told the *Washington Post:* "It's what America's about, for God's sake. Our royalty is show business. We don't get kings and queens." She was a shrewd commentator.

On the evening of July 3, on Governors Island at the tip of Manhattan, the president appeared at a ceremony to relight the statue's torch. Immediately before Reagan's remarks, Frank Sinatra sang a song. His choice was fitting—"The House I Live In"—about brotherhood and tolerance. But it also evoked a political past that Sinatra and Reagan might have preferred to forget. Sinatra had recorded the song in a film shot in the late 1940s, when he was a fighting liberal. (Reagan, of course, was a liberal then, too. But when Sinatra protested the House Un-American Activities Committee investigations of Hollywood, Reagan volunteered as a secret FBI informer.) "The House I Live In" was

associated with the old left. Its lyricist was Abel Meeropol, the
adoptive father of the children of Julius and Ethel Rosenberg, the
left-wing couple executed on spy charges. Now the song was sung
by the ex-liberal Sinatra as a statement of unambiguous patriotism.

Then, as the president pressed a button, a laser beam lit the
torch. The crowd sang "America the Beautiful." The therapeutic
power of nostalgia seemed proved. The faces of the Reagans were
superimposed on the image of the radiant statue. They had
reached an apotheosis, at least for the moment.

The heyday of Reaganism as a spectacle of optimism lasted
roughly two years, from the Olympics to the Statue of Liberty
centennial. On November 6, 1986, the Republicans lost the Senate. Three days earlier, a Lebanese magazine, *Al-Shiraa,* reported
that the United States had secretly sold arms to Iran—the beginning of the Iran-contra scandal.

If the scandal had not intervened, the promotion of Reagan as
icon (and, implicitly, neokitsch as an aesthetic) would have accelerated. On his seventy-sixth birthday, February 6, 1987, an
hour-long syndicated television special, "Reagan's Way," was
scheduled for broadcast. (The title evoked Sinatra's signature
song, "My Way.") The film was produced by Daniel Selznick, son
of the famous Hollywood producer, David O. Selznick, and friend
of Nancy Reagan. But all the advertisers, once eager to place their
products in close proximity to Reagan, withdrew—"because of
the Iranian thing," explained Sidney Love, the program's distrib-
utor. The cancellation of "Reagan's Way" ratified the cancellation of a short-lived mood that was supposed to be permanent.

Where was the hero? To many right-wingers, Lieutenant Colonel Oliver North, on the witness stand at the Iran-contra hearings,

was the fantasy eerily come to life—the hostage rescuer as patriot. North was the sequel to end all sequels. This troubled Vietnam veteran (who had spent weeks in the Bethesda Naval Hospital for psychiatric care) testified that America had lost the Vietnam War because it had been betrayed by politicians and the press at home. He upheld the values of the traditional family, spoke of the need for discipline, claimed that the ends justified the means, and challenged the terrorist, Abu Nidal, to a *mano-a-mano* duel. This was no unclouded optimist, no Reagan. North's vision was of a world teetering on the edge of chaos; extreme measures were needed. In filmic terms he seemed to be Robert Walker, the seductive psycho in *Strangers on a Train,* playing Jimmy Stewart, the populist tribune in *Mr. Smith Goes to Washington.* The transmutation of the hero from the screen to the White House situation room broke through the boundary of dreams; the fantasy was a premonition of policy. Rambo was America's kitsch Caligari.

Another current that flourished under Reagan was that of evangelism. It was more than simply a religious expression; it was political and cultural, too. Reagan's chief contribution to this development was encouragement. "I endorse you," he told a convention of right-wing religious broadcasters. Though he claimed to be "born again" and occasionally regaled visitors with stream-of-consciousness chat about Armageddon, Reagan's attachment to the creed seemed entirely political and rhetorical. As he noted during the 1984 campaign, he never attended church because of fear of terrorist attack. His children showed no evidence of religious training or interest, though Patti did marry her yoga instructor.

The cultural explosion of the evangelicals was partly made possible by modern telecommunications. There were television shows, cable networks, radio stations, "Christian" pop singers like Amy Grant, and "Christian" record labels. Novel means advanced the old-time religion. Though some "Christian" music was presented in the form of MTV-like videos, the chief style was kitsch. For example, the mainstay programming of the Christian Broadcasting Network was not "The 700 Club," the talk show hosted by the network's owner, the Reverend Pat Robertson, but old television series from the 1950s. Apparently, kitsch in black and white was traditional culture.

The enemy, according to the religious right, was a demonic secular humanism, which encompassed most of contemporary American culture. Curiously, Reagan and Reaganism were seen as standing apart, somehow untainted. The president, of course, rhetorically supported the religious-right agenda, lending it legitimacy. But the movement's acceptance of him went beyond the political. To them, he was a cultural hero. The fundamentalists assailed the popular culture as profane, but a creature of neokitsch was seen as sacred. Perhaps because Reagan seemed to fit the category of black-and-white kitsch, he was regarded as a defender of the traditional. The host of "Death Valley Days" and "General Electric Theater" was the moral guardian of My Little Margie and Lassie.

The neokitsch aesthetic—the true Reaganite aesthetic—had few self-conscious exponents (apart from Ron Reagan). It was ironic that it did not claim advocates among those who argued most strongly for the return to the past as the source of virtue and cultural coherence. It was even more revealing that the so-called traditionalists neglected to sustain a criticism of Reaganite culture.

The intellectual traditionalists who emerged as apologists for Reaganism in the 1980s mostly kept their distance from Pat Robertson's presidential ambition in 1988. They were prophets who neglected to claim at least some of the credit that was due them. The Robertson campaign certainly had an independent existence, separate even from much of the conservative movement. But the cultural conservatives' incantatory calls for "traditional" values and their denunciations of modern secular society had helped create an atmosphere in which Robertson flourished.

William Bennett, the secretary of education, was perhaps the administration's champion of this order of conservatives. In his 1984 encyclical, "To Reclaim a Legacy," issued when he was chairman of the National Endowment for the Humanities, Bennett urged the teaching of the classics as an antidote to the cancer of "relativism." He viewed students as passive receptacles into which would be poured the great works of Western civilization. These works he viewed as capsules of pure, unalterable truth. But Bennett never bothered to say which parts of which texts were particularly pertinent, and why. He merely argued on behalf of the classics. In his view, amalgamation was enough to create both philosophical and theological consistency. He did not comprehend the conflict-ridden origins of what has come to be the traditional. Nor did he understand how the concept of the traditional emerged, or its widely varying applications. Nor did he appreciate that an immersion in the classics might reveal that the ancients were not a unified school of thought; that a real grasp of their teachings might better explain today's factiousness without providing a way to escape it. Bennett aimed to impose classic "intellectual authority," but he had a rearguard view of the classics. He devalued the past by his ahistoricism. His failure of understanding derived from his contempt for the present. And his prejudice in favor of absolute values set him against experience in general.

Bennett considered his philosophy to be the essence of Americanism. "Our central values as a free people and the central values of the Judeo-Christian tradition are flesh of the flesh, blood of the blood," said William Bennett. But the courtesy of "the Judeo-Christian tradition" had no theological merit. And the definition of American republicanism in the liturgy of the Roman Catholic Church was a bizarre confusion of realms.

George Will, the conservative columnist, was Bennett's intellectual mentor. Will fancied himself a Burkean, a defender of tradition, but he was more a form of Burke's nightmare, ruled by metaphysical fixations. Will's love of country was mostly expressed as a loathing for much of its culture. The "political culture of affluent consumer societies," he sneered in *The Morning After,* undermined the ability of democracies to "summon the will" to confront communism.

"The late twentieth century," wrote the self-styled American Tory, "needs what the mid-nineteenth century had, a Matthew Arnold to insist that everything connected with culture, from literature through science, depends upon a network of received authority." One need look no farther than Will to find the "received authority."

He despised almost all contemporary trends. "We need a literature of cheerful sociability," he wrote. Nothing critical, bleak, or tragic like, say, Hawthorne, Melville, or Twain?

Will also advanced his expertise in art. He derided Jackson Pollack's "canvases covered with drips" and "fads of nonrepresentational art" as "substanceless . . . effortless." Those who sought to appreciate such art had a "contempt for mind." But the contempt was all Will's. In his views on culture, Will neatly fit a basic Arnoldian category—the philistine.

Allan Bloom, the University of Chicago philosopher and author of *The Closing of the American Mind,* was of the cultural conservative school. He blamed the country's social and political problems on what he claimed was its dominant philosophy—"relativism"—which he traced to Machiavelli, Nietzsche, and Heidegger. The chief expression of this philosophy, which Bloom found most irritating, was rock and roll—"Mick Jagger tarting it up on the stage is all that we brought back from the voyage to the underworld." In Bloom's treatise on the cultural and philosophical impoverishment of America, especially of its young people, he never once mentioned the American pragmatists, William James or Charles Peirce. (Bloom did, however, devote a paragraph to dismissing Oliver Wendell Holmes.) Presumably, Nietzsche and Heidegger had a greater influence. America was really not much on Bloom's mind. To the extent it was, he was revolted by it.

Though Reagan frequently referred to Franklin D. Roosevelt, the hero of his youth, he never catalyzed a deep cultural outpouring similar to that of the New Deal era, which was integral to the transformations the New Deal wrought in American life. Reagan himself lived in the shadow of Roosevelt, and never cast one as long.

The New Deal was first of all premised on a belief in the public realm, which suggested that the artist could give voice to and help shape the national experience. But there was no rigid formula. The aesthetic was pluralistic, reflecting a diverse country; regionalism flourished. Just as the New Deal was a coalition of outsid-

ers—immigrants, minorities, urban laborers, yeoman farmers
—the art of the period attempted to give expression to their lives
and hopes. The tone was usually optimistic, sometimes sentimental, rarely celebratory. Hard work and struggle were clear motifs.
Tradition was cultivated; folkloric and mythic elements clearly
appeared in painting (Wood, Benton) and music (Copland).

But the interest in the past was not self-consuming. The effort
by artists to document reality, to describe it as closely as possible,
was intense. And this was not a clinical search for the empirical.
Social realism was driven by an impulse to reveal the authentic
—an aesthetic of commitment and innocence. Its doubly distilled
product may be *Let Us Now Praise Famous Men,* written by James
Agee, with photographs by Walker Evans, begun in 1936 and
completed in 1941, an unsparing portrait of three families of
southern sharecroppers. "Above all else; in God's name don't
think of it as Art," wrote Agee. He did not want the reader
diverted by attention paid to the literary construction, but to
convey directly experience and feeling and fact.

The aesthetic of the Reagan years, unlike that of the Roosevelt
era, was premised first of all on a disbelief in the public realm.
Belief in a common good was seen by many conservatives as a
pathology, a dangerous liberal attitude that needed to be searched
out and destroyed. The artistic imagination, along with everything
else, was to be privatized, a matter for the Glorious Free Market
to sort out.

But more than money was involved in setting value. The dominant Reaganite aesthetic was built upon the older generation's
pop-cult memories, which included Reagan. The new was almost
exclusively a pastiche of the old. And yet, while a quasi-official
premium was placed on "cheerful sociability," the only original

characters in the pantheon of Reaganite culture were the uncheerful parvenus from "Dynasty" and the unsociable heroes from the "time to go to war" movies.

The contrast with the New Deal years could not have been starker. There was no spontaneous burst of truly original artistic creation that somehow could be seen as part of the larger changes Reagan sought. Where was his John Steinbeck? Clifford Odets? Robert Sherwood? William Saroyan? Nelson Algren? Or Aaron Copland? Or Ben Shahn? Thomas Hart Benton? Grant Wood? Or Walker Evans? Dorothea Lange? Or taken from the other side, where was his D'Annunzio, Ezra Pound, or Céline? However one critically judged the works of each of these artists, it was undeniable that they had existed.

Under Reagan, there were only a scattered few who were part of the temper of the time and yet did not personally possess the reservoir of past kitsch from which to draw. Their metallic superficiality lacked a nostalgic warmth; their overweening self-regard was matched by their artistic thinness. They may not have been attracted to Reaganism, but simply reflected certain of its currents. In the future, they might develop into something quite different; in the Reagan era, however, they produced culture lite.

In literature, perhaps the best representative was Bret Easton Ellis, in his early twenties, author of *Less Than Zero,* a portrait of the pointless, drug-filled lives of affluent youth in Los Angeles: *Home Front* twenty years later, but lacking Patti Davis's sense of larger questions. Also absent in Ellis was any moral sense of literary vocation. "I guess," he said, "I'm writing about—it always sounds so grandiose—about chronicling this generation. I'm not really out to change someone's consciousness, because I think writers are primarily entertainers."

In art, perhaps the best representative was Julian Schnabel, in his mid-thirties, avidly promoted by his art dealers and wildly self-promoting (claiming his "peers" to be "Duccio, Giotto, and Van Gogh"), but possessing "no talent as a draftsman: the weak lumpish silhouettes, the kitsch-expressionist faces with their poached-egg eyes, the clumsy line, and the inability to relate a form to the space around it by the energy of its contour were all there from the beginning," according to Robert Hughes in the *New Republic.*

Schnabel's friend, Jeff Koons, a former commodities broker on Wall Street, used his skill as a salesman to promote himself into a hot artist. His stainless-steel-coated kitsch objects, such as a statue of Bob Hope, fetched prices of up to seventy-five thousand dollars apiece. His buyers were almost exclusively the parvenus of Wall Street, desperate for material signs of their status. "The great artists of the future," Koons told *Manhattan, Inc.,* "are going to be the great negotiators."

Perhaps the popular writers of the 1980s who matched the minor proletarian novelists of the 1930s were those, such as Judith Krantz and Sidney Sheldon, who depicted the adventures of American parvenus in the world of Eurotrash as kitsch romance. Pulp anti-Communist fiction was another popular genre, typified by Tom Clancy's *Red Storm Rising,* about World War III, filled with banal military verisimilitude. But neither the ham-handed Clancy nor the breathless Krantz were the equals of such serious proletarian novelists of the 1930s as Jack Conroy or Edward Dahlberg—or even the Communist Party literary gatekeeper, Mike Gold.

Moreover, nothing written by conservatives in the 1980s approached the standards of the literary Southern Agrarians in the

1930s. It was telling that one of those Southern Agrarians, Robert Penn Warren, was selected by the Reagan administration as the first national poet laureate. The appointment was an homage to Warren—and the past. He deserved whatever honors came his way, but the one bestowed by the Reagan administration reflected more on his lifelong accomplishments than it did on the cultural promise of Reaganism.

Far more enlightening about the dominant aesthetic of the Reagan era than the largely rhetorical effort to evoke the New Deal or the cranky complaints of the cultural conservatives was the controversy surrounding *Amerika*—at fifteen hours the single longest neokitsch extravaganza of the 1980s.

Brandon Stoddard, the ABC entertainment chief, the modulated voice of the boardroom, stepped forward to explain that this phantasmagorical melodrama about jackbooted Russians stomping on Heartland USA, a treatment that was a figment of the right-wing imagination, was really about broad, undebatable questions such as "freedom and responsibility and the American character." That is, it was about everything and, therefore, nothing. It was a civics lesson in neokitsch.

During the *Amerika* dispute, Jeane Kirkpatrick, the administration's former United Nations ambassador, extended her polemics to the cultural sphere. In a review delivered at an appropriate venue—the Low-Intensity Warfare Conference of January 1986, sponsored by the Defense Department—she made the case that *Amerika* was crucial to national security: "I was shocked, by the way, by the ABC story concerning that *Amerika* series and the possibility of its withdrawal. That's a very interesting example of a successful effort to persuade us not to defend ourselves. . . . And I am particularly interested, of course, personally, with the symbolic and ideological debate, because those happen to be the instruments that I wield, not guns or planes or something."

Amerika, however, was not withdrawn because of pressure; it was broadcast precisely as a result of right-wing lobbying. But Kirkpatrick viewed success as failure. It was apparently important for her to regard her faction as the last of the just. Kirkpatrick's aesthetic judgment showed as steely a regard for the bottom line as Louis B. Mayer. But her bottom line was not profit; it was ideological ratings points. The notion that *Amerika* was disposable kitsch produced to satisfy the extremists of the president's party was not within her powers to discern. But Kirkpatrick's comments did clarify her understanding of the proper relationship of culture to politics: obedient servant.

On that subject, Donald Wrye, the scriptwriter of *Amerika,* offered the perspective from Sunset Boulevard: "This isn't a little political science course. This film is not intended to be a civics lesson. You know, it's an entertainment." In other words, the fifteen-hour program had no moral, political, or artistic seriousness. It was merely a cynical diversion. And the Soviet occupation of the United States? That, said Wrye, was just a "story device."

The concept of the "story device" explained more than *Amerika.* It went far to explain the dramaturgy of Reaganism. In Reagan's hands, contextless bits of popular culture became story devices, illustrations of his myths. The "story device" was preferred over the fact, which always has the unfortunate habit of speaking for itself. The odd phrase lifted from a movie, or an old song lyric, however, required the pop-cult pol. Story devices, like *Amerika,* provided Reagan with grist for "the symbolic and ideological debate," as Kirkpatrick put it. But what happened when another story device was called for?

The ideologues who clamored for *Amerika* had the notion that the happy ending to the Reagan presidency would be a bleak, windswept landscape on the other side of which lay the evil empire's forces in strategic retreat. That ending, however, proved a disaster in sneak previews at Geneva and Reykjavik. The studio (Howard Baker's White House) demanded that the leading man give the audience what it wanted. And Reagan gave them another spectacle—the Washington summit. Optimism was momentarily buoyed by the appearance of Mikhail Gorbachev. That's entertainment!

The failure of Reagan's presidency to inspire artists, writers, and musicians was a simple failure: it was because his ideal of beauty was uninspiring. Neokitsch, by its nature, is two-dimensional, cut off from the original sources of artistic creation, and thus from passion, insight, and grandeur.

Ironically, the neokitsch aesthetic would have been impossible without the inspirational aesthetic of the New Deal years. From it, Reagan gleaned his model of confidence, his storehouse of popular sentiments and common references. But the neokitsch effect was the opposite of the New Deal's. At best, it was morning in America. At worst, it was twilight in Amerika. There was an art to it, but it was a shallow art.

Notes for "The Reagan Legacy," by Thomas Byrne Edsall

1. See *Economic Report of the President, January 1987* (Washington, D.C.: Government Printing Office), pp. 69–70.

2. U.S. Bureau of the Census, *Household After-Tax Income: 1985*, Series P-23, no. 151 (Washington, D.C.: Government Printing Office, June 1987), and prior reports from 1980 through 1984 on the same subject. This issue will be explored in more detail further on in the chapter.

3. *Economic Report of the President, January 1987*, pp. 280–81; Robert J. Samuelson, "The American Jobs Machine," *Newsweek*, February 23, 1987, p. 57; "Increasing Incidence of Low-Wage Employment in the U.S.," an unpublished paper by Barry Bluestone of the University of Massachusetts–Boston, and Bennett Harrison of the Massachusetts Institute of Technology.

4. See, for example, *Public Opinion*, March–April 1987, pp. 21–33; Kay Lehman Schlozman, ed., *Elections In America* (Boston: Allen & Unwin, 1987), tables on pp. 311–20; "Report on Democratic Defection," a study by the Analysis Group for the Michigan House Democratic Campaign Committee, New Haven, Conn., 1985.

5. One of the most interesting expositions of the pressures of the international marketplace on domestic politics is in a forthcoming paper, " 'Reaganism' After Reagan," by Joshua Cohen and Joel Rogers, of MIT and the University of Wisconsin, respectively. (To appear in Ralph Miliband and Leo Panitch, eds., *The Socialist Register 1988* (London: Merlin Press).

6. See *Economic Report of the President, January 1987*.

7. Congressional Budget Office, "Major Legislative Changes in Human Resources Programs Since January 1981," staff memorandum, Washington, D.C., August 1983; John L. Palmer and Isabel V. Sawhill, eds., *The Reagan Experiment* (Washington, D.C.: Urban Institute Press, 1982); Thomas Byrne Edsall, *The New Politics of Inequality* (New York: W. W. Norton & Co., 1984).

8. See Joint Committee on Taxation, *General Explanation of the Economic Recovery Tax Act of 1981* (Washington, D.C.: Government Printing Office, 1981).

9. All unemployment data is from the *Economic Report of the President, February 1983* (Washington, D.C.: Government Printing Office).

10. See Edsall, *The New Politics;* Martin P. Wattenberg, "Realignment Without Party Revitalization," paper delivered at the American Association for Public Opinion Research, McAfee, N.J., 1985; and Frederick T. Steeper, of Market Opinion Research, and John R. Petrocik, UCLA, "New Coalitions in 1988," June 1987, a version of an article to be published in *Public Opinion.*

11. For data on the decline in competitive House districts, I have used statistics developed by David W. Brady and Bernard Grofman in "The Decline in Electoral Competition and the Swing Ratio in U.S. House Elections: 1850–1980," a paper delivered at the 1987 American Political Science Association meeting in Chicago, and "Elections as Democratic Institutions," a chapter by Walter Dean Burnham in *Elections in America.*

12. Federal Election Commission press release "Political Party Figures for '86 Elections," May 31, 1987. 999 E Street NW, Washington, D.C. 20463.

13. The data was distributed by Richard Wirthlin, president of the Wirthlin Group, at the 1987 American Political Science Association meeting in Chicago.

14. Material on the composition of state legislatures was supplied by the National Conference of State Legislatures, 444 North Capitol Street NW, Washington, D.C. 20001.

15. *Economic Report of the President, February 1983* (Washington, D.C.: Government Printing Office), p. 195.

16. See chapter by Warren E. Miller, "The Election of 1984 and the Future of American Politics," in *Elections in America,* pp. 315–20; and Wattenberg, *Ronald Reagan and the Polarization of American Electoral Politics,* forthcoming.

17. Samuel Lubell, *The Future of American Politics,* rev. ed. (Garden City, N.Y.: Doubleday/Anchor Books, 1955), pp. 212, 214.

18. Wattenberg, "The Hollow Realignment: Partisan Change in a Candidate-Centered Era," a paper delivered at the 1985 American Political Science Association meeting in New Orleans, based on data from the National Election Studies.

19. Date supplied by Martin Wattenberg of the Political Science Department at the University of California–Irvine.

20. See Thomas E. Cavanaugh, "Changes in American Voter Turnout, 1964–76," *Political Science Quarterly,* Spring 1981; and Edsall, *The New Politics of Inequality.*

21. A. James Reichley, *Religion in American Life* (Washington, D.C.: Brookings Institution, 1985), pp. 278–79.

22. James L. Guth, "Political Converts: Partisan Realignment Among Southern Baptist Ministers," in *Election Politics,* Winter 1985–86 (published by the Institute for Government and Politics, Washington, D.C.).

23. Reichley, *Religion in American Life,* pp. 269–75.

24. Steeper and Petrocik, "New Coalitions in 1988."

25. Peter F. Galderisi and Michael S. Lyons, "Realignment Past and Present," in *The Politics of Realignment: Party Change in the Mountain West,* ed. Galderisi, Lyons, Randy T. Simmons, and John G. Francis (Boulder, Colo.: Westview Press, 1987), p. 3.

26. Patrick H. Caddell, "An Analysis of the Presidential General Election Circumstances Confronting the Democratic Party in 1988," a report prepared for IMPAC, an organization of Democratic fund-raisers, January 1, 1987.

27. Based on data distributed by Richard Wirthlin at the 1987 American Political Science Association meeting in Chicago.

28. Jeanie R. Stanley, "Party Realignment in the States: Texas in the 1980s," a paper delivered at the 1987 American Political Science Association meeting in Chicago.

29. Edsall, *Washington Post,* September 7, 1987, p. A16.

30. Stanley B. Greenberg, in "Report on Democratic Defection."

31. U.S. Department of Labor, *Handbook of Labor Statistics,* December 1980, p. 412, and current data provided in interviews with the staff.

32. U.S. Bureau of the Census, *Statistical Abstract of the United States, 1987* (Washington, D.C.: Government Printing Office), pp. 408–09; and William Serrin, *New York Times,* October 27, 1985, p. 4E. The *Statistical Abstract* is also the source of data on racial trends in the union movement; see p. 409.

33. There have been many excellent news articles on this broad subject, including: Peter Perl, *Washington Post,* September 6 and 13, p. H1 both days; William Serrin, *New York Times,* October 27, 1985, p. 4E; A. H. Raskin, *New York Times,* June 15, 1986, p. F1; Alex Kotlowitz, *Wall Street Journal,* October 13, 1986, p. 6; Chris Spolar, *Washington Post,* June 21, 1987, p. D1; Kenneth R. Noble, *New York Times,* July 9, 1985, p. A14. See also the text of a speech by Janet L. Norwood, commissioner of labor statistics for the Bureau of Labor Statistics, entitled "The Future of Employment," given at the Institute of Industrial Relations, UCLA, October 18, 1986.

34. See articles in the *Washington Post* by Howard Kurtz, February 28, 1986, p. A9; by Marjorie Hyer, April 20, 1985, p. G10; by Don Oberdorfer, May 2, 1985, p. A17; and by Mary Thornton, November 8, 1985, p. A21.

35. Alan Murray, *Wall Street Journal,* March 25, 1987, p. 1.

36. Edsall, *Washington Post,* September 12, 1982, p. H1; September 13, p. D7; October 9, 1982, p. A1.

37. Federal Election Commission release, May 21, 1987.

38. Edsall, *Washington Post,* July 17, 1987, p. A1.

39. See tables accompanying Miller chapter in *Elections in America;* and Figure 13-5 in John E. Chubb and Paul E. Peterson, eds., *The New Directions in American Politics* (Washington, D.C.: Brookings Institution, 1985), p. 388; *Public Opinion,* March–April 1987, pp. 21–40.

40. *Economic Report of the President, January 1987,* pp. 246, 278, 281; Robert J. Samuelson, *Washington Post,* September 9, 1987, p. F1.

41. U.S. Bureau of the Census, *Estimating After-Tax Money Income Distribution,* Series P-23, no. 126 (Washington, D.C.: Government Printing Office, August 1983); and *Household After-Tax Income: 1985,* Series P-23, no. 151, June 1987.

42. Ibid. The income groups in Tables 3 and 5—the bottom 40 percent, the 21st through 60th percentiles, the 41st through 80th percentiles, the top 40 percent, and the top 10 percent—are based on census data. This data provides the median income for each of the groups described in the tables.

43. For a sampling of some of the arguments, see Robert J. Samuelson, "The Two-Tiered Nation," *Washington Post,* August 19, 1987, p. D1; Frank Levy, *Dollars and Dreams: The Changing American Income Distribution* (New York: Basic Books, 1987); Sheldon Danziger and Peter Gottschalk, "How Have Families with Children Been Faring?" a paper prepared for the Joint Economic Committee, U.S. Congress, November 1985; Warren Brookes, numerous articles in the *Washington Times,* including "Is Family Income Down?" November 17, 1986, p. D1, and "The American Dream Is Back," August 31, 1987, p. D1; "Fairness vs. Politics of Envy," *Human Events,* January 25, 1986, p. 16; and "Low Pay Jobs: The Big Lie," *Wall Street Journal,* March 24, 1987, editorial page; Marvin H. Kosters, "New Arguments About America's New Jobs," *Public Opinion,* August 1987, p. 44; Spencer Rich, "Average Family's Income Up Little Over 11 Years," *Washington Post,* August 25, 1986, p. A1; Barry Bluestone and Bennett Harrison, "Increasing Incidence of Low-Wage Employment in the U.S.," unpublished paper from the forthcoming book, *The Great U-Turn* (Basic Books); Katherine L. Bradbury, "The Shrinking Middle Class," *New England Economic Review,* September–October 1986, p. 41; McKinley L. Blackburn and David E. Bloom, "Family Income Inequality in the United States: 1967–1984," paper delivered at the 1986 meeting of the Industrial Relations Research Association.

44. See note 41.

45. See note 40.

46. Frank S. Levy and Richard C. Michel, "The Economic Future of the Baby Boom," a report for the Joint Economic Committee of the U.S. Congress, December 5, 1985.

47. Michael deCourcy Hinds, *New York Times Real Estate Report,* September 13, 1987, p. 19.

48. U.S. Bureau of the Census, *Statistical Abstract of the United States, 1987,* p. 443; Levy, *Dollars and Dreams,* pp. 180–81; "Smaller Slices of the Pie," a report by the Center on Budget and Policy Priorities, Washington, D.C., November 1985.

49. "Bureau of Labor Statistics Previews the Economy of the Year 2000," released by the bureau June 25, 1987.

Contributors

Sidney Blumenthal is a staff writer for the *Washington Post.* He was the national political correspondent for the *New Republic* from 1983 to 1985, and is the author of *The Permanent Campaign* and *The Rise of the Counter-Establishment.*

Lincoln Caplan is a frequent contributor to the *New Yorker.* He has written for the *Washington Post,* the *Los Angeles Times,* and the *New York Times.* He is the author of *The Insanity Defense and the Trial of John W. Hinckley, Jr.* and *The Tenth Justice: The Solicitor General and the Rule of Law.* He is a graduate of Harvard Law School and the recipient of the Silver Gavel Award of the American Bar Association.

Thomas Byrne Edsall is a political reporter for the *Washington Post.* He has written for the *New York Review of Books,* the *New Republic,* the *Washington Monthly,* the *Nation,* and *Dissent.* He is the author of *The New Politics of Inequality* and *Power and Money: Writing About Politics.*

David Ignatius is the editor of the "Outlook" section of the *Washington Post.* From 1980 to 1983, he covered the Middle East for the *Wall Street Journal.* He has written for the *New York Times Magazine,* the *Washington Monthly,* and *Foreign Affairs,* and is the author of *Agents of Innocence.*

John Judis is a senior editor of *In These Times.* He has written for the *New Republic,* the *New York Times Magazine, Progressive,* and *Commonweal.* He is the author of *William F. Buckley, Jr.: Patron Saint of the Conservatives.*

Robert Kuttner is the economics correspondent of the *New Republic* and a columnist for *Business Week* and the *Boston Globe.* He is the author of *The Life of the Party, Revolt of the Haves,* and *The Economic Illusion,* which was nominated for the National Book Critics Circle Award.

William Schneider is a resident fellow at the American Enterprise Institute in Washington, D.C., and a contributing editor to the *Los Angeles Times, National Journal,* the *Atlantic,* and *Public Opinion.* He has taught political science at Harvard University and has been a national fellow of the Hoover Institution at Stanford University. Schneider is coauthor of *The Confidence Gap: Business, Labor, and Government in the Public Mind.*

Index